D0386877

THE GREAT DIVE

THE GREAT DIVERGENCE

AMERICA'S GROWING INEQUALITY CRISIS
AND WHAT WE CAN DO ABOUT IT

TIMOTHY NOAH
ILLUSTRATIONS BY CATHERINE MULBRANDON

BLOOMSBURY PRESS
NEW YORK   BERLIN   LONDON   SYDNEY

Copyright © 2012 by Timothy Noah
Illustrations copyright © 2012 by Catherine Mulbrandon

All rights reserved. No part of this book may be used or reproduced in any manner
whatsoever without written permission from the publisher except in the case of
brief quotations embodied in critical articles or reviews. For information address
Bloomsbury Press, 175 Fifth Avenue, New York, NY 10010.

Published by Bloomsbury Press, New York

All papers used by Bloomsbury Press are natural, recyclable products made
from wood grown in well-managed forests. The manufacturing processes
conform to the environmental regulations of the country of origin.

LIBRARY OF CONGRESS CATALOGING-IN-PUBLICATION DATA

Noah, Timothy.
The great divergence : America's growing inequality crisis and what we can do
about it / Timothy Noah.—1st U.S. ed.
p.   cm.
ISBN: 978-1-60819-633-3
1. Income distribution—United States. 2. Wealth—United States.
3. Poverty—United States. 4. Equality—United States. 5. United States—
Economic conditions. 6. United States—Economic policy. I. Title.
HC110.I5N63 2012
339.2'20973—dc23
2011048447

First U.S. edition 2012

1 3 5 7 9 10 8 6 4 2

Typeset by Westchester Book Group
Printed in the U.S.A. by Quad/Graphics, Fairfield, Pennsylvania

For Robert and Marian Noah

Contents

Introduction   1
  1. Paradise Lost   10
  2. Going Up   28
  3. Usual Suspects   44
  4. Teeming Shores   60
  5. *Kudoka* and the College Premium   75
  6. Offshore   94
  7. Unequal Government   108
  8. The Fall of Detroit   125
  9. Rise of the Stinking Rich   144
10. Why It Matters   164
11. What to Do   179
     Acknowledgments   197
     Notes   201
     Index   249

Introduction

The fact is that income inequality is real;
it's been rising for more than twenty-five years.

—President George W. Bush, January 2007

DURING THE PAST THIRTY-THREE YEARS the difference in America between being rich and being middle class became much more pronounced. People with high incomes consumed an ever-larger share of the nation's total income, while people in the middle saw their share shrink. For most of this time the phenomenon attracted little attention from the general public and the press because it occurred in increments over one third of a century. During the previous five decades—from the early 1930s through most of the 1970s—the precise opposite had occurred. The share of the nation's income that went to the wealthy had either shrunk or remained stable. At the first signs, during the early 1980s, that this was no longer happening, economists figured they were witnessing a fluke, an inexplicable but temporary phenomenon, or perhaps an artifact of faulty statistics. But they weren't. A democratization of incomes that Americans had long taken for granted as a happy fact of modern life was reversing itself. Eventually it was the steady growth in income inequality that Americans took for granted. The divergent fortunes of the rich and the middle class became such a fact of everyday life that people seldom noticed it, except perhaps to observe now and then with a shrug that life was unfair.

1

There were signs that this indifference was beginning to evaporate in the fall of 2011, when protestors turned up on Wall Street waving signs that said WE ARE THE BOTTOM 99 PERCENT. As I write, it's too early to say whether the Occupy Wall Street movement will have any lasting positive effect, but certainly the topic is becoming more difficult to ignore.

"I am 21 and scared of what the future will bring," read one testimonial posted online by a protester. "I work full time with no benefits and I am actively looking for a second job, because I am barely making it. I worry every month that I will not be able to afford rent. I am afraid of what will happen if I get sick. I am afraid I will never be able to go back to school." Another read: "My parents have worked hard their entire lives as small business owners. In hard times they ALWAYS paid their employees before themselves. They would like to retire soon, but can't afford to stay in the modest ranch house they have lived in for 35 years. We are currently making renovations to our house so they can move in and avoid Section 8 [low-income] housing." The day before these statements appeared on the Web, the *New York Times* evaluated for its more affluent readers the pluses and minuses of Kohler's new $6,400 luxury Numi toilet, which featured two flushing modes, an automatically rising toilet lid, and stereophonic sound.

We tend to think of the United States as a place that has grown more equal over time, not less, and in the most obvious ways that's true. When the republic was founded, African Americans were still held in bondage and were defined in the Constitution as representing three fifths of a human being. Only adult white male property owners could vote. Over the next two centuries full citizenship rights were extended gradually to people who didn't own property, to blacks, to women, and to Native Americans. In recent years, gay activists have fought at the state level for the right to same-sex marriage, and they've prevailed, at this writing, in six states and the District of Columbia. It seems just a matter of time before this right is extended in the rest of the country. Difficult to enforce, the principle that all men and women are equal before the law is even more difficult to refute. All the groups mentioned here experienced setbacks in their pursuit of legal equality, some lasting as long as a century. Few people belonging to any of these groups would argue that this pursuit ends with the removal of explicit legal barriers. Still, most would likely agree that over the long haul legal obstacles to full and equal participation in American life tend to diminish.

It was once possible to make a similar argument with respect to economic obstacles. As late as 1979, the prevailing view among economists was that incomes in any advanced industrial democracy would inevitably become more equal or remain stable in their distribution. They certainly wouldn't become more *un*equal. That sorry fate was reserved for societies at an earlier stage of development or where the dictatorial powers of the state preserved privilege for the few at the expense of the many. In civilized, mature, and free nations, the gaps between rich, middle class, and poor did not increase.

That seemed the logical lesson to draw from U.S. history. The country's transformation from an agrarian society to an industrial one during the late nineteenth and early twentieth centuries had created a period of extreme economic inequality—one whose ramifications can still be glimpsed by, say, pairing a visit to George Vanderbilt's 125,000-acre Biltmore Estate in Ashville, North Carolina, with a trip to the Tenement Museum on Manhattan's Lower East Side. But from the early 1930s through the early 1970s, incomes became more equal, and remained so, while the industrial economy lost none of its rude vitality. As the 1970s progressed, that vitality diminished, but income distribution remained unchanged. "As measured in the official data," the Princeton economist Alan Blinder wrote in 1980, "income inequality was just about the same in 1977 . . . as it was in 1947."[1] What Blinder couldn't know (because he didn't have more recent data) was that this was already beginning to change. Starting in 1979, incomes once again began to grow unequal. When the economy recovered in 1983, incomes grew even more unequal. They have continued growing more unequal to this day.

The United States is not the only advanced industrialized democracy where incomes have become more unequal in recent decades. The trend is global. A 2008 report by the Organisation for Economic Co-operation and Development, which represents thirty-four market-oriented democracies, concluded that since the mid-1980s, income inequality had increased in two thirds of the twenty-four OECD countries for which data were available, which included most of the world's leading industrial democracies.[2] But the level and growth rate of income inequality in the United States has been particularly extreme.

There are various ways to measure income distribution, and by all of them the United States ranks at or near the bottom in terms of equality. The most common measure, the Gini coefficient, is named for an

Italian statistician named Corrado Gini (1884–1965).[3] It measures distribution—of income or anything else—on a scale that goes from 0 to 1. Let's imagine, for instance, that we had fifty marbles to distribute among fifty children. Perfect equality of distribution would be if each child got one marble. The Gini coefficient would then be 0. Perfect inequality of distribution would be if one especially pushy child ended up with all fifty marbles. The Gini coefficient would then be 1.[4] As of 2005, the United States' Gini coefficient was 0.38, which on the income-equality scale ranked this country twenty-seventh of the thirty OECD nations for which data were available. The only countries with more unequal income distribution were Portugal (0.42), Turkey (0.43), and Mexico (0.47). The same relative rankings were achieved when you calculated the ratio of the highest income below the threshold for the top 10 percent to the highest income below the threshold for the bottom 10 percent. The United States dropped to twenty-ninth place (just above Mexico) when you calculated the ratio of median income to the highest income below the threshold for the bottom 10 percent. When you calculated the percentage of national income that went to the top 1 percent, the United States was the undisputed champion. Its measured income distribution was more unequal than that of any other OECD nation.[5] As of 2007 (i.e., right before the 2008 financial crisis), America's richest 1 percent possessed nearly 24 percent of the nation's pretax income, a statistic that gave new meaning to the expression "Can you spare a quarter?" (I include capital gains as part of income, and will do so whenever possible throughout this book.) In 2008, the last year for which data are available, the recession drove the richest 1 percent's income share down to 21 percent.[6] To judge from Wall Street's record bonuses and corporate America's surging profitability in the years following the 2008 financial crisis, income share for the top 1 percent will resume its upward climb momentarily, if it hasn't already. We already know from census data that in 2010 income share for the bottom 40 percent fell and that the poverty rate climbed to its highest point in nearly two decades.[7]

In addition to having an unusually high *level* of income inequality, the United States has seen income inequality increase at a much faster *rate* than most other countries. Among the twenty-four OECD countries for which Gini-coefficient change can be measured from the mid-1980s to the mid-aughts, only Finland, Portugal, and New Zealand experienced a faster growth rate in income inequality. Of these, only Portugal ended up with a Gini rating worse than the United States'. Another important point of comparison is that some OECD countries saw income inequality *decline* during this period. France, Greece, Ireland, Spain, and Turkey all saw their Gini ratings go *down* (though the OECD report's data for Ireland and Spain didn't extend beyond 2000). That proves it is not woven into the laws of economics that an advanced industrial democracy must, during the present epoch, see its income-inequality level fall, or even stay the same. Some of these countries are becoming more economically egalitarian, not less, just as the United States did for much of the twentieth century.[8]

Many changes in the global economy are making incomes less equal in many countries outside the United States, but the income-inequality trend of the past three decades has been unusually fierce here in the world's richest nation. Americans usually invoke the term "American exceptionalism" to describe what it is that makes our country so much more blessed than all others. But American exceptionalism can also describe ingrained aspects of our country's economy, or government, or character, that put us at a disadvantage on the world stage. Income inequality is one of the more notable ways that the United States differs, in ways we can only regret, even from nations that resemble us more than they do not.

The Nobel Prize–winning economist Paul Krugman of Princeton (and the *New York Times* op-ed page) termed the age of inequality "the Great Divergence" in his 2007 book *The Conscience of a Liberal*. It has existed for my entire adult life. I graduated from college and moved to Washington, D.C., in 1980, one year after the Great Divergence began. Today I'm a middle-aged man with two nearly grown children. For thirty-two years I've covered politics and policy in the nation's capital for a variety of newspapers and magazines, and quite a lot has changed. When I started out, I typed my stories on an IBM Selectric. My editor scribbled changes in pencil and handed the story to a composer (sometimes me), who tapped the keys of a typesetting machine that groaned and shuddered as it turned the story into a long column of type on a glue-backed white sheet. The white sheet was then pasted onto large posterboards called "mechanicals" and shipped off to a printing press. The Soviet Union was an indestructible adversary, China was a poverty-ridden curiosity making its first baby steps toward joining the community of nations, and everybody thought sending Stinger missile launchers to Afghan rebels was a swell idea. Foreign policy intellectuals furrowed their brows over Eurocommunism, and feminists still believed they had a decent shot at adding an Equal Rights Amendment to the Constitution. It was a different reality. But incomes were growing more unequal in America then, and they continue to grow more unequal in America today. That story hasn't changed at all.

What did change over the years were the speculative explanations as to *why* incomes were becoming more unequal. It was Ronald Reagan's fault. No, it was the inevitable result of a maturing global economy. No, it was caused by computers. No, it was caused by the twin epidemics of teenage pregnancy and divorce. Some people denied the Great Divergence was happening at all. Others said it was a fleeting phenomenon. Still others said all would be well once the economy became more productive (i.e., once there was a significant increase in output per hour worked). As time went on, the favored hypotheses kept changing. It was maddening. How can we address the problem if we don't even know what the problem *is*?

Gradually, however, a body of academic work, mainly by economists but also by political scientists and sociologists, has begun to accumulate. This book is an attempt to synthesize the best of that work for non-experts who would like to know, at long last, what's been happening to the economy, especially in the United States. Economists are often treated skeptically by the public at large, mainly because it usually sees them when they're on TV attempting to predict the future. But while the economics profession isn't much better at soothsaying than any other, it performs an enormously valuable, greatly underappreciated service in documenting and interpreting the past. Economic trends are hard to interpret in real time because doing so requires data, and the best and most complete data sets often aren't available for five or ten years. By the time they are available, the world has moved on to fretting about newer trends. As a result, when the day arrives for us to understand better, say, the oil shocks of 1973, or the recession of 1982–83, we are preoccupied with trying to figure out the tech boom of the late 1990s or the housing bubble of the aughts. By "we," I mean all of American society but especially my own fraternity of political and policy-wonk journalists. History isn't news. But the Great Divergence has been going on for so long that it manages to be both. It's history because it began when Jimmy Carter was in the White House. It's also news because it's continuing while Barack Obama is president.

The scholars who have struggled to understand why income inequality is growing so much worse in the United States than in other countries have their share of disagreements, and in the coming pages I'll air some of them. Probably the biggest is between those who believe that higher education and the advent of computers played a significant role in creating income inequality in the United States and those who believe the only factor that matters was the stratospheric income growth enjoyed by the top 1 percent, and especially the top 0.1 percent and even the top 0.01 percent. But any considered review of the income-inequality trend dating back to 1979 should, I think, reveal that all of these factors played significant roles, albeit at different stages.

The income gap between people who hold college degrees and people who never advanced beyond high school grew dramatically in the 1980s. (More recently, that gap has stopped growing, while the gap between people who hold graduate degrees and people who do not has opened up.) The computer-driven hollowing-out of traditional middle class jobs was especially fierce during the 1980s; then it eased up during the 1990s; then it resumed during the aughts. The huge increase in income shares at the top began around 1979 but accelerated in the 1990s and then continued unabated. I find it most useful to think of the Great Divergence as not a single trend, but as two. It's not at all clear that the "upper tail" trend of ever-growing high incomes has much to do with the more complex societal changes plaguing the middle class. Just because two bad things happen at the same time doesn't mean they have a common cause.

What impressed me most in researching the Great Divergence wasn't how much disagreement there was among the experts, but how much consensus. This book is an attempt to present that consensus as fair-mindedly as possible. For too long, it seems to me, the Great Divergence has been treated as a debating point in heated ideological battles rather than a historical phenomenon of long standing that's interesting and important in and of itself. We used to live in an age of growing income equality. Now we live in an age of growing income inequality. How do we measure it? What accounted for the change? Why has it continued for so long? What does it mean for the future of democracy and civil society?

I'll begin my inquiry with an account of how income inequality first came to be measured in the United States during the early part of the twentieth century. Next I'll relate what scholars, politicians, and others made of that inequality as it dissipated from the 1930s through most of the 1970s and then reversed course to grow with a vengeance. In chapter 2 I'll set aside the question of income inequality to consider why Americans believe their country has more upward mobility relative to other nations than it actually does. In chapter 3 I'll dismiss some plausible causes of income inequality that turn out to have no relevance at all, and examine how living standards have changed for the middle class. In chapters 4, 5, and 6 I'll weigh, successively, the varying relevance of several possible factors—immigration, computers, education, trade, and globalization—in contributing to income inequality. In chapter 7 I'll examine the important role played by government policy in creating income inequality—a role that economists long pooh-poohed, but that is now being seen, increasingly, as central. An important case study in government's role as income distributor is how it influenced the rise and fall of the labor movement, which I'll examine at some length in chapter 8. In chapter 9 I'll consider the enormous changes at the upper end of the income distribution, fueled by the evolution of the corporate and financial worlds and largely unchecked by government. Finally, I'll step back and try to explain to hard-core skeptics why growing income inequality is worth caring about.

President George W. Bush, obviously no socialist, is not among these skeptics, as the epigraph for this chapter makes plain. Unfortunately, the only cause of the income gap he was willing to consider, while addressing this topic before an audience in New York's financial district, was the education gap. Bush's breezy indifference to the accumulation of income share at the very top, which has almost nothing to do with educational differences, may have helped polarize academic debate about what caused the Great Divergence.

I will also suggest some policies that might help reverse the trend of inequality and establish greater income equality. These are offered with few illusions that most will be politically feasible in the near future, but with the hope that as time passes and voters familiarize themselves with the story of how the age of inequality came into being they will become more amenable to effecting significant change.

For now, I believe, our country's principal task with respect to the Great Divergence is to learn more about these past three decades of American economic history. I don't think it's possible to read this history and not feel an enormous sense of urgency about the way this country is changing and our need to get it back on the right track. There is a tradition in our not-too-distant past of fellowship and decency and shared commitment to fair play, a feeling that when the country prospers, everyone should prosper. That tradition has been slipping away, and hardness and mutual suspicion and belief in markets as the infallible measure of all things have taken its place. That's a legacy of the Great Divergence. What follows is a history of an era we have not yet left behind. I offer it in the hope that we will soon see its end.

1

Paradise Lost

IN 1915, A RANGY, SOFT-SPOKEN STATISTICIAN named Willford I. King, age thirty-five, published *The Wealth and Income of the People of the United States*. The United States was displacing Great Britain as the world's wealthiest industrial nation, but detailed information about how incomes were distributed was not yet readily available; the federal government wouldn't start collecting such data in any systematic way until the late 1930s. Though King is largely forgotten today, his book was recognized in its time as an important landmark. *The Survey*, a leading journal affiliated with the Progressive movement, called it "the best and the most comprehensive attempt yet made to state wealth and income conditions in the United States." Two decades later, an analysis prepared by a Commerce Department official for the nonprofit National Bureau of Economic Research, then (as now) a leader in the study of income distribution (though better known today as the official arbiter of when recessions begin and end), would identify King's book as "the pioneer work" in the field.[1]

"If there has been an increase in the riches of the nation as a whole," King asked in his book's first chapter, "has the increase been distributed to all classes of the population, or have the benefits been monopolized by a favored few?" Mostly the latter, it turned out. Incomes had risen across the board, but King calculated that as of 1910 the richest 1 percent possessed about 15 percent of the nation's income. A more authoritative contemporary calculation puts the figure slightly higher, at about 18 percent.[2] This was the era during which public alarm at the accumulated riches of America's wealthiest families—the Rockefellers, the Vanderbilts, the Carnegies—prompted ratification, in 1913, of the

Sixteenth Amendment to the Constitution, which created the modern income tax. The socialist movement was approaching its historic peak, a wave of anarchist bombings was about to terrorize the nation's industrialists, and President Woodrow Wilson's attorney general, A. Mitchell Palmer, would soon stage (after an anarchist bombed his own home) brutal raids on radicals of every stripe. In American history, there has never been a time when class warfare seemed more imminent.

That was when the richest 1 percent accounted for 18 percent of the nation's income. By 2007, their share would balloon to 24 percent, an increase of roughly a third.[3]

Perhaps it strikes you as odd that the "pioneer work" measuring income distribution in the United States didn't appear until 139 years after Thomas Jefferson wrote into America's founding document that "all men are created equal." But it wasn't until the Progressive era that rigorous analysis of meticulously assembled statistical data came to dominate the study of economics, government, and sociology, all newly rechristened "social sciences." Nobody embraced the new zest for statistical research more wholeheartedly than King. "If you are curious to ascertain how many days of labor it took to build the pyramids," King wrote in 1917, "how many germs you consumed at this morning's breakfast, or how many times per page Shakespeare used the word 'and,' rest assured that the data are awaiting your examination."[4]

Another reason why income distribution received little attention prior to the Progressive era was that egalitarians outside the labor movement seldom gave much thought to incomes as a measure of equality. In an agrarian economy, a man's dignity and economic worth weren't determined by his income; they were determined by whether he was free and able to own property. Property allowed families to live by the fruits of their labors; lack of property reduced families to servitude. In the early years of the republic a man couldn't even vote if he didn't own property.

Michael J. Thompson, an intellectual historian of inequality in America, identifies Langton Byllesby's *Observations on the Sources and Effects of Unequal Wealth*, published in 1826, as "the first sustained analysis of economic inequality in America." But Byllesby didn't write about income. He wrote about property, the just distribution of which was, in Byllesby's view, being corrupted in the cities by the first stirrings of industrialism. Farmers resented bankers because they substituted an intangible and, they believed, illegitimate form of wealth (capital) for a tangible one (land).

By the mid-nineteenth century, the American industrial revolution was well under way, creating unprecedented levels of income inequality (and simultaneously, we'll learn in the next chapter, extraordinary opportunities for upward mobility). But reformers and even radicals, Thompson argues, continued to frame the issue as one of unequal distribution of property. Their dissent was against industrialization itself. As late as 1907, President Theodore Roosevelt denounced not "malefactors of great income" but "malefactors of great *wealth*."[5]

Only in the Progressive era were reformers finally ready to make peace with industrial production as a permanent reality. Urban workers didn't feed their families with crops grown on plots of land. They fed them by buying food. "Income is the best single criterion of economic welfare," King wrote in *The Wealth and Income of the People of the United States*. In 1915 this still required explanation.

> Wealth is a better safeguard against disaster. It sometimes is a more effective source of power. But, in every day experience, no other quest is carried on so assiduously as that for the maximum income. Income will obtain the necessities, comforts, and luxuries of life. It will, if saved, lead to the added advantages of wealth.[6]

King's book grew out of research he performed as a graduate student under the supervision of Richard T. Ely, a nationally prominent economist. Ely wasn't just King's academic mentor; he was the reason King had become an economist. As an undergraduate at the University of Nebraska, King would later recall in an autobiographical sketch, he found economics "mildly interesting, but by no means thrilling." He took only a single class in the subject. But after graduating, King taught high school science in Iowa and was asked to teach a class in economics. Boning up at the public library, King discovered Ely's books and was bowled over by "the simplicity of presentation and the clarity of the style." King decided that economics was his own true calling and enrolled in the graduate program at the University of Wisconsin, where Ely chaired the economics department.[7]

Ely was an influential figure in the Progressive movement. (Among his admirers were Roosevelt and Wisconsin governor—later senator—Robert La Follette.) Ely was a founder of the American Economic Association and one of the originators of "the Wisconsin Idea," which called on the university to contribute its expertise wherever possible to improve governance at the state and federal levels. It was Ely's view, King recalled in his informal précis of his life, that "if the University was to serve the State, its actions must be based, not upon emotions, but upon knowledge. It was this program of action, based upon research, that made Wisconsin famous as the leader among the progressive states of the union."

Ely favored a larger role for government in the regulation of business. But although sometimes identified as a socialist, Ely opposed socialism, and so did his protégé King. Redistributing income to the poor, King wrote in *The Wealth and Income of the People of the United States*, "would merely mean more rapid multiplication of the lowest and least desirable classes," who remained, "from the reproductive standpoint, on the low plane of their four-footed ancestors." Also like Ely, King was a Malthusian who believed in population control. Income inequality in the United States could be addressed, King wrote, by limiting immigration (King deplored "low-standard alien invaders") and by discouraging excessive breeding among the poor ("eugenists are just beginning to impress upon us the absurd folly of breeding great troops of paupers, defectives and criminals to be a burden upon organized society").[8]

King's casual embrace of nativism and eugenics, plainly abhorrent today, put him well within the mainstream of Progressive thought at the time. The Progressives resented the support that immigrants gave to urban political machines and worried that they were taking low-wage jobs away from native-born Americans. Less loftily, they convinced themselves that southern and eastern European stock was genetically inferior to that of northern Europe. The Progressive movement produced numerous pseudoscientific studies "proving" the undesirability of these darker-skinned Europeans as U.S. citizens, and with a few exceptions (the settlement-house leader Jane Addams was one) they sought to keep them out. In 1917 they would successfully push through Congress an immigration literacy test, passed over President Woodrow Wilson's veto. When that failed to do the job, they would, during the 1920s, get Congress to enact two successive bills imposing strict quotas on southern and eastern Europeans that persisted into the 1960s. One of the Progressives' leading lights on this issue was the sociologist Edward A. Ross, who coined the term "race suicide" to describe how undesirable stock would outbreed and crowd out the superior Anglo-Saxon race. Ross, too, taught at the University of Wisconsin.[9]

Although King shared the Progressives' crude prejudices, he was too careful a researcher to pretend that the inflow of immigrants or the fecundity of the poor played much role in skewing income distribution.

> The greatest force in the last three decades making for income concentration has been the successful organization of monster corporations. The promoters and manipulators of these concerns have received, as their share of the spoils, permanent income claims, in the shape of securities, large enough to make Croesus appear like a pauper.[10]

King's only solace for readers (and himself) was that incomes in the United States were more equal than in Prussia, France, and the United Kingdom. A century later, such comfort is no longer available. Today, incomes in the United States are more *unequal* than in Germany, France, and the United Kingdom.

Two years after publishing his book, King left Wisconsin for Washington, D.C., to become a government statistician, but in 1920 he left that job to continue his research into income distribution in New York City at the newly created National Bureau of Economic Research. The NBER was a perfect embodiment of the Progressive era's conviction that rational expertise was the best tool to address social problems. It owed its existence to a friendly dispute about income distribution in the United States that arose in 1916 between a conservative named Malcolm Rorty, who worked as a statistician for the American Telegraph and Telephone Company, and a liberal economist named Nahum Stone, who worked as a labor arbitrator. Stone had written about income distribution for a socialist monthly, and Rorty, who disagreed with Stone's conclusions but admired the quality of his scholarship, invited him to lunch. "Would it not be a great step forward," Rorty proposed, "if we had an organization that devoted itself to fact finding on controversial economic subjects of great public interest?" Funds were secured from the Carnegie Corporation and the Commonwealth Fund, and an Episcopal seminary set aside office space in lower Manhattan.[11]

The NBER's first project, published in 1921, was a two-volume survey of the distribution of income in the United States. King and three other staff economists, using significantly better data than had been available to King six years earlier, concluded that in 1918 the richest 1 percent received 14 percent of the national income—one percentage point less than King's earlier calculation for 1910. A contemporary recalculation puts the figure at about 16 percent, down from 18 percent in 1913. The Great War had made incomes somewhat more equal, as wars tend to do. In a follow-up analysis, published in 1930, an NBER report listing King as sole author carried the analysis forward to 1926. Here King found that the richest 1 percent, after seeing its share of the national income decline during the war and in the years immediately following, had subsequently rebounded and in 1926 received 13 percent of the national income. King underestimated that rebound, remembered by history as the Roaring Twenties. We now know that the richest 1 percent's share of the national income in 1926 was about 20 percent. By 1928 it was about 24 percent.[12]

In his 1931 book *Only Yesterday*, the popular historian Frederick Lewis Allen described vividly the country's mood at the height of the 1920s bull market.

> The American could spin wonderful dreams—of a romantic day when he would sell his Westinghouse common at a fabulous price and live in a great house and have a fleet of shining cars and loll at ease on the sands of Palm Beach. And when he looked toward the future of his country, he could envision an America set free—not from graft, nor from crime, nor from war, nor from control by Wall Street, nor from irreligion, nor from lust, for the utopias of an earlier day left him for the most part skeptical or indifferent; he envisioned an America set free from poverty and toil.

To embrace the fantasy of a poverty-free America, one had to be unaware that during the 1920s the bottom 95 percent saw its proportion of the nation's income drop from 72 percent to 64 percent.[13] The bigger problem, of course, was that economic catastrophe loomed for just about everyone. Why did people believe otherwise? Partly because financial experts *told* them to. In August 1929 the investor and Democratic National Committee chairman John J. Raskob published, in the *Ladies' Home Journal*, an article titled "Everybody Ought to be Rich." In mid-October Yale's Irving Fisher—the most eminent economist of the era—pronounced, "Stock prices have reached what looks like a permanently high plateau." Mere days later, the stock market crashed and the Great Depression began.

By this time King had left the NBER for a professorship in economics at New York University. Although he was initially sympathetic to President

Franklin Roosevelt, King tacked steadily rightward in his politics as FDR expanded Washington's role in the economy. One reason may be that King was in demand to provide research to businesses and business-oriented groups like the National Association of Manufacturers. "If the W.P.A. and the labor [unions] remain strong enough to keep control of the Government," King confided in private correspondence in 1939, "I suspect that we may just as well reconcile ourselves to the advent of a fascist dictatorship in due course of time." King railed against top income tax rates (too high); the capital gains tax and corporate income tax (shouldn't exist); and the minimum wage ("dangerous"). Upon retiring from NYU in 1945, King became chairman of the Committee for Constitutional Government, an anti–New Deal organization originally founded to oppose Roosevelt's 1937 court-packing scheme, which outraged King.

Well before he died in 1962 at age eighty-two, King saw his legacy eclipsed by the work of a Russian émigré who in 1927 had succeeded King at the NBER and in 1971 would win the Nobel Prize in economics. His name was Simon Kuznets, and among his many lasting contributions to economics was the creation of the analytic foundation for the study of income inequality. Kuznets had (and continues to have) legions of admirers in the economics profession. King was not one of them. In a 1940 letter to one of the NBER's directors, King quarreled with what he termed Kuznets's "assumption . . . that environment and luck are the principal determinants of a persons [sic] success or failure in life." He concluded, "It is a shame that the Bureau is putting out such twaddle." The outraged tone carried more than a whiff of professional jealousy.[14] Kuznets was already sufficiently eminent that the Commerce Department had invited him to create the government's official yardsticks for national income, a discipline that King had virtually invented. Kuznets ended up formulating, among other indicators, the most widely used measurement of all—what we call today "gross domestic product."

Kuznets saw income inequality as a U-shaped cycle. An economy began in a primitive state, operating at the subsistence level; it was egalitarian but poor. Incomes became less egalitarian with more advanced agricultural development, and a lot less egalitarian with the advent of industrialization and urbanization. But as a modern economy evolved beyond industrialization's initial disruptive phase, the trend reversed itself and incomes became more equal. The eventual result would be a mature economy that was egalitarian *and* prosperous. Although he never put it so loftily, Kuznets in effect posited that growing equality of incomes was the mark of an advanced civilization. This conceit was elegant, stirring, and at odds with the existing paradigm, developed by the nineteenth-century French-Italian economist Vilfredo Pareto, that the shape of income distribution did not change over time.

Kuznets believed that income distribution *did* change shape, and he was right.[15] But he was wrong in believing that after the initial inegalitarian phase of industrialization incomes would only grow more equal. Or rather, that conclusion is wrong today. It fit the data perfectly in 1954, when Kuznets formulated it in a speech he gave at a Detroit meeting of the American Economic Association, of which he was president. It described the reality Kuznets had known for most of his adult life. It described the world created after the 1929 crash, and especially after the United States entered World War II.[16]

"In the United States," Kuznets said in his 1954 speech,

in the distribution of income among families (excluding single individuals), the shares of the two lowest quintiles [i.e., the bottom 40 percent] rise from 13½ percent in 1929 to 18 percent in the years after the second world war (average of 1944, 1946, 1947, and 1950); whereas the share of the top quintile [i.e., the top 20 percent] declines from 55 to 44 percent, and that of the top 5 percent from 31 to 20 percent.

Families whose incomes were lower than the U.S. average were *increasing* their share of the national income, while families whose incomes were higher than the U.S. average were *decreasing* their share. That calculation excluded income tax, which in the postwar years Kuznets cited never had a top rate lower than 86 percent. It also excluded redistribution of federal tax dollars downward in the form of welfare payments or other "free assistance." Kuznets observed the same pattern, timed a little differently, in the United Kingdom and Germany. In all three countries, incomes were becoming more equal as economic growth boomed.

There were two reasons, Kuznets said, to find this counterintuitive. The first was that, for all practical purposes, the only people who had any savings were those with the highest incomes. Over time this higher concentration of wealth could be expected to create a higher concentration of income at the top. But it hadn't. The second reason was that as industrialization moved more people from rural to urban areas, rural areas got poorer and urban areas got richer. Why didn't that create more inequality?

Kuznets concluded that these factors had been outweighed by other considerations. One was "the dynamism of a growing and free economic society." The same families didn't necessarily occupy, say, the top 5 percent in incomes over multiple generations. Old fortunes were dissipated, and new fortunes sprang up to take their place. Another countervailing circumstance was that various government actions had worked to limit the concentration of wealth, either indirectly by permitting higher levels of inflation (which eroded the value of existing wealth) or directly through such policies as rent control and ceilings on long-term interest rates (which slowed wealth's accumulation). Even when such government actions were not intended to redistribute income, Kuznets wrote, they nonetheless reflected "the view of society on the long-term utility of wide income inequalities. *This view is a vital force that would operate in democratic societies even if there were no counteracting factors* [italics mine]." Democratic societies did not deem it wise to allow income differences to become too extreme.[17]

In the political environment of today, where growing income disparities are often taken in stride and the inheritance tax is rechristened the "death tax," it may surprise some that mainstream American opinion during the mid-twentieth century considered the prospect of growing income inequality to be unacceptably antidemocratic. A dozen years before Kuznets gave his speech, President Roosevelt had actually proposed, at a time of "grave national danger, when all excess income should go to win the war," that "no American citizen ought to have a net income, after he has paid his taxes, of more than $25,000."[18] In 2011 President Obama got called a socialist for wanting to raise the marginal tax on people making more than $250,000 to not quite 40 percent (i.e., 39.6 percent on every dollar earned above $250,000). In 1942 Roosevelt wanted to raise the marginal tax on people making more than today's equivalent (after inflation) of about $345,000 to 100 percent. FDR wanted to bookend the minimum wage he'd created a decade earlier with a new maximum wage. Congress didn't let him, but the idea won popular support. Such was the lingering political culture in the sleepy Eisenhower era during which Kuznets gave his speech. Kuznets could take it for granted that fully industrialized democracies would never allow income disparities to get out of hand.

Cultural historians often snicker at the drab conventionality of mid-century America—Levittown, bowling leagues, *The Adventures of Ozzie and Harriet*. But, assuming you were white, male, heterosexual, not of draft age, and Christian—a lot of assumptions, to be sure, but none of them economic—there probably was no better time to hold membership in America's middle class. Prosperity mostly reigned from 1945 to 1973, and for a half century encompassing the Great Depression, World War II, and the three decades that followed, incomes became more equal and stayed that way. In a landmark 1992 paper, the economic historians Claudia Goldin (of Harvard and the NBER) and Robert A. Margo (then of Vanderbilt, now of Boston University) termed this midcentury era "the Great Compression."[19] Others have simply called it "the Golden Age."

The five-decade trend of growing and then stable income equality merits close examination because it represents a path that would be abandoned in the late 1970s—a path so seemingly inevitable that Kuznets could conclude that was just how life was in any mature, democratically governed economy. If you are American and older than thirty-three, this more egalitarian world was one you once lived in. Today it has vanished, like Brigadoon.

Incomes started growing more equal, according to Goldin and Margo, in 1934. Comparing wages for white-collar clerks working for railroads and in factories with those for unskilled manual laborers in the same workplaces,[20] Goldin and Margo found that during the first few years of the Depression incomes for the two occupations became more *unequal*. But after 1933 the trend reversed itself. The likely reason, they said, was the National Industrial Recovery Act (passed in June 1933), which created a federal minimum wage eventually set at twenty-five cents per hour (the equivalent of $4.33 per hour today) and a maximum work-week eventually set at forty-four hours—two policies that Willford King, despite his interest in income distribution, had opposed. The Supreme Court ruled the NIRA unconstitutional in 1935, but the Fair Labor Standards Act reinstated the minimum wage in 1938. Goldin and Margo further noted that Kuznets had earlier shown that the top 5 percent saw a decline in its share of national income between the 1929 crash and 1941, the year the United States entered the war, from 30 percent to 26 percent. (A contemporary calculation has it dropping from 36 percent to 30 percent.)[21] King, too, noticed as early as 1938 that incomes were "materially more equal" than before the crash.[22]

Goldin and Margo had to admit that the evidence about the Great Depression was a bit murky. On the one hand, the rich clearly lost income. On the other hand, middle-class incomes fell and a high level of unemployment (which peaked at 25 percent) hit those at the bottom of the income scale especially hard. Unemployment reduces wages to zero, and when there's more of it at the bottom (as is nearly always the case), that increases income inequality. In addition, just because the *trend* during the Depression was toward greater income equality, that doesn't mean that income distribution in *any given year* was notably egalitarian. Goldin and Margo calculated that wage inequality (expressed as the mathematical relationship between the ninetieth percentile and the tenth percentile) was worse in 1940 than it would later be in 1985, after the trend toward greater income inequality was well under way. But an important difference to remember is that in 1940 incomes were becoming *more* equal, while by 1985 they were becoming *less* so.

A more dramatic shift toward greater income equality occurred after U.S. entry into World War II. Goldin and Margo looked at census-based wage data for males age eighteen to sixty-four working full-time; self-employed workers were excluded because the 1940 census didn't include earnings information for this group. Comparing the ninetieth percentile to the tenth percentile—rich to poor—they found that between 1940 and 1950 the wage difference shrank by 35 percent. Comparing the ninetieth percentile to the median (i.e., the fiftieth percentile)—rich to middle class—they found that the wage difference shrank by 20 percent. Comparing the median to the tenth percentile—middle class to poor—they found the wage difference shrank by 15 percent. The college premium—the wage gap between those whose formal education ended with high school graduation and those who went on to graduate from college—shrank by 13 percent. (The college premium would increase again in the 1950s, but not enough to bring it back to the 1940 level.) Members of the professions (doctors, lawyers, etc.) lost 14 percent of their earnings edge over all nonfarm workers, and common laborers gained 21 percent on all nonfarm workers. There was even a decrease in inequality *within* demographic groups. Wage dispersion shrank 32 percent for white-collar workers. Keep in mind that this was a decade not when the economy declined, as it did during the Depression, but when the economy *recovered*, albeit under the unusual circumstance of the nation mobilizing to fight a world war.

Some of the change was surely attributable to the war itself. Goldin and Margo gave much credit to the National War Labor Board, which administered wage controls and did its best to impose labor peace between 1942 and 1945. Most of the rules imposed by the NWLB had the effect of reducing wage inequality; for instance, any employer could raise wages to forty cents an hour without NWLB approval, and to fifty cents an hour with approval only at the regional level. When an exception was granted to a particular rule, it was usually to address the problem of "substandard" wages. Another likely factor was the labor scarcity created by the wartime draft. In manufacturing, production and nonsupervisory (i.e., blue-collar) workers saw their wages more than double between 1940 and 1949, with the biggest bump during the war.

What's harder to explain is why incomes continued to become more equal after V-J Day. One possible reason may be postwar increases in the hourly minimum wage, from thirty cents during the war (up from the initial twenty-five cents) to forty cents immediately after the war to seventy-five cents (the equivalent of seven dollars today, only twenty-five cents less than the current minimum wage) in 1950. But Goldin and Margo found that the equalizing trend for the poor compared to the middle class (tenth to fiftieth percentile) *slowed down* after the war, while the equalizing trend for the middle class compared to the rich (fiftieth percentile to ninetieth) remained just as robust. Part of the answer to this riddle, they concluded, was that supply exceeded demand for college-educated (skilled) workers while it did not for high school graduates (less-skilled workers). The market for the college-educated tightened up in the 1950s, but the market for high school graduates did, too. Another part of the answer, surely, is that the American labor movement reached the zenith of its power during the 1950s. (More on this in chapter 8.)

Incomes stopped converging around 1952. But what happened next is in many ways even more remarkable. Although incomes ceased becoming *more* equal, they didn't start becoming *less* equal (as they had during the 1920s after World War I). The income ratios stayed more or less the same. For instance, in 1952 the share of national income going to the top 10 percent was 33 percent. In 1962 it was 34 percent. In 1972 it was . . . 34 percent.[23] The rich were getting richer, but not disproportionately to everyone else.

Writing in 1952, Frederick Lewis Allen observed, "The enormous lead of the well-to-do in the economic race has been considerably reduced."

Forty or fifty years ago the countryman in a metropolis was visibly a "hayseed"; the purchaser of inexpensive men's clothing was betrayed by his tight-waisted jackets and bulbous-toed shoes. Today the difference in appearance between a steelworker (or a clerk) and a high executive is hardly noticeable to the casual eye . . . In the early years of the century there was a hierarchy of automobiles. At the top were such imported cars as the Rolls-Royce, Mercedes-Benz, and Isotta Fraschini; to possess one of these was a mark of lively wealth. There was also an American aristocracy of the Pierce-Arrow, Peerless, and Packard. Then came group after group, in descending scale, till you reached the homely Model-T Ford. Today, except for a few survivals such as the obstinately rectangular Rolls-Royces of the old school, and a few such oddities such as the new British sports cars . . . there is a comparative absence of class groupings.[24]

Goldin and Margo quoted the MIT economist Lester Thurow saying that the wage differentials of the Depression and World War II "became the new standard of relative deprivation and were regarded as 'just' even after the egalitarian pressures of World War II had disappeared. Basically, the same differentials exist to this day." Thurow said that in 1975. He couldn't say the same in 1986. By then, the share of national income going to the top 10 percent was no longer 33 or 34 percent. It was 41 percent.

It was, President Reagan insisted, morning in America. In one of the most effective political TV ads ever conceived, aired during Reagan's 1984 reelection campaign, gauzy early-morning images of Americans at work and play and gentle pastoral music provided the background for the following recitation.

It's morning again in America. Today, more men and women will go to work than ever before in our country's history. With interest rates and inflation down, more people are buying new homes, and our new families can have confidence in the future. America today is prouder and stronger and better. Why would we want to return to where we were less than four short years ago?

Never mind that two years earlier unemployment had risen higher than it had since the Great Depression. Never mind that at 7.2 percent, unemployment in November 1984 was only slightly lower than in November 1980, when it was 7.5 percent. The economy was in recovery. But the Golden Age was over.

The first sign of trouble had been stagnation of the median income. In October 1973 the Arab members of the Organization of Arab Petroleum Exporting Countries retaliated against U.S. support for Israel during the Yom Kippur War by imposing an embargo that quadrupled the price of oil. The immediate result was a sixteen-month recession and a simultaneous upsurge in inflation, an unusually hideous combination dubbed "stagflation." After the recession ended, in March 1975, the median income was expected to resume a brisk upward climb. But it didn't. Median income, which more than doubled between 1947 and 1973, would rise by less than one quarter between 1973 and 2004. During the decade after the oil embargo it actually went *down*. (Remember that these calculations, here and throughout this book, are in "real" income, i.e., with inflation factored out.) Median income would drop again during the first decade of the twenty-first century.

That incomes were stagnating for middle-class Americans wasn't immediately recognized as an *inequality* problem because incomes were also stagnating for more affluent Americans. From 1971 to 1979 the college premium dropped by about one third for recent college graduates.[25] (I'll explain why in chapter 5.) Corporate profits had been in decline since the mid-1960s, and per capita GDP growth had dropped from about 3 percent in the late 1960s and early 1970s to below 1 percent during the late 1970s.[26] The share of national income going to the richest 1 percent had slipped from about 11 percent in 1965 to about 9 percent in 1975, and it stayed there for three more years. Even if you could get a raise, it had to be pretty big to keep up with inflation, which averaged more than 9 percent during the second half of the 1970s. This was largely due to oil prices, which continued to rise briskly even after the oil embargo was halted early in 1974.[27] In short, the economy was lousy for everyone. All Ronald Reagan really had to do to win the 1980 general election was say the following (in his debate with President Jimmy Carter):

When he was a candidate in 1976, President Carter invented a thing he called the misery index. He added the rate of unemployment and the rate of inflation, and it came, at that time, to 12.5% under President

Ford. He said that no man with that size misery index has a right to seek reelection to the Presidency. Today, by his own decision, the misery index is in excess of 20%.[28]

Even as Reagan was reciting this, some of the dire economic circumstances were beginning to recede, but only for the affluent. In the late 1970s the college premium started to rise again, and after faltering in the early 1980s it began a steep climb. The richest 1 percent's income share began to increase in 1979.[29] Misery index or no misery index, eco-

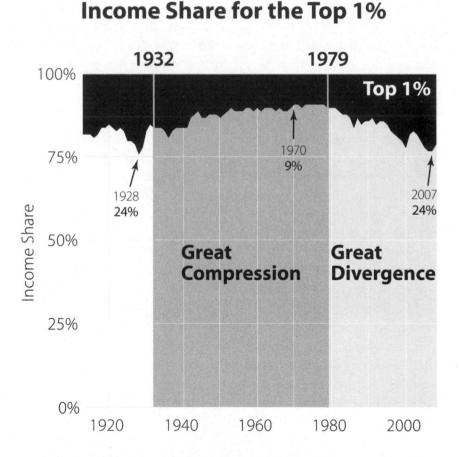

Top 1 percent income share includes capital gains. Source: Facundo Alvaredo, Tony Atkinson, Thomas Piketty, and Emmanuel Saez, "The World Top Incomes Database."

nomic conditions were getting a little better. But they were only getting better for incomes above the median. For the average middle-class American, nothing was getting better.

The economic fortunes of the middle class and the affluent never converged again.

Income inequality in the United States grew through the 1980s, slackened briefly at the end of the 1990s, and then resumed with a vengeance in the aughts. Princeton's Paul Krugman had Goldin and Margo's "Great Compression" in mind when he labeled this epoch the Great Divergence. It's generally understood that we live in a time of growing income inequality, but "the ordinary person is not really aware of how big it is," Krugman says.[30] During the late 1980s and the late 1990s, the United States experienced two unprecedentedly long periods of sustained economic growth: the "seven fat years" and the "long boom." Yet from 1980 to 2005, *80 percent* of the total increase in Americans' income went to the top 1 percent. When you factor in federal (including corporate) taxes; the monetary value of employer-sponsored health insurance; employer contributions to Social Security, Medicare, and federal unemployment insurance; and all federal benefits, the top 1 percent still received fully *36 percent* of the nation's total increase.[31] Economic growth was more sluggish in the aughts, and median income, as noted earlier, declined. But the decade saw productivity increase by about 20 percent. Yet none of that increase translated into wage growth for the average working-age family, an outcome that left many economists scratching their heads. By one calculation, during the economic expansion of 2002–07 two thirds of the total increase in Americans' income went to the top 1 percent.[32]

When signs first emerged in the early 1980s that the Great Compression had reversed course, the economics profession was initially inclined to ignore them. "Some questioned whether the facts would stand up to closer scrutiny," Goldin and Lawrence F. Katz write in their 2008 book, *The Race Between Education and Technology*. One person who spotted the trend early was Thomas Byrne Edsall, a *Washington Post* reporter (now a professor of journalism at Columbia) who published, in 1984, a prescient book titled *The New Politics of Inequality*. Even when economists finally accepted that incomes were indeed diverging, they were slow to accept Edsall's argument that the trend had a lot to do with politics. Edsall saw a significant erosion of the power of those on the bottom half of the economic spectrum, an erosion of the power not only of the poor but of those in the working and middle classes. At the same time, there has been a sharp increase in the power of economic elites, of those who fall in the top 15 percent of the income distribution.[33]

In retrospect, this trend looks pretty hard to miss. But economists are congenitally resistant to believing that government policies can have significant long-term, or what economists call "secular," effects. And identifying precisely *which* government policies guided the change is something that economists and political scientists are still arguing about. (More on that in chapter 8.)

Perhaps we would know more about the Great Divergence, one third of a century after its advent, if the general topic of income distribution inspired less squeamishness. "I was once told by the head of a prestigious think tank in Washington, D.C.," wrote Branko Milanovic, lead economist at the World Bank's research division, in his 2011 book *The Haves and the Have-Nots: A Brief and Idiosyncratic History of Global Inequality*,

> that the think tank's board was very unlikely to fund any work that had *income* or *wealth inequality* in its title. Yes, they would finance anything to do with poverty alleviation, but inequality was an altogether different matter. Why? Because "my" concern with the poverty of some people actually projects me in a very nice, warm glow: I am ready to use my money to help them. Charity is a good thing; a lot of egos are boosted by it and many ethical points earned even when only tiny amounts are given to the poor. But inequality is different: Every mention of it raises in fact the issue of the appropriateness or legitimacy of my income. Perhaps my charity will not be seen so very favorably, if somebody argued that my income was acquired unjustly or illegally. Thus, it's better to pass inequality in silence.

Milanovic went on to report that even the cosmopolitan World Bank "refused to call its flagship report on the topic a report on inequality: It was, more tamely, called a report on 'equity' instead."[34]

All my life I've heard Latin America described as a failed society (or collection of failed societies) because of its grotesque maldistribution of wealth. Peasants in rags beg for food outside the high walls of opulent villas, and so on. But according to the Central Intelligence Agency (whose patriotism I hesitate to question), income distribution in the United States is now more unequal than in Uruguay, Nicaragua, Guyana, and Venezuela, and roughly on par with Argentina.[35] Income inequality is actually declining in Latin America even as it continues to increase in the United States.[36] Economically speaking, the richest nation on Earth is starting to resemble a banana republic. The main difference is that the United States is big enough to maintain geographic distance between the villa-dweller and the beggar. As Ralston Thorpe tells his St. Paul's classmate, the investment banker Sherman McCoy, in Tom Wolfe's 1987 novel *The Bonfire of the Vanities*: "You've got to insulate, insulate, insulate."

Why do Americans tolerate this troubling state of affairs? The biggest likely reason is our enduring belief in upward mobility. Economic inequality is less troubling if you live in a country where any child, no matter how humble his or her origins, can grow up to be president. This idea lies at the heart of the notion of American exceptionalism. It defines the American dream. But as we'll see in the next chapter, the United States no longer sets much of an example for the rest of the world in rags-to-riches opportunity. The American dream is less attainable than it once was. And it was never as attainable as many people wanted to believe.

2

Going Up

*Dick left the counting-room, hardly knowing whether he stood on
his head or his heels, so overjoyed was he at the sudden change in
his fortunes. Ten dollars a week was to him a fortune, and three
times as much as he had expected to obtain at first . . . It was
indeed a bright prospect for a boy who, only a year before, could
neither read nor write, and depended for a night's lodging upon the
chance hospitality of an alley-way or old wagon.*

—Horatio Alger Jr., *Ragged Dick*, 1868

UPWARD MOBILITY IS AMERICA'S CREED. Circumstances at the bottom
might be hard, but a plucky young bootblack with his eye on the main
chance can rise in the world through hard work. Americans believe this
more fervently than do citizens of other advanced industrial democracies. But the limited data we have show that we demonstrate it less than
most of those other countries do. The United States today is no longer,
by international standards, a land notably rich in opportunities to move
up the income ladder.

A survey of twenty-seven nations conducted from 1998 to 2001 asked
participants whether they agreed with the statement "People are rewarded
for intelligence and skill." The country with the highest proportion answering in the affirmative was the United States (69 percent), compared
to a median among all countries of about 40 percent. Similarly, more

than 60 percent of Americans agreed that "people get rewarded for their effort," compared to an international median of less than 40 percent. When participants were asked whether coming from a wealthy family was "essential" or "very important" to getting ahead, the percentage of American affirmatives was much lower than the international median: 19 percent versus 28 percent.[1]

The nonprofit Pew Charitable Trusts sponsored a U.S. poll on income mobility in March 2009, when the country was enduring the worst recession since the Great Depression. Thirty-nine percent of the respondents agreed with the statement that it was common for someone in the United States to start out poor and become rich. A poll taken six years before by the Gallup organization found that 31 percent of Americans expected to get rich themselves before they die, with "rich" defined by respondents (according to the median) as an income of $120,000 per year (roughly in the top 10 percent). Among those age eighteen to twenty-nine, 51 percent expected to get rich.[2]

Economic reality does not match these expectations. Only 6 percent of Americans born at the bottom of the heap (defined as the lowest fifth in income distribution, i.e., those whose family incomes go up to about $25,000) ever make it in adulthood to the top (defined as the highest fifth in income distribution, i.e., those whose family incomes are above $100,000).[3] The most striking finding about upward mobility in contemporary America concerns the relationship between who your parents are and how much money you can expect to make. Parentage is a greater determinant of a man's future earnings than it is of his height and weight.[4] Height and weight are influenced by the genes passed from parents to children. Future earnings are not. But you wouldn't know that from available data on economic mobility in the United States.

The extent to which people at different levels in a society change their economic circumstances is not easy to measure. Rather than use a single yardstick, economists and sociologists use two.

Absolute mobility is the simpler but less useful measurement. Let's say I earn $30,000 a year today. If, ten years from now, I earn, in today's dollars, the equivalent of $40,000, I will have achieved absolute upward mobility because I increased my income by one third. That's certainly better than not increasing my income at all or experiencing a drop in income. But my absolute upward mobility doesn't indicate whether I've improved my station in life, because it doesn't take into account what was happening during those ten years to everyone else.

To gauge that, we need to look at *relative mobility*. Let's say that while I was increasing my income by *one third*, everybody who made more money than me increased *their* incomes by *two thirds*. In that instance, my *absolute* upward mobility went *up* but my *relative* upward mobility went *down*, because my economic position *relative to everybody else* declined.

The trouble with absolute mobility, and even to some extent relative mobility, is that a significant number of people will move up or down the income scale not because of larger forces in the economy but because they are in a particular phase of life. When you begin your working life, you probably make less money than you can expect to later on. First you're in school, making little or no money. Then you take an entry-level job, making an entry-level wage. Simply acquire a paying job—any job— and you've achieved both absolute *and* relative upward mobility because before you had no income and now you have some. Later, as you acquire experience and skill, your boss may give you more responsibility and pay you more, or you may use that experience and skill to secure a higher-paying job somewhere else. You will thereby achieve upward absolute mobility and possibly (depending how much more you get paid) upward relative mobility, too. Eventually you will retire and live off Social Security and (if you're lucky) a pension. That probably means your income will go down, and you will experience downward mobility in absolute terms and possibly also in relative terms. Through all these ups and downs, the structure of the economy didn't necessarily change. *You* changed. Not every worker follows this life cycle, but enough do to limit the usefulness of data concerning either absolute or relative mobility.

One solution to this problem is to take a much longer view. How much did your father earn relative to his contemporaries? How much do you earn relative to yours? Compare these two calculations, either for comparable periods in your father's life and yours, or over the entire course of both lifetimes, and you have a measure of *intergenerational mobility*. This is the best way to measure mobility, not only because it takes a longer view but also because it reflects the way most people actually think about upward mobility. A Vietnamese immigrant working as a seamstress might hope to earn enough to send herself to law school. Much more likely, though, she'll hope to send her daughter to law school. We all want a better life, but what we most want—and can more plausibly aspire to through hard work—is a better life for our children. Immigrants are believed to achieve very brisk upward mobility, partly because merely coming to the United States demonstrates that they have initiative, and partly because immigrants usually start at the very bottom, where there's nowhere to go but up. Unfortunately, none of the analysis that follows compares the economic status of immigrants to that of their parents in their countries of origin, because very little such cross-country data are available. Since America is the world's wealthiest country, we can assume that nearly all immigrants earn considerably more in the United States than their parents were able to earn in their country of origin. That's typically why they come. Anecdotal evidence suggests, however, that immigrants' *relative* position in the United States is often *lower* than their parents' *relative* position in the country of origin.

According to Julia B. Isaacs of Washington's Brookings Institution, 67 percent of us have more income, after inflation, than our parents had (absolute mobility), and about a third of us end up more prosperous relative to our fellow Americans than our parents were (relative mobility).[5] You more likely than not will outearn your parents. And you've got a one in three shot at making more money compared to your contemporaries than your parents made compared to theirs. But the greater likelihood is that your relative position will be merely as good as, or possibly worse than, your parents'. Intergenerational upward relative mobility from one generation to the next certainly occurs in the United States. But it isn't the norm.

Most of what we know about long-term income-mobility trends in the United States during the previous half century comes from the University of Michigan's Panel Study of Income Dynamics, a longitudinal study of more than nine thousand families from across the continental United States begun in 1968. The PSID is the world's longest-running "panel survey" of nationally representative households. (A panel survey is a longitudinal study in which respondents are interviewed at regular intervals.) PSID participants are interviewed once a year, typically by phone; the response rate has been above 96 percent since 1969. Now old enough to include data on three or four generations, the survey covers a variety of topics of interest to scholars in the fields of health, psychology, and sociology, but its principal task is to collect data on income, wealth, consumption, employment, and other economic matters. It is especially useful for measuring intergenerational income mobility.[6]

What does the PSID reveal about the trend in intergenerational mobility since 1968? It depends on whom you ask, but Isabel Sawhill, an economist at the Brookings Institution, sees a rough consensus that mobility
either leveled off or declined somewhat. "Personally," she told me in an
interview, "I believe that it has slipped."[7]

In a 2006 paper Chul-In Lee and Gary Solon, economists at Konkuk
University in Seoul, South Korea, and the University of Michigan, respectively, looked at PSID income data for men and women born between
1952 and 1975. Rather than compare children's incomes to those of their
parents, they looked at incomes for this entire cohort starting at the age
of twenty-five. Since that gave them a group whose ages varied from
twenty-five to forty-eight (their data only went up through 2000), they
calculated a way to control the income numbers according to where in
his or her life cycle any particular person happened to be. Their conclusion: "Intergenerational income mobility in the United States has not
changed dramatically over the last two decades."[8]

But in a 2009 paper, Katharine Bradbury and Jane Katz of the Federal
Reserve of Boston looked at PSID income data from 1967 to 2004 and
concluded that "by most measures" mobility was lower in the 1990s and
early 2000s than it had been during the 1970s. These declines were
small, they conceded, but "the fact that so many different measures all
move down suggests that a decline, not just leveling, did occur." Bradbury and Katz found the most pronounced decline in mobility among
those starting near the bottom of the income scale. The percentage of
families who were able to move out of the bottom 10 percent, they found,
was 51 percent between 1968 and 1978. That dropped to 46 percent between 1993 and 2003.[9]

The PSID data, then, provide a somewhat muddy picture as to whether
economic mobility stayed the same in recent decades or declined somewhat. But the PSID's snapshot was absolutely clear in another respect: It
enabled scholars to discover that they had previously underestimated, to
a significant degree, the extent to which, in the words of Gary Solon,
"income status is transmitted from one generation to the next." We may
be roughly as mobile a society as we used to be, give or take, but we aren't
nearly so mobile a society as we once thought we were.

A 1992 paper by Solon,[10] derived from the PSID numbers, changed
the economics profession's view of an index that economists call "intergenerational income elasticity" but that I'll call "income heritability." (I

don't mean heritability in the biological sense, of course; the phenomenon I'm describing merely apes biological heredity.) If your parents' income bore *no* probabilistic relation to your income, which is to say that you were just as likely to earn as much or as little as anybody born into a different family, then your income status heritability would be zero percent. If your parents' income were *entirely* determinative of your income, which is to say that no matter how much of a genius or screw-up you were you were nonetheless destined to earn a fixed amount based entirely on how much your parents earned, then your income heritability would be 100 percent. Real life exists between those two poles. Your parents' income will likely have at least *some* influence on your income because that income is partly the result of various tangible and intangible personal characteristics that you share with them through nature or nurture. But the more your parents' income varies from the average (either higher or lower), the less likely it is that yours will vary to the same degree, because of the phenomenon that statisticians call "regression to the mean." Nature abhors an outlier. Income heritability is, broadly speaking, a measure of how much you're likely to regress from your parents' relative income toward the average income of all Americans.

Previously, studies had shown income heritability to be less than 20 percent, which didn't seem too bad. Eighty percent of your economic destiny was in your hands (or at least out of your parents' hands). Perhaps you're familiar with the following lines from William Ernest Henley's "Invictus," an oft-quoted inspirational poem from the nineteenth century: "I am the master of my fate:/I am the captain of my soul." Before 1992 it was possible for Americans to believe, with respect to income, a relatively minor variation: *I am the master of 80 percent of my fate/I am the captain of 80 percent of my soul.* Or as the University of Chicago economist Gary S. Becker, a Nobel laureate, put it in a 1988 speech to the American Economic Association, "In every country with data that I have seen . . . low earnings as well as high earnings are not strongly transmitted from fathers to sons."[11]

Trouble was, Solon pointed out in his 1992 paper, the relatively sparse estimates that Becker and others were relying on to judge income heritability in the United States were "based on error-ridden data, unrepresentative samples, or both." When Solon recalculated based on PSID data, he found income heritability to be at least 40 percent "and possibly higher." *I am the master of 60 percent of my fate.*

Or possibly: *I am the master of 40–50 percent of my fate.* In 2001 Bhashkar Mazumder, an economist with the Federal Reserve Bank of Chicago, recalculated income heritability matching census data to Social Security data, which allowed him to compare parent-child incomes over a greater number of years. He found that income heritability was more like 50 to 60 percent. Mazumder later recalculated Solon's PSID-based findings applying a more elaborate statistical weighting procedure than Solon had used and found that income heritability was about 60 percent. Then, in a 2004 study, Mazumder approached the question from a different angle, examining the correlation in incomes among siblings, using longitudinal survey data collected by the U.S. Bureau of Labor Statistics. That put income heritability at about 50 percent. "The sibling correlation in economic outcomes and human capital are larger than the sibling correlation in a variety of other outcomes including some measures of physical attributes," Mazumder wrote. He found the notional heritability of income to approximate the literal heritability of height. Most strikingly, Mazumder found that income among brothers actually correlated more closely than height and weight. *I am less the master of my fate than I am of my body mass index.*[12]

It's important to remember that the mobility trend for Americans as a whole is not necessarily a trend for every subgroup in America. Upward mobility for women has accelerated in recent decades. The trend doesn't show up in intergenerational family income data because it's a lot easier for a contemporary woman to outearn her mother, who lived at a time when society provided far fewer economic opportunities to women, than it is for her to outearn her father, who faced no gender barriers at all. Upward mobility for African Americans has lagged behind upward mobility for whites. One especially disturbing 2008 analysis by the Brookings Institution's Isaacs compared PSID income data from parents in the late 1960s with PSID income data from their children in the late 1990s. Isaacs found that the *majority* of black children born into the middle fifth of family incomes—dead center of the middle class, where incomes (in 2006 dollars) range from $48,800 to $65,100—ended up with lower incomes than their parents had, corrected for inflation. Fully 45 percent fell all the way to the bottom income fifth (below $33,800). By comparison only one third of whites born into the middle income fifth ended up with incomes equal to or below that of their parents, and only 16 percent tumbled all the way down to the bottom income fifth. Where these white children's parents mostly saw their children become better off economically than they had been, these black children's parents mostly saw their children become worse off. This was not the future Martin Luther King Jr. had in mind in 1963 when he stood on the steps of the Lincoln Memorial and shared his dream of racial equality.[13]

To summarize the society-wide trend: Upward mobility in the United States is not as brisk as economists once believed it was. There's some evidence that it has slowed since the 1970s. Certainly it hasn't accelerated. Now let's look at how the United States stacks up against traditionally class-bound nations of western Europe—what we once called the Old World.

Short answer: very poorly. A 2007 study by the Organisation for Economic Co-operation and Development combined a number of previous estimates and found income heritability to be greater (and economic mobility therefore lower) in the United States than in Demark, Australia, Norway, Finland, Canada, Sweden, Germany, Spain, and France. Italy was a little bit less mobile than the United States, and the United Kingdom brought up the rear. This ranking was based on a somewhat conservative U.S. estimate of 47 percent income heritability;[14] Mazumder of the Chicago Fed, we've just seen, puts it at 50 to 60 percent, which would rank the United States either tied with the United Kingdom for last place or dead last *after* the United Kingdom. *Almost (arguably every) comparably developed nation for which we have data offers greater income mobility than the United States.* A common American criticism of the "socialist" countries of western and particularly northern Europe is that by providing guaranteed health care and a social safety net for the poor and unemployed that is more comprehensive than the one in the United States, these nations diminish their economies' ability to create economic opportunity. That argument is refuted by the evidence presented here that western and northern European countries provide, in fact, *greater* opportunity than the United States to move up the economic ladder.

It's especially surprising that Canada should experience more intergenerational economic mobility than the United States. The two countries are, after all, similar in more ways than one can count. The most significant way they differ (at least for the purposes of this discussion) is that the United States is richer, with a per capita gross domestic product

Income Heritability by Country

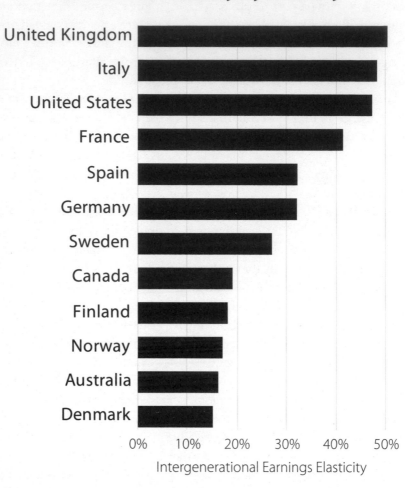

Intergenerational Earnings Elasticity

Source: Anna Cristina D'Addio, "Intergenerational Transmission of Disadvantage: Mobility or Immobility Across Generations? A Review of the Evidence for OECD Countries," Social, Employment, and Migration Working Paper 52 (Paris: OECD, 2007), 33.

that's 20 percent higher. Most migration between the two is from Canada to the United States, not the other way around. How can *Canada* be the land of greater opportunity for lowborn strivers?

Miles Corak, an economist at the University of Ottawa, examined this puzzle in a 2010 paper. Canada's lesser income heritability is no statistical quirk. Examining several existing mobility studies using "particularly high-quality data," Corak found that Canada is "up to *three times* more mobile than the United States [italics mine]." The difference arises from disparities at the top and bottom of the income scale. If a father is in the bottom tenth of U.S. incomes (less than about $12,000 today), Corak found, his son has a 22 percent likelihood of ending up in the bottom tenth. If a father is in Canada's bottom income tenth, his son's likelihood of ending up in the bottom tenth is 16 percent. At the other end of the income scale, if a father is in the top tenth of U.S. incomes (more than $133,000 today), his son has a 26 percent chance of ending up in the top tenth. If a father is in Canada's top income tenth, his son's likelihood of ending up in the top tenth is 18 percent.[15]

Corak, whose Canada paper was sponsored by the Pew Charitable Trusts' Economic Mobility Project, looked at the Pew poll cited at the beginning of this chapter and found that even though Canada was demonstrably more economically mobile than the United States, you were less likely to *believe* that the likelihood of your financial success depended on your parents' income if you lived in the United States (42 percent) than if you lived in Canada (57 percent).[16]

Why do Americans overestimate the extent to which their society fosters upward mobility? As we've seen, *even economists* exaggerated American upward mobility until Solon set them straight two decades ago. Clearly the United States lags the other industrialized democracies in offering opportunities for upward mobility. Why do Americans resist knowing that?

Partly because an everyday egalitarianism is embedded in the very language we speak. Henry Fairlie was a young political journalist in England when he coined, in 1955, the term "the Establishment" to describe the matrix of political, cultural, business, and other leaders who controlled England through the informal, and largely unconscious, exercise of social power.[17] A decade later Fairlie emigrated to the United States. Remembering his arrival in a 1983 essay for the *New Republic* titled "Why I Love America," Fairlie reminisced about the jolt he initially experienced whenever Americans greeted him.

> One spring day, shortly after my arrival in America, I was walking down the long, broad street of a suburb . . . The only other person on the street was a small boy on a tricycle. As I passed him, he said, "Hi!"—just like

that. No four-year-old boy had ever addressed me without an introduction before. Yet here was this one, with his cheerful "Hi!" Recovering
from the culture shock, I tried to look down stonily at his flaxen head,
but instead, involuntarily, I found myself saying in return: "Well—hi!"
He pedaled off, apparently satisfied. He had begun my Americanization.

Fairlie came from a country, he wrote, where you could tell a person's
social class by whether he greeted you with "Hallo!" or "Hello!" or "Hullo,"
or indeed whether he greeted you at all. But in America,

> anyone can say "Hi!" Anyone does. Shortly after my encounter with
> the boy, I called on the then Suffragan Bishop of Washington. Did he
> greet me as the Archbishop of Canterbury would have done? No. He
> said, "Hi, Henry!" I put it down to an aberration, an excess of Episco-
> palian latitudinarianism. But what about my first meeting with Lyn-
> don B. Johnson, the President of the United States, the Emperor of
> the Free World, before whom, like a Burgher of Calais, a halter round
> my neck, I would have sunk to my knees, pleading for a loan for my
> country? He held out the largest hand in Christendom, and said, "Hi,
> Henry!"

What Fairlie describes is a society that demonstrates in a thousand
informal ways its distaste for class divisions. But to dislike such divisions is not the same thing as to abolish them.

Another reason why Americans resist knowing that income mobility
in the United States is unexceptional is the enduring influence of two
American writers. Neither author is much read anymore, but one of them
remains a household name, while the other coined a phrase whose fame
long outlived his own. The two writers formed their views about opportunity during the American industrial revolution of the late nineteenth and
early twentieth centuries, when unprecedented income inequality could
plausibly be called the price our society paid for unprecedented upward
mobility. They were two sides of the same coin. Many Americans want to
believe that's still true, but it isn't.

The writers were Horatio Alger Jr. and James Truslow Adams. Alger
wrote *Ragged Dick* (1868), *Luck and Pluck* (1869), and other dime novels
for boys about getting ahead through virtue and hard work. To call these
books popular would be an understatement: fully 5 percent of all the

books checked out of the Muncie, Indiana, public library between November 1891 and December 1902 were authored by Alger. Adams was a more cerebral fellow who wrote books of American history, one of which (*The Epic of America*, 1931) introduced the phrase "the American dream" to our national discourse. Writing at the start of the Great Depression, Adams envisioned not "a dream of motor cars and high wages merely," but rather "a dream of a social order in which each man and each woman shall be able to attain to the fullest stature of which they are innately capable, and be recognized by others for what they are, regardless of the fortuitous circumstances of birth or position."

Born a half century apart, neither Alger nor Adams could claim to have risen from the bottom. Both were born into well-established families whose American roots dated to the early seventeenth century. Alger could trace his lineage to three Pilgrims who in 1621 sailed to Plymouth Plantation on the *Fortune*, the second English ship to arrive there.[18] Adams—no relation to the presidential Adamses—was descended from a man who arrived in Maryland in 1638 as an indentured servant and within three years possessed 185 acres.[19] Alger's father was a Unitarian minister, Adams's a stockbroker. Both fathers were men of good breeding and education who struggled to make ends meet but were able—at a time when well over 90 percent of the population didn't finish high school—to obtain higher education for their sons. Alger went to Harvard, and Adams went to Brooklyn Polytechnic and, briefly, Yale. Both sons initially followed their fathers into the ministry and finance, respectively, before becoming full-time writers.

Each author became, in his own way, highly successful, but the upward trajectory of these two literary careers would make poor material for a Horatio Alger tale. The circumstances of Alger's job change are especially problematic. At thirty-four he vacated the pulpit abruptly when he was charged with "the abominable and revolting crime of unnatural familiarity with Boys." Alger did not dispute the accusation, which was based on the testimony of two teenage boys in his parish, ages thirteen and fifteen, who said Alger had molested them, and on rumors that he'd abused other youths in similar fashion. After confessing his guilt privately to William James, the founding father of American psychology, Alger never spoke of it again.[20] Adams left Wall Street under less lurid circumstances. He simply disliked the work and resolved to stop once he amassed $100,000. Reviewing his accounts on his thirty-fifth birthday,

he concluded he'd achieved his goal—the equivalent of about $2 million
in current dollars—and resigned the following day.[21] Adams spent much
of his subsequent life abroad and wrote *The Epic of America* in London.

Alger and Adams celebrated America's unprecedented capacity for
upward mobility, but neither writer idealized his country to anything
like the extent that would later be credited to the name Horatio Alger
and the phrase "the American dream." Alger worked into his later juvenile fiction much moralizing against the robber barons' self-dealing and
cruel treatment of the downtrodden. "He has done more harm than he
can ever repair," a character in Alger's 1889 novel, *Luke Walton*, laments
about a villain modeled on the Gilded Age stock manipulator Jay Gould.[22]
Adams deplored America's tendency to celebrate "business and money-
making and material improvement as good in themselves" and its refusal
"to look on the seamy and sordid realities of any situation in which we
found ourselves." He complained that Americans were inclined "to think
manners undemocratic, and a cultivated mind a hindrance to success, a
sign of inefficient effeminacy." Many aspects of commercial culture ap-
palled Adams. "The use of our most beautiful scenery for the advertising
of products," he wrote, was a "symptom of "our slipping down from
civilized standards of life." Adams even complained about America's
maldistribution of wealth.[23]

But neither writer had much taste for radical politics. Alger was essentially a mugwump—a good-government Republican distrustful of machine politics and Free Silver populism. Adams was a Tory-minded political
independent who became a severe critic of President Franklin Roosevelt's New Deal, which he deemed financially irresponsible. When Roosevelt and Congress compelled the railroads to set aside funds for
pensions, Adams fumed (in a private letter) that the president was out
to "punish . . . the honest stockholder and investor." For Adams, the
American dream was not about altering economic outcomes but about
providing economic opportunities, a distinction that was "difficult . . . for
the European upper classes to interpret adequately." It wasn't woven into
their history.[24]

It's impossible to understand Adams's and Alger's vision of America
as the land of opportunity without considering how different the country of their youth was from the one we know today. Joseph P. Ferrie, a
professor of economics at Northwestern, has scrutinized census records
for information about fathers and sons between 1850 (the year Alger

turned eighteen) and 1920 (twenty-one years after Alger's death and the year Adams turned forty-two; Adams would coin "the American dream" eleven years later).[25] Since income data are unavailable, Ferrie looked instead at occupational data from the U.S. census, dividing all jobs into four categories: white-collar worker, farmer, skilled or semiskilled worker, and unskilled worker. Ferrie then compared father-son data from the nineteenth and early twentieth centuries to some comparable father-son data covering the second half of the twentieth century. The twentieth-century data came from the U.S. Bureau of Labor Statistics. To keep both data sets consistent, Ferrie limited his inquiry to white, native-born males.[26]

Ferrie figured that if your father was a farmer and you were a white-collar worker, you were doing better than your dad. That wasn't always the case back in the late nineteenth and early twentieth centuries (farmers sometimes made pretty good money), but in most instances it was. He also made some technical adjustments to allow for the different occupational structures of the two eras. He found that the equivalent of 41 percent of farmers' sons advanced to white-collar jobs between 1880 and 1900, compared to 32 percent between 1950 and 1973. Between horse-and-buggy days and the interstate-highway era, American society had become significantly less mobile. Ferrie's conclusion held up when he looked at all four job categories, and when he compared other stretches of the late nineteenth century to other stretches of the late twentieth.

These findings are striking because the 1950s and 1960s were a period—the last period, it turned out—of rising intergenerational mobility in the United States.[27] The postwar economy was booming, and men born during the Great Depression and World War II were enjoying opportunities that their fathers could scarcely imagine. Even so, their rise in fortune was not as great as that enjoyed by the generations of workers who lived during Horatio Alger's lifetime and James T. Adams's youth and early manhood. That was, of course, an era when America was industrializing and urbanizing at breakneck speed. During that time, the loftiest rhetoric about the land of opportunity—rhetoric that shapes American opinion still—struck closer to the truth than it has since.

Adams wrote in *The Epic of America* that the dream of living "unhampered by the barriers which had slowly been erected in older civilizations" was "realized more fully in actual life [in the United States] than anywhere else." Was that a fantasy? Probably not in Adams's lifetime. It certainly aligns with what Northwestern's Ferrie and Jason Long, an associate professor of economics at Colby College, found when they compared mobility during the late nineteenth century in the United States and Great Britain. Although England was still the richest industrial country in the world, the United States offered considerably more opportunity. In Britain, for example, 51 percent of the sons of unskilled laborers moved up to skilled and semiskilled labor or better. In the United States fully 81 percent did. Such findings confirmed Alexis de Tocqueville's observation while touring America in the 1830s that whereas in the "aristocratic nations" of Europe "families remain for centuries in the same condition," in "democratic nations" like the United States "new families are constantly springing up, others are constantly falling away, and all that remain change their condition." Long and Ferrie noted Karl Marx's observation in 1865 that it would be difficult for class consciousness to develop in America because "the position of wage laborer is for a very large part of the American people but a probational state, which they are sure to leave within a longer or shorter term." But by the late twentieth century, Tocqueville's admiration and Marx's resignation were no longer justified. U.S. and British data pairing fathers' occupations in the 1950s to sons' occupations in the early 1970s showed that the levels of intergenerational mobility in the United States and Britain had become virtually indistinguishable.[28]

One legacy of Alger and Adams is that Americans today are a bit hazy about the difference between how much upward mobility is possible and how much is likely. Barack Obama's presidency demonstrates that a black man, raised by a mother with meager financial means, can grow up to be president. When one reviews Obama's life story, his trajectory doesn't seem all that remarkable because (regardless of what you may think about his performance in office) Obama is and for a long time has been a remarkable man. But how many other black children growing up in financially stressed households can rationally aspire to the same fate? How many *white* children growing up in *prosperous* households can rationally aspire to the same fate? How many children, black or white, can match both Obama's talents and Obama's luck? (Luck is another notable factor that put Obama in the White House, to at least the same extent as it did for his forty-three predecessors.)

Perhaps there is a benefit to lacking a realistic understanding about your odds of improving your relative position in society. Excessive optimism is, James Fallows argues in his 1989 book *More Like Us: Making America Great Again*, a major driver of the U.S. economy. Paraphrasing the Harvard psychologist David McClelland's 1961 book *The Achieving Society*, Fallows writes that a society in which "people routinely overestimated their chances for success," in which entrepreneurs "launched ventures that by rational standards were likely to fail," was a society that, collectively and over the long term, would invent more, innovate more, and succeed more. The positive cast Fallows puts to this mindset—one that connects McClelland's thinking to Adams's American dream—is that McClelland described a society in which people did not know their place.

A more jaundiced view of Americans' obdurate, "Invictus"-type belief that we are all masters of our fate is expressed in Barbara Ehrenreich's 2009 book *Bright-Sided: How Positive Thinking Is Undermining America*. What if you *don't* achieve your most unrealistic goals, as most of us won't? "Always," Ehrenreich writes, "in a hissed undertone, there is the darker message that if you don't have all that you want, if you feel sick, discouraged, or defeated, you have only yourself to blame." The American reluctance to regard disappointing outcomes as anything other than failed personal agency, Ehrenreich argues, is not only painful to the spirit; it is also an obstacle to constructive forms of collective action such as forming a labor union or organizing a political movement.

I won't attempt to resolve the conflict between Fallows's view and Ehrenreich's; they both capture an important truth. My interest is in a particular consequence of Americans' overconfidence in upward mobility. It has become the rationale for indifference toward income inequality—a rationale built on a demonstrably false premise. Now that we've seen that America doesn't provide opportunity to anything like the extent that Alger and Adams believed (or what Americans have come to believe they believed), let's turn our attention back to the Great Divergence and start to consider what might be driving American incomes apart.

3

Usual Suspects

MOST DISCUSSION ABOUT INEQUALITY in the United States focuses on race or gender. Our society has a conspicuous history of treating blacks differently from whites and women differently from men. Black/white and male/female inequalities in income persist to this day. The median annual income for black households ($32,068) is 38 percent lower than for white households ($51,846). The median annual income for women working full-time ($36,931) is 23 percent lower than for men working full-time ($47,715).[1]

Much disagreement exists over the extent to which these imbalances result from lingering racism and sexism; from more complex matters of sociology and biology; or from some combination of these and perhaps other factors. But we need not delve into that anguished and heated debate, because the Great Divergence can't be blamed on either race or gender. To contribute to the growth in income inequality over the past three decades, the income gaps between blacks and whites and between women and men would have to have grown. But they didn't.

The black/white gap in median family income remained essentially the same. It's a mere four percentage points smaller today than it was in 1980.[2] This lack of progress is, to say the least, dismaying. Back in 1980 most of us expected (or at least hoped) that the next three decades would narrow significantly the very large income gulf between whites and blacks. "That the black middle class will continue to grow is beyond dispute," *Time* magazine declared boldly in a 1974 cover story. It *did* grow after 1974, but at a much slower rate than before, and the growth was disproportionately at the lower end. One complicating factor was that at the very moment blacks were entering it, the middle class was starting to shrink. (More about that in chapter 5.)

The failure of the white/black income gap to diminish during the past thirty years indicates that something in American society went terribly wrong (or *stayed* terribly wrong). Yet the persistent disparity between white and black incomes can't be a contributing factor to the Great Divergence if that disparity didn't *grow* after 1979. And even if it had grown, there would be a limit to how much impact it could have on the national trend, because African Americans constitute only 13 percent of the U.S. population. Persistent black/white income inequality is an important story, but it's a different story from the one this book will relate.

Women constitute half the U.S. population, and any trend affecting them will have a major impact on the country as a whole. But the unequal treatment of women can't be causing the Great Divergence because during the past three decades the male/female wage gap shrank by nearly half. In 1980 the median annual income for women working full-time was not 23 percent less than men's, as it is today, but 40 percent less.[3] Most of these gains occurred in the 1980s and early 1990s, but there's every reason to believe the male/female income gap will continue to narrow in the future, because in the United States women are becoming better educated than men.[4]

The feminization of higher education is one of the more striking sociological trends of recent decades. Starting in the early 1980s, female undergraduates began to outnumber male undergraduates at colleges and universities. The female-to-male ratio is currently 57 percent to 43 percent. Starting in 2009, the majority of doctoral degrees awarded in the United States went to women. The female-to-male graduate-student ratio is now 59 percent to 41 percent.[5] These numbers may puzzle some, but anyone familiar with girls' long-standing superior performance in elementary, middle, and high school will likelier wonder what took women so long to achieve dominance at the college and grad-school levels. Girls, according to the Berkeley sociologist Claude Fischer, do better in school because, on average, they are better at "self-control, paying attention, not getting into trouble, eagerness to learn, and so on."[6]

Every biennial survey of the National Assessment of Educational Progress, which measures educational achievement for fourth, eighth, and twelfth graders, has observed girls outperforming boys in reading—the single most essential educational skill—going back to when the NAEP first started collecting national data in 1969.[7] A 2006 study by the Harvard economists Claudia Goldin and Lawrence Katz and Ilyana Kuziemko (then a Harvard graduate student, now an assistant professor of economics at Princeton) found that as far back as 1957, when there were about 50 percent more male undergrads than female ones, the high school rank of the median girl in the state of Wisconsin was about 21 percent higher than the high school rank of the median boy. There's no reason to think that girls in Wisconsin were notably smarter relative to boys than girls in the rest of the country, and indeed comparable national data for 1972 and 1992 put girls' advantage in high school rank in the same ballpark (17 and 16 percent). In addition, girls have had higher high school graduation rates going back to the early twentieth century.[8]

If girls had long outperformed boys in high school as far back as the 1950s, why were they so much less likely than boys to go to college? Do you really have to ask? Societal expectations about realizing girls' academic and occupational potential were dismally low in the 1950s. "Women are not expected to grow up to find out who they are, to choose their human identity," Betty Friedan wrote in her 1963 book *The Feminine Mystique*. "Anatomy is woman's destiny." Friedan's book and the feminist movement that gradually came into being—with a strong assist by the Food and Drug Administration's 1960 approval of the first birth-control pill—altered that destiny.

Although growing percentages of women (even married women) joined the workforce throughout the twentieth century, as recently as 1970 most women still didn't work; their participation in the civilian labor force was 43 percent. By 1980 that rate had risen to 52 percent, and since 1990 it's hovered around 60 percent.[9] Harvard's Goldin observed a particularly dramatic change in women's attitudes toward work around 1970, partly in reaction against the previous generation's experience. Women born during the Great Depression "anticipated brief and intermittent employment in various jobs, not generally in a career." That turned out to be a miscalculation. These women ended up working much more than they expected to, yet they didn't advance much. They had jobs but not careers.

It was different for the baby-boom generation that succeeded them. These young women, Goldin found, "more accurately anticipated their future work lives" and therefore took greater care to "plan for careers rather than jobs" by acquiring the necessary skills. Goldin called women's collective decision to prepare for and then embark on career paths that were previously limited, in large part, to men a "quiet revolution." Its effects began to be felt in the late 1970s, and it was "quiet" because growth in the percentage of married women who worked was actually slower than it had been during the 1930s, 1940s, and the Friedan-lamented 1950s. Broad numerical measurements didn't capture the quiet revolution because it wasn't about whether women should work. It was about what sort of work women should perform, and about finding ways to make it happen. Getting more women into college was an essential first step. So where previously, for instance, girls had been more reluctant than boys to take high school math and science classes, by 1992 girls were taking about as much math and science as boys were (while simultaneously taking more foreign languages than boys). A historic math-science skills gap favoring boys over girls dwindled.[10] The removal of this academic barrier helped boost women's college attendance and their likelihood of staying in college long enough to get a degree. Eventually the male undergrad majority gave way to a (smaller) female undergrad majority.[11]

African Americans have not contributed to the Great Divergence, but they've certainly experienced it. The black middle class (which starts out less prosperous than its white counterpart) has fallen behind just as the white middle class has. With women, it's a bit different. Women have not contributed to the Great Divergence, and they have also, by some significant measures, avoided its effects. This is illustrated on the next page by a bar graph by David Autor, an MIT labor economist.

During the past three decades, women outperformed men in the workforce at all skill levels. Both men and women (in the aggregate) moved out of moderately skilled jobs (secretary, retail sales representative, steelworker, etc.)—women more rapidly than men. But women were much more likely than men to shift upward into higher-skilled jobs—from information technology engineer and personnel manager on up through various high-paying professions that require graduate degrees (doctor, lawyer, etc.).[12]

These findings reflect feminism's victories in the workplace, but they also reflect something else: diminishing job opportunities for working-class males. The journalist Hanna Rosin, writing in the *Atlantic* in 2010, observed that three quarters of the jobs lost during the 2007–09

Changes in occupational employment shares by education and sex, 1979–2007

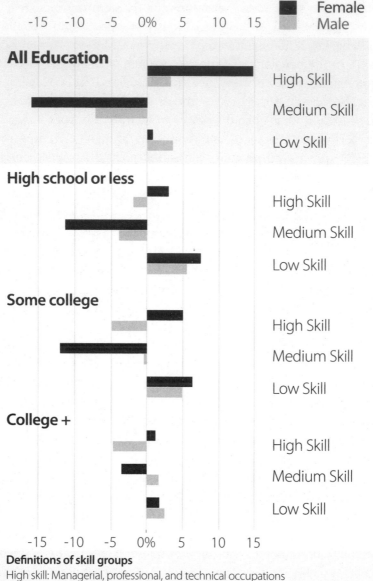

Definitions of skill groups
High skill: Managerial, professional, and technical occupations
Medium skill: Sales, office/admin, production, and operators
Low skill: Protective service, food prep, janitorial/cleaning, personal care/services

Source: David Autor, "The Polarization of Job Opportunities in the U.S. Labor Market: Implications for Employment and Earnings" (Washington, Center for American Progress, April 2010), 10. Autor's source was data from the Census Bureau's Current Population Survey.

recession had been held by men. "The worst-hit industries," she wrote, "were overwhelmingly male and deeply identified with macho: construction, manufacturing, high finance." Picking through this wreckage, Rosin wondered, "What if the modern, postindustrial economy is simply more congenial to women than to men?"[13]

That might seem counterintuitive at a time when the top of the economic heap is overwhelmingly male. Every year *Forbes* magazine compiles a list of the four hundred richest Americans. In 2010 only forty-two of these four hundred (all of them worth at least $1 billion) were women, and thirty-eight of the forty-two got rich by inheriting money from their fathers or their husbands. But most of us don't live at the top of the heap. Between 1979 and 2009 the median income for males working full-time rose, after inflation, a mere 2 percent. For women the comparable figure was 22 percent. The median male income was still well above the median female income. But women were closing the gap, partly because their incomes were rising and partly because men's incomes weren't. Indeed, compared to 1973, when middle incomes first began to stagnate, the male median income has *declined* somewhat. (The Great Divergence didn't commence until 1979 because for much of the 1970s upper incomes were stagnating, too.)

The culture began to wonder whether men had any use at all. "We're finished," Gaz, a laid-off steelworker, tells his friend in the popular 1997 film *The Full Monty*. "A few years and men won't exist, except in a zoo or something. We're not needed no more, are we? Obsolete. Dinosaurs. Yesterday's news." Desperate for work, Gaz joins forces with five other out-of-work men to mount a strip show. Weirdly, the film was a comedy. In 2000, when it was adapted into a hit Broadway musical, the setting was effortlessly transferred from Sheffield, England, to Buffalo, New York. Men's economic decline is a worldwide phenomenon.

One way women have *not* avoided the Great Divergence's effects is by creating families with men. The fact that women's median income remains, after historic gains, 23 percent lower than men's means the economic fortunes of families typically remain disproportionately dependent on what dads earn, even when the moms work, too. (And the moms typically *do* work; since the early 1990s, the labor participation rate of married women in their thirties has exceeded 70 percent among high school graduates.)[14] Between 1979 and 2010, real median family income increased by about 10 percent, with most of that increase occurring during

the tech boom of the late 1990s. By comparison, during the prior thirty-
year period, between 1949 and 1979, real median family income doubled.[15] Another way of putting it is that the typical family's income has
increased during the Great Divergence at one tenth the speed it did
during the Great Compression.

In practical terms, typical family incomes may actually have dwindled.
Bob Davis and David Wessel of the *Wall Street Journal* calculated the
number of hours the average person had to work to buy various items in
1973, when the median family income halted its upward climb, compared
to 1996, when it started to creep up again.[16] They found that many things
(a one-pound chicken breast; a movie ticket; a Zenith nineteen-inch color
TV; a five-minute phone call from Dallas to Seattle) required fewer person-
hours to acquire in 1996. Where once, for instance, the purchase of an
American Airlines round-trip ticket from New York to Los Angeles had
required the average person to work 9.6 days, by 1996 the average person
had to work only 3.9 days. But the really big things all required more
person-hours. An obstetrician's childbirth fee cost the average person 15
days' labor in 1996, compared to 8.6 days in 1973. A year's tuition at
Brown cost 8.5 months, compared to 4.3 months. The average price of a car
(including financing) cost 9.5 months, compared to 6.2 months. And the
median price of a house in Des Moines cost 3.2 years compared to 2.3
years.[17]

In 2003 Elizabeth Warren, the Harvard law professor appointed by
President Barack Obama to set up the Consumer Financial Protection
Bureau (and subsequently a U.S. Senate candidate in Massachusetts),
made a similar calculation. Appliances, food, and clothing were all cheaper,
she found, and families were spending close to five hundred dollars more
on the various electronic amenities that had been largely unavailable in the
early 1970s—cable TV, computers, et cetera. But when you factored in
mortgage payments, car payments, taxes, health insurance, and day-care
bills, Warren calculated that "today's dual-income families have *less* discre-
tionary income—and less money to put away for a rainy day—than the
single-income family of a generation ago."[18]

In their 1998 book, *Prosperity*, Davis and Wessel examined the lives
of two families a generation apart in age, the Kerleys and the Blentlingers,
to shed some light on how middle-class life had changed since 1973.
Both families were from Chattanooga, Tennessee, and both occupied
"the middle of the middle class." The Kerley family lived on one income,

that of Dennis Kerley, a high school graduate who as a young man in the early 1970s worked while his wife, Ann, stayed home to raise their three kids. The Blentlingers lived on two incomes, those of Jim Blentlinger and his wife, Ann-Marie, college graduates who entered the workforce in the early 1990s. By the end of that decade they had two kids. When the Kerleys, in 1973, looked back on their parents' lives and their own childhoods, they considered themselves better off. But when Wessel, in the late 1990s, asked Ann-Marie Blentlinger's father, Herb Hooper, to predict Ann Marie and Jim's future, he answered, "They'll have to work as hard as [my wife] and I have worked, but they won't have the income to show for it."

Back in 1973, Dennis Kerley, twenty-five, was a factory worker in a Du-Pont textile plant. The job was dull, but the pay was good enough to earn him close to the median for married couples. Although the plant had been a nonunion shop for fifteen years, the company still kept wages reasonably high, in part to counter the threat of new organizing drives. When DuPont laid Dennis off for ten months he never bothered to look for other work because he felt certain he'd eventually get rehired, which he was. The Kerleys kept a weekly budget and economized where necessary (drinking iced tea, for instance, because it was cheaper than Coke, and hanging the wash on a clothesline rather than purchasing a dryer). But during his childhood in the 1950s Dennis had experienced much harsher privation, sometimes living in a home without hot running water. During her childhood, Ann had slept two or three to a bed. The Kerleys' kids never endured anything like that level of hardship. In their rented house they had a double-door refrigerator, a hi-fi, and a twenty-one-inch color TV. In 1976 they bought their own three-bedroom house.

Twenty-three years later, the Blentlingers lived somewhat better than the Kerleys had at the same stage in their lives, but only because both Blentlingers worked. (They also "rel[ied] on easy credit far more than the Kerleys did in the early 1970s," Davis and Wessel noted, and at one point ran up a $2,000 Visa debt.) Neither of the Blentlingers earned as much as Dennis Kerley had (adjusted for inflation) in the mid-1970s. Jim Blentlinger, who at twenty-nine had acquired an associate's degree in computer-aided design and mechanical engineering, began his career designing restaurant layouts for a small restaurant-supply business. But that company went bust a year after he arrived. Next Jim was a stock clerk and then salesman at an office-supply firm. He quit that job

nine months later to take a better-paying computer-aided design job
with an air-conditioning manufacturer. But the office was a long com-
mute from home, so after not quite ten months he took a better-paying
job closer in with an engineering company. Ann-Marie Blentlinger
wanted to quit her job as a seventh-grade teacher so she could stay home
with their young kids and save three hundred dollars a month in day care.
She thought maybe she could work at home to make up some of the difference in income. But in the end the family couldn't swing that financially. The Blentlingers bought their first house in 1995; like the house
the Kerleys bought in 1976, it had three bedrooms. Unlike the Kerleys,
the Blentlingers needed some parental help to make the purchase. Ann-
Marie's parents contributed four thousand dollars toward the down
payment.

In the summer of 2011 I checked in on the Blentlingers to see how
the twenty-first century was treating them. The good news was that they
had graduated from "the middle of the middle class." They now pulled
down a combined income that put them in the highest fifth (or "quintile") of all American households, and higher, too, than the median for
families with two incomes. In 2004 they moved into a larger, newly built
house closer to Ann-Marie's parents. Their older son, Matthew, graduated from high school in the spring of 2011 and enrolled at his mother's
alma mater, the University of Tennessee, Knoxville. Merit scholarships
from the state and from a retirement community Matthew had worked
for, combined with a tuition break granted to children of public school
teachers, meant Matthew could enter his first year of college without
taking out a student loan. Ann-Marie now had a master's degree in education, which boosted her income, and was teaching sixth graders at a
different school. Jim got himself certified by Microsoft as a computer
systems engineer and, after a brief spell working for the local electric
company, settled into a job that made use of his expertise in both design
and engineering. When we spoke by phone Jim had begun his tenth
year with the firm. The only debt the couple carried was their thirty-year
mortgage and payments for their car, which was a year away from being
owned free and clear.

The bad news—bad as an indicator for the health of the U.S. economy, though not at all bad for the Blentlingers themselves—was that
the Blentlingers achieved upward mobility in large part by taking leave
of the private-sector economy. Ann-Marie had long been a government

employee as a public school teacher; in 2002 Jim became a government employee at the federal level by going to work for the Tennessee Valley Authority, the regional utility created by President Franklin Roosevelt in 1933. The TVA, though no longer government-subsidized, is still government-owned, and its employees enjoy job protections that reward seniority to a greater degree than is typically found in private companies. Jim also has something currently available to fewer than 10 percent of all private sector employees: a union. Jim says he's received some merit raises along the way, but that most of his pay increases came by way of seniority rules. When Jim first arrived at the TVA, his job was to teach classes that trained TVA employees in computer-aided design. He trained perhaps fifty or sixty people a week. A few years later, as the economy started to slacken, the TVA shifted its training to the Internet, and Jim was redeployed to create videos that train TVA employees by the thousands. Entering the federal workforce has been a boon to Jim and his family, but it's not a realistic option for most people because non-military jobs with the U.S. government represent only about 1 percent of all jobs in the United States.[19]

Women's increased presence in the labor force has, from an economic point of view, quite obviously benefited women, their families, and the country as a whole. Had the majority of married women of childbearing age chosen to stay at home, the post-1973 stagnation of male incomes would have had much more dire consequences for the middle class. But women's growing economic independence has also destabilized the middle class in three important ways.

Greater Risk of Job Loss

When both husband and wife work, the likelihood that a family will lose all its income through job loss is half as great as it would be if only the husband worked. If Dad gets laid off, Mom can still pull in some cash (though probably not as much as Dad did). That enhances the family's stability. But it's also true that when both husband and wife work, the likelihood is *doubled* that a family breadwinner will suffer job loss, thereby depriving a family of a substantial portion of its income. If Mom gets laid off, the family can quickly find it difficult to pay the mortgage, meet car payments, or cover college tuition. That reduces the family's stability.

After 1970 the likelihood that any individual would suffer a family income loss of 50 percent or more rose from 7 percent to more than 14 percent. Somewhat more surprisingly, among families that suffered income loss in any given year, the median drop rose from 27 percent in 1970 to 38 percent in 2002, even though most two-parent families were now relying on two incomes instead of one.[20]

The stagnation of middle-class incomes since the early 1970s means that middle-income people are already living pretty close to the edge financially just to cover the basics. Food and clothing are cheaper, but shelter, transportation, health care, and higher education are much more expensive. As a consequence, for middle-income families a job loss can easily push a family into serious debt or even bankruptcy. And, in fact, consumer debt and bankruptcy rates have exploded during the Great Divergence. Since 1968, Warren calculates, credit card debt has increased sixtyfold. Between 1979 and 2002—well *before* the collapse of the housing boom of the aughts—foreclosures increased by a factor of nearly 15. Between 1980 and 2006—*before* the last recession hit—nonbusiness bankruptcies increased more than fourfold on a per capita basis.[21]

These trends are part of what the Yale political scientist Jacob Hacker identified as "the great risk shift." In a 2006 book of that name, Hacker argued that corporations and the government have been off-loading economic risk onto individuals. The most familiar example is pensions. Since 1981 the proportion of large- and medium-sized companies offering fixed-benefit pensions has dropped from more than 80 percent to less than one third. Instead of receiving a guaranteed pension from the company, employees today typically acquire a personalized 401(k) plan that exposes their retirement fund to financial risk in the event of a market downturn. Hacker also noted the widespread substitution of company employees with company contractors. Where taxicab drivers once were employed by cab companies, by 2006 most of them leased their cabs from cab companies, an arrangement that required them to acquire their own gasoline and their own auto insurance and to take the losses when business was slow.[22]

Shifts in Marriage Patterns

People like to procreate with people like themselves. Biologists refer to this as "assortative mating." One particularly strong affinity is economic.

People tend to marry people whose incomes are at roughly the same level as their own. Back when women didn't typically have professional careers, the opportunities for a male lawyer on his way to making partner to marry a female lawyer on her way to making partner were few and far between. (There were also some ugly social prejudices against women pursuing careers usually limited to males.) So instead the male lawyer married a woman he met at the country club, or perhaps the daughter of a senior partner—that is, someone from a "good family" but with very little earning potential of her own. If he married a co-worker, it was likely to be his secretary or the head of the typing pool—again, not anyone likely ever to earn anywhere near what he did, assuming she planned to keep working at all.

As more women came to hold high-paying jobs, that dynamic changed. Today, colleges, professional schools, and the lower rungs of the professions and the corporate world have lots of women, making it much easier for, say, one aspiring anesthesiologist to marry another. Between 1960 and 2003, the likelihood that spouses would share comparable levels of schooling ("educational homogamy") increased by more than 25 percent, according to a 2005 study by Christine R. Schwartz and Robert D. Mare, sociologists at the University of California, Los Angeles.[23] During the same period, the likelihood that highly educated women would continue to work after marriage was also increasing. These two trends meant that a significant number of women were able to double their husbands' family income the moment they said, "I do." Indeed, more than one researcher has suggested that what we might call the Jane Austen Paradigm—economic competition among women for men ("It is a truth universally acknowledged, that a single man in possession of a good fortune must be in want of a wife")—is giving way to economic competition among men *and* women for mates ("It is a truth universally acknowledged, that a single man in possession of a high salary must be in want of a wife with an equally high or higher salary, and vice versa").

That has implications for income distribution—not the distribution between women and men, but rather the distribution between families that enjoy the benefits of combining two high incomes and families that don't have even one high earner. "Are marriages becoming more equal at the expense of economic equality across families?" asked Schwartz in a 2010 paper. (By then she had moved on to the University of Wisconsin.) She concluded the answer was yes. Among married couples in the

United States, Schwarz calculated, earnings inequality would, from 1967 to 2005, be 25 percent to 30 percent lower were it not for that period's growing correlation between spouses' incomes.[24]

The Rise in Single Parenthood

Earlier in this chapter I noted that during the Great Divergence family incomes increased by only 10 percent, even though families during this period were much likelier than they previously were to rely on two salaries, and even though women's incomes were gaining on men's. Part of the reason was a rise in single-parent households, which in most instances meant a woman raising children without a husband or male partner. Just as the *Atlantic*'s Hanna Rosin and *The Full Monty*'s Gaz wonder whether the modern, postindustrial economy has much use for men, so might we wonder about the modern, postindustrial family.

The declining economic value of men as Ward Cleaver–style breadwinners is a significant reason for the rise in single parenthood. As male incomes became less reliable and social taboos were loosened against divorce and out-of-wedlock birth, women became less inclined to marry, or stay married to, the fathers of their children. Between 1970 and 2004, the proportion of U.S. children living with one parent jumped from 12 percent to more than 26 percent. The social consequences of this trend are much debated, but the economic consequence is not: Single-parent families typically have less income than two-parent families. "Single mothers seldom command high wages," observed David Ellwood and Christopher Jencks, both of Harvard's Kennedy School of Government, in a 2004 paper. "They also find it unusually difficult to work long hours."[25]

The basic problem single mothers face is that while men may no longer be necessary economically, they still tend to be helpful. Two incomes are better than one, even if the man's income is no higher than it would have been back in 1973. Forty percent of single-mother families have incomes below the poverty line, compared to only 8 percent of two-income families. Another way of putting this is that the child of a single mother is five times as likely as the child of a two-parent family to grow up poor. And while single parenthood has become more common all over the world, the rate of single-parent families that are in or near poverty is significantly higher in the United States than in western Europe.

In America fully 50 percent of single-parent families are in or near poverty, compared to 44 percent in the United Kingdom, 34 percent in Germany, 27 percent in France, and 17 percent in Denmark. Single mothers are especially vulnerable to the "risk shift" described by Yale's Hacker. According to Elizabeth Warren, during the first two decades of the Great Divergence the number of single mothers in bankruptcy increased by more than 600 percent. Single mothers are now more likely to file for bankruptcy than the elderly, divorced men, members of ethnic minorities, and inhabitants of low-income neighborhoods.[26]

Do greater financial risk, increased assortative mating, and the rise of single-parent households—all by-products of women's growing clout in the economy—contribute to the Great Divergence? In the case of economic risk, the answer is yes in the abstract—families at greater risk of going bankrupt are by definition at greater risk of lowering their income. But if the reason for their instability is that they rely on more income than they once did (from two sources rather than one), it would seem perverse to blame the Great Divergence on two-income families. Assortative mating clearly *did* contribute to the Great Divergence. But since income-based assortative mating has also been on the rise abroad—one study has it rising within OECD countries from 33 percent to 40 percent during the past two decades—it seems doubtful that assortative mating did much to make the Great Divergence so much worse in the United States than income-inequality trends in other industrialized democracies.[27] As for single parenthood, its contribution to the Great Divergence must be judged minimal because it increased mostly before 1980, when the Great Divergence was just getting under way. By the early 1990s, the growth in single-parent households halted altogether, and though it resumed in the aughts the rate of growth was significantly slower.[28]

Another consideration is that single parenthood is today less damaging economically than it was at the start of the Great Divergence. "That's mostly because the percentage of women who are actually working who are single parents went up," Jencks told me. In a 2008 paper, three Harvard sociologists concluded that the two-thirds rise in income inequality among families with children from 1975 to 2005 could not be attributed to divorce and out-of-wedlock births. "Single parenthood increased inequality," they conceded, "but the income gap was closed by mothers who entered the labor force." One trend canceled the effects of another (at least in the aggregate).[29]

While we're on the topic of single- versus two-parent households, we ought to consider what a "household" is.

Stephen J. Rose is a labor economist at Georgetown University best known for publishing, since the 1970s, successive editions of *Social Stratification in the United States*, a pamphlet and poster much revered by the left that depict economic inequality in the United States. In his 2010 book *Rebound: Why America Will Emerge Stronger from the Financial Crisis*, Rose wrote that the second edition of his pamphlet got "the inequality debate started in full force." But during the subsequent three decades he came to believe that worries about rising income inequality and a disappearing middle class were overblown. Rose built his case largely on the notion that the Census Bureau's preferred metric—"median household income"—was misleading.

The trouble, Rose wrote, was that households varied greatly in composition and size. A household might consist of a single young man just starting out on his own or an elderly widow in retirement. Neither would likely enjoy a high income, but that would be a function of mere circumstance (the young man was just beginning his climb up the greasy pole; the retired widow no longer worked at all) and need (neither was likely to be responsible for any children). Another problem, Rose suggested, was that some households were bigger than others. Couples tended to have larger household incomes than single people, but that was because they likely collected two paychecks rather than one. The proportion of Americans living alone had for various reasons increased over time; that needed to be taken into account, too. Finally, Rose argued, one had to count as income the rising employer share of health insurance premiums. Correcting for all these factors, Rose calculated that between 1979 and 2007 median household income actually grew not by 15 percent, as reported by the Census Bureau, but by 33 percent.

That was the good news. The bad news: Even with these new calculations, Rose couldn't deny the existence of a Great Divergence. Median income was still growing at one third the rate it had between 1949 and 1979. "Under all circumstances," he wrote, "inequality has risen considerably, and this is a bad thing for America. Those at the bottom of the income ladder have benefited only minimally from the significant gains in overall production over the past three decades." The Census Bureau routinely recalculates the three-decade inequality trend using "equivalence-adjusted" numbers that take into account family size; the fact that children consume less than adults; efficiencies of scale as families grow; and the fact that a first child incurs greater expenses for a single parent than for a two-parent household. When all these factors are plugged in, the overall inequality level is indeed lower. But the rate at which inequality has grown is *faster*.[30]

Back, then, to the drawing board. The Great Divergence did not result from societal prejudice against women or blacks. Some changes in family dynamics contributed to it, but not to an extent that explains why inequality has grown so much worse in the United States than in other industrialized democracies. Could it be that we're dividing the population into the wrong subgroups? Rather than consider gender and race, or today's two-income families versus the single-income families of the past, lets consider the impact made by people who inhabit, but were not born in, the United States: immigrants, both legal and undocumented.

4
Teeming Shores

In June 1970, when I was twelve, my family moved from New York to California. We didn't know it at the time, but our migration came at the tail end of a historic trend that predated California's entry into the union. Starting with the 1848 Gold Rush (which prompted Congress to grant statehood), California had been a place whose population grew mainly because people from other parts of the United States picked up and moved there. In the 1870s, Hoosiers tired of the cold and settled Pasadena. In the 1930s, Okies fled the Dust Bowl and followed Route 66 to the Central Valley. In the 1950s, engineers descended on South Bay to create an aerospace industry. My family's migration came about because my dad was a TV producer, and for about a decade most television production had been shifting from New York City to Los Angeles.

After 1970, people kept coming to California, and new industries continued to sprout there (most notably in Northern California's Silicon Valley). But the engine of population growth ceased to be native-born Americans like me leaving one part of the United States for another. Instead, California's population grew mainly because of people like Maria Andrade.

Born and raised in a little town called Jaripo in the Mexican state of Michoacán, Maria was nine when she emigrated to California in 1974. Her father, a farm laborer, had come to the United States a few years before on a guest worker visa and had managed to obtain permanent residency. Maria, her mother, and her six siblings joined him in French Camp, in the Central Valley. One of her first days at school Maria was approached by some girls who asked her name; not understanding the language and thinking "they were saying bad words to me," she wept. "You come to a different country not knowing many things, " she recalls today, "especially the language." Weekends she would join her father to work in the fields. During her senior year in high school she married a farm worker named Rafael Andrade, and by 1991 the two of them were running a farm labor contracting business, hiring workers to pick tomatoes, cherries, and asparagus. They bought a house in Stockton and sent their kids to college at Sacramento State. "We were blessed to come to this country," Maria Andrade says today.[1]

The 1970s upsurge in immigration was especially dramatic in California, but it was happening elsewhere in the United States, too. The catalyst was the Immigration and Nationality Act of 1965, which eased immigration restrictions generally and restrictions affecting non-Europeans in particular. It is one of the least discussed and most lastingly important components to President Lyndon Johnson's Great Society program. It changed the face of America.[2]

About a million people immigrate to the United States each year, not counting undocumented immigrants, of whom there was a net annual increase of about 500,000 prior to the 2007–09 recession.[3] As a result, the foreign-born proportion of the U.S. population is about 13 percent. In 1965, when the immigration law was enacted, the foreign-born made up about 5 percent. That was a historic low.

The highest-ever percentage of foreign-born people living in the United States was reached in 1890 and 1910, when immigration pushed it to 15 percent. After 1910 the foreign-born proportion entered six decades of decline.[4] It dwindled not because foreigners lost interest in migrating to the United States, but rather because the immigration wave of the late nineteenth and early twentieth centuries created a formidable backlash. The huddled masses welcomed by the poet Emma Lazarus in 1883 ("Give me your tired, your poor . . .") were not welcomed by most native-born Americans. That's why she wrote her famous poem in the first place.

That America is a nation of immigrants is regularly heralded in patriotic speeches. But Americans have always been more inclined to celebrate immigration in the past tense than in the present. While it's been occurring, it has typically been judged at best a nuisance and at worst a menace. In his 2002 book *Dividing Lines: The Politics of Immigration Control in America*, the University of Oregon political scientist Daniel Tichenor notes that even the Founding Fathers could be cranky on the subject. Benjamin Franklin groused about Pennsylvania's "Palatine boors"— German-speaking immigrants—who "will shortly be so numerous as to Germanize us instead of our Anglifying them," a broadside that, according to the historian Edmund S. Morgan, "was as politically incorrect in 1751 as it would be today." Thomas Jefferson professed in 1787 that "it would be a miracle" if immigrants managed to embrace the "temperate liberty" necessary to sustain the young republic.[5]

During the United States' first century, nothing much came of such complaints; indeed, in less sour moods Franklin and Jefferson both strongly favored immigration. The sole significant attempt to curb immigration was President John Adams's Alien and Sedition Acts of 1798, which extended the citizenship residency requirement from five years to fourteen and made it easier for the executive to deport resident aliens. Even these laws were aimed less at immigrants than at the opposing Democratic-Republican Party, forerunner to today's Democratic Party, with which—even then—immigrants were allied. The various restrictions were mostly done away with under Adams's Democrat-Republican successor, Jefferson.

America's laissez-faire policy toward immigration began to change in the latter half of the nineteenth century. Growing native resentment against Chinese immigrants, who had started entering the country at midcentury as low-wage "coolies" hired to build the railroads, led to a series of laws severely restricting entry of Chinese immigrants. These restrictions were subsequently extended first to Japanese immigrants and later to virtually all Asian immigrants. In public discussion of Chinese immigrants, economic anxiety quickly spiraled into xenophobia, with Senator William Morris Stewart of Nevada denigrating the Chinese as "pagans in religion" and Horace Greeley, editor of the *New York Tribune*, denouncing the Chinese as "uncivilized, unclean, and filthy beyond all conception."[6] "Asiatics" were understood to be an "inferior race," in the words of California governor Henry Haight.

The next groups to attract hostile attention were southern and eastern Europeans, who accounted for more than 75 percent of the 8 million European immigrants who entered the United States during the first decade of the twentieth century. Here, too, the underlying worry was economic. Samuel Gompers, president of the American Federation of Labor, supported restricting their admission to ward off "low wages and bad working conditions" for native-born workers. And as with the Chinese, pocketbook concerns gave way to crude racial and cultural prejudice. Here is how President-to-be Woodrow Wilson put it in his multivolume *History of the American People,* published in 1902, the year he became president of Princeton University.

> Throughout the [nineteenth] century men of the sturdy stocks of the north of Europe had made up the main strain of foreign blood which was every year added to the vital working force of the country, or else men of the Latin-Gallic stocks of France and northern Italy; but now there came multitudes of men of the lowest class from the south of Italy and men of the meaner sort out of Hungary and Poland, men out of the ranks where there was neither skill nor energy nor any initiative of quick intelligence; and they came in numbers which increased from year to year, as if the countries of the south of Europe were disburdening themselves of the more sordid and hapless elements of their population.

The southern and eastern Europeans were, Wilson wrote, even worse than the Chinese, "as workmen if not as citizens."[7]

Wilson's vicious cultural stereotyping demonstrated that resistance to eastern and southern European immigrants bore the imprimatur of the academic elite, a distinction not present in the earlier resistance to the Chinese. It was also reflective of the dark strain within the Progressive movement discussed in chapter 1. The Progressives' fervent belief in scientific expertise aided the cause of good government in many areas—food safety, financial regulation, and public education, for instance—but when it came to immigration the Progressives fell hard for the pseudoscience of eugenics, which assigned superior and inferior qualities to the cultures of various regions based on what was presumed to be their genetic inheritance.

A Cornell economist named Jeremiah Jenks, appointed to a congressional commission created to formulate a properly scientific response to the immigration problem, weighed in with a *Dictionary of Races or Peoples* (authored principally by an anthropologist who worked as his staff assistant). Published in 1911 by the Senate Committee on Immigration, the dictionary rendered authoritative-sounding distinctions between, for instance, northern Italians ("cool, deliberate, patient, practical") and southern Italians (a "long-headed, dark, 'Mediterranean' race of short stature" who were "excitable, impulsive, highly imaginative, [and] impracticable," and who demonstrated "little adaptability to highly organized society").[8]

Combining such findings with an assertion that the United States already suffered an "oversupply of unskilled labor," the commission recommended that the U.S. government require immigrants to pass a literacy test. Congress imposed such a test in 1917 over the veto of President Wilson. (Since entering politics, Wilson had backed away from his earlier blanket condemnation—Italians, Hungarians, and Poles being regular visitors to the polls.) The test required immigrants sixteen and over to demonstrate that they could read "not less than thirty nor more than forty words in ordinary use, printed in plainly legible type in some one of the various languages or dialects of immigrants."

The expectation was that a literacy test would (in the words of a long-time supporter, Massachusetts senator Henry Cabot Lodge) "bear most heavily" on southern and eastern Europeans "and very lightly, or not at all, upon English-speaking emigrants or Germans, Scandinavians, and French." But the test didn't weed out the swarthy undesirables in anything like the hoped-for numbers. Rather than reconsider their view that southern and eastern Europeans were inherently inferior, anti-immigrant groups resolved to further restrict their entry by imposing numerical quotas. Two quota laws ensued in 1921 and 1924, passed by Congress and signed into law by Presidents Warren G. Harding and Calvin Coolidge. The second and tougher of the two laws limited annual immigration to 2 percent of the number of each nationality already residing in the United States. This was calculated not from the 1920 census, but from the 1890 census, which predated the migration surge from southern and eastern Europe. The desired effect was achieved. Where during the teens southern and eastern Europeans admitted to the United States had numbered 3.4 million, by the 1930s that had dropped to 130,000. Immigration from northern and western Europe dropped too, but far less drastically, from about 1 million during the teens to 200,000 during the 1930s.

Even before the literacy test and the quotas were enacted into law, the *New Republic* predicted that "freedom of migration from one country to another" was "one of the elements of nineteenth century liberalism that is fated to disappear." In the United States it didn't disappear, but it did diminish. In 1910 the foreign-born proportion of the U.S. population was 15 percent. It then dropped to 13 percent in 1920, 12 percent in 1930, 9 percent in 1940, and eventually all the way down down to 5 percent in 1970.[9] Not even the knowledge of Adolf Hitler's mass murder of Jews during World War II could persuade the U.S. government to lift the quotas. Although President Franklin D. Roosevelt made a small refugee relief effort at the insistence of his Jewish treasury secretary, Henry Morgenthau Jr., resistance to mounting any large-scale effort was considerable both on Capitol Hill and within Roosevelt's own State Department.[10]

After the war a succession of presidents found ways to admit more refugees, but overall immigration numbers stayed low. The quota system favoring western Europeans became an embarrassment, based as it was on eugenics theories discredited when Nazi Germany carried them through to their logical conclusion. The quotas were also a diplomatic hindrance in cultivating Cold War allies. In Congress, conservative committee chairmen from the South and the West resisted dismantling the quotas. The 1952 McCarran-Walter Act, remembered today for restricting entry of foreigners deemed subversive, tinkered with the quotas but did not eliminate them. Given the United States's leadership role in containing Soviet expansion, though, it seemed only a matter of time before the quotas would be removed.

That moment arrived in 1965. In the aftermath of President John F. Kennedy's assassination, his successor, Lyndon Johnson, pushed through a string of ambitious civil rights bills, including the Civil Rights Act of 1964 and the Voting Rights Act of 1965. Although Johnson had previously voted for the McCarran-Walter Act, his aides Jack Valenti and Bill Moyers convinced him that the national-origin immigration quotas were a civil rights issue, too. The law that resulted eliminated the national quotas and all remaining formal limits on Asian immigration and replaced these with two hemispheric quotas: 170,000 visas for the East and 120,000 visas for the West. The combined total, 290,000, approximated the number being issued at the time the bill was passed. (The hemispheric quotas would be repealed in the 1970s, but the combined ceiling remained.) Exceptions were made for close relatives of people living in the

United States and for political refugees, but even so the bill wasn't expected to increase immigration much. Various versions of the family-reunification provision had been on the books since 1924, and there was a rough limit of 17,400 visas for all refugees. The stated goal was a fairer allocation of visas, not a larger one. The main beneficiaries, one leading congressional sponsor of the bill predicted, would be European.

In fact, the law's passage enabled immigration to increase substantially, and the main beneficiaries turned out to be principally Latin Americans and Asians, who today represent more than 80 percent of the nation's foreign-born. One reason was that the family-reunification provisions were significantly more generous than they'd ever been before. For example, adult brothers, adult sisters, and married adult children (along with their families) had previously been given low priority. Under the 1965 law they were given much higher priority. Latinos and Asians worked the system to their advantage. The first wave of immigrants would establish a beachhead in the United States, then bring relatives over; those relatives in turn would bring more relatives over, in a process that came to be known as "chaining." U.S. officials failed to anticipate this because previous immigration restrictions left them without a yardstick to measure the demand to emigrate from Asia and Mexico (Mexicans represented the largest portion of Latino immigrants). The Asian barrier has been discussed; the barrier for Mexicans was that entry was mainly limited to participation in a guest worker ("bracero") program dating back to the 1940s and finally eliminated, under pressure from U.S. labor groups, around the time the immigration bill passed. With the bracero program gone, those who couldn't secure legal immigration entered the United States illegally in growing numbers. Between 1965 and 1970, the number of undocumented aliens who were apprehended and deported—a small fraction of the total—tripled. Between 1961 and 1964, that number had remained stable.

Another reason the 1965 law led to more immigration than anticipated was that the limits on refugees were either overridden or ignored. The very day President Johnson signed the bill into law he promised refuge to political opponents of the Cuban dictator Fidel Castro, who had abruptly invited them to leave. Their number exceeded the new law's annual allotment for *all* refugee preferences. President Richard Nixon brought in thousands of Czech refugees from the 1968 Soviet crackdown against the "Prague Spring," again greatly exceeding the existing allotment. The fall of Saigon in 1975 prompted the rescue of 130,000 Vietnamese, Cambodians, and Laotians. And so on.

Today a little more than half of the foreign-born population in the United States hails from Mexico and Central and South America. Mexico alone represents 30 percent, well ahead of the next-most-common country of origin, China, which represents 5 percent. Twenty-eight percent of the foreign-born are estimated to be undocumented aliens, and the majority of these hail from Mexico. Although a substantial minority of immigrants are highly skilled, most are not as well educated as native-born Americans. One third never finished high school, compared to 13 percent of the native-born. Immigrants are also much likelier than the native-born to be poor. Fully 17 percent of foreign-born families (and 23 percent of foreign-born Latinos) have incomes that put them below the official poverty line (about $22,000 per year for a family of four). The comparable proportion for native-born families is 9 percent. The poorest foreign-born families, unsurprisingly, tend to be the most recent arrivals.[11] In view of these facts, it's logical to wonder whether immigration, today within striking distance of its historic peak, is driving down wages.

It wouldn't be the first time. There's broad agreement among economic historians that immigration at the end of the nineteenth century and the beginning of the twentieth did indeed lower wages for unskilled workers. Samuel Gompers wasn't imagining things. Claudia Goldin calculated that during these peak years a 1 percent increase in the foreign-born proportion of any given city's population lowered wages for unskilled workers by 1 to 1.5 percent. Immigration's impact on industries that were particular magnets for the foreign-born was even greater. Among laborers engaged in manufacturing men's clothing, for instance, a 1 percent increase in the foreign-born proportion of a city's population lowered wages by 1.5 to 3 percent.[12] Surveying the economic literature in 2006, the economists Timothy Hatton (of Australian National University and the University of Essex) and Jeffrey Williamson (of Harvard) calculated that in 1910 unskilled wages in the United States would have been about 9 to 14 percent higher had there been no immigration between 1870 and 1910.[13]

Did the Great Compression, the long and prosperous midcentury period during which incomes became more equal and stayed that way,

owe a debt to the immigration restrictions imposed in the 1920s? The
Nobel Prize–winning economist Paul Samuelson thought so. "By keeping labor supply down," he wrote in his bestselling economics textbook,
a restrictive immigration policy "tends to keep wages high."[14] Less than
a decade after the 1965 immigration law reopened the spigot, middle-
class incomes were stagnating, and by 1979 inequality was increasing.
It's therefore logical to suspect that the Great Divergence was the product
of legal and undocumented immigrants yearning to breathe free. But the
best available evidence indicates that immigration's impact on the income-
inequality boom was actually somewhat modest.

Immigrants are generally understood to contribute to economic growth.
A 1997 study by the National Academy of Sciences estimated that their
contribution to GDP might be as high as $10 billion each year. Immi-
grants do draw on taxpayer dollars to receive social services, but the
NAS study calculated that over a lifetime an immigrant would pay
$80,000 more in taxes than he received in benefits.[15] "Immigrants have
contributed to job growth in three main ways," concluded a 2003 study
by the Federal Reserve Bank of Dallas. "They fill an increasing share of
jobs overall, they take jobs in labor-scarce regions, and they fill the types
of jobs native workers often shun."

Economic growth is a wonderful thing. But it won't ease income inequality if only a trifling amount of the gains ends up in the hands of
ordinary Americans. The Dallas Fed study calculated that although the
foreign-born were only 14 percent of the labor force, they accounted for
a slender majority of all the job growth between 1996 and 2002.[16] That
immigrants perform more of society's newly created jobs than the native-
born speaks well of their enterprise, but is it really good news for the
native-born? Are these truly jobs that native-born Americans don't want?
What impact does immigrants' seeming willingness to take just about
any job at just about any wage have on wages overall?

In 1990 the economist David Card (then at Princeton, now at Berkeley) rather ingeniously posed this question in the context of the Mariel
boatlift. On April 20, 1980, Castro declared that any Cuban who wanted
to emigrate to the United States could do so from the Cuban port of
Mariel. Between May and October of that year, 125,000 mostly poorly
educated, low-wage Cuban workers (along with some criminals and lu-
natics Castro freed from Cuba's prisons and mental hospitals) made the

ocean voyage to Miami. Half of them remained in Miami, increasing its labor force by 7 percent. Because of its suddenness, its size, and its geographic confinement, the boatlift created a seemingly perfect laboratory in which to observe the effect of immigration on the labor market.

The Marielitos certainly made their presence known. President Jimmy Carter declared a state of emergency in Florida and diverted navy ships from Guantánamo to assist the Coast Guard. Miami's city government commandeered the Orange Bowl Stadium and turned it into a giant homeless shelter for the refugees. In one year homicides went up by 50 percent and robberies went up 75 percent.[17] Had the same economic dynamic existed that Goldin observed for the years around the turn of the twentieth century, the Marielitos' arrival would have lowered wages for Miami's unskilled laborers by somewhere between 7 and 11 percent. But Card observed *no impact on wages at all* (except on the Marielitos themselves), *even among unskilled native-born workers.*[18] Although unemployment in Miami jumped from 5 to 7 percent between April and July 1980, that followed a national trend; the country was in a recession that bottomed out in July. The boatlift had nothing to do with it. If a massive, sudden exodus like the Mariel boatlift didn't affect the target city's labor market, it seems doubtful that much change would be observed in other cities and regions where immigration has been more gradual and diffuse. Indeed, cities where immigrants cluster tend to be *more* prosperous than other cities, not less.

But George Borjas, an economics professor at Harvard's Kennedy School of Government (and a Cuban immigrant himself), says looking at individual cities or regions is the wrong approach. We live in a highly mobile society, Borjas points out, and it's only logical that immigrants would be drawn to areas with booming economies. Immigration *looks* like it is creating opportunity, he wrote in 2004,[19] but what's really happening is that immigrants are moving to places where they have the best odds of getting a decent-paying job. Once a place starts to become saturated with cheap immigrant labor, Borjas explains, the unskilled American workers who compete with immigrants for jobs no longer move there. (Or if they already live there, they move away to seek better pay.)

Instead of looking at the effects of immigration on isolated labor markets like New York or Los Angeles, Borjas gathered data at the national level, sorted workers according to their skill levels and their experience, and made some calculations about what native-born workers would earn had there been no immigration between 1980 and 2000. This is more difficult than you might suppose, because modern markets adjust quickly to the price of labor. A company that spends less to pay workers performing one function may find it has more to pay workers performing another function. A native-born high school student who in an earlier era would have dropped out to become, say, a meatpacker—a job that today is dominated by immigrants—might observe that meatpacking doesn't pay what it used to, and choose instead to graduate, thereby improving his chances of getting a better-paying job. There are other variables as well. Nonetheless, Borjas constructed a mathematical model—one that has received wide if not unanimous acceptance among experts in the field—and found that between 1980 and 2000, immigration reduced the income of native-born high school dropouts ("who roughly correspond to the poorest tenth of the workforce") by 7.4 percent over the entire period. That works out to a reduction of not quite 0.4 percent per year, and puts current immigration's dampening effect on unskilled salaries within range of what it was during the peak immigration years of the late nineteenth and early twentieth centuries.[20]

If immigrants are today lowering unskilled wages at a rate comparable to that of nativism's heyday, doesn't that contradict my earlier statement that immigration's impact on the Great Divergence has been comparatively modest? Actually, no. One hundred years ago, the term "unskilled labor" described practically the entire industrial workforce. The social movement to provide a high school education to the American masses was in its infancy. (More on that in the next chapter.) An overwhelming majority didn't even *attend* high school, much less graduate from it. Fewer than 20 percent of all fifteen- to eighteen-year-olds were enrolled in any high school, public or private.[21] To say, then, that immigration lowered wages for unskilled workers by 9 to 14 percent was to say that immigration lowered wages for nearly every industrial worker in America.

Today, however, "unskilled labor," if defined as the country's pool of high school dropouts, is comparatively small. Only 15 percent of all adults age twenty-five or older lack a high school diploma or an equivalent GED. Among U.S. workers age twenty-five or older who never graduated high school, *nearly half* are immigrants, most of them from Mexico and Central America.[22] Granted, high school dropouts are a uniquely vulnerable population. They are the poorest Americans. But there aren't that many of them. Indeed, Borjas points out in his 1999 book, *Heaven's Door: Immigration Policy and the American Economy*, that in the modern era high school dropouts may not even constitute the full universe of the group we ought to consider "unskilled." Because today's employers demand college degrees to at least the same extent that employers of a century ago demanded high school degrees, many experts currently define "unskilled labor" to include not only high school dropouts, but also high school graduates who never went on to college. For this latter group, immigration since 1980 has had virtually no impact on wages.[23]

The Great Divergence is not principally a story about the poor. People whose incomes put them in the bottom 20 percent have seen their share of the nation's income decline, but the blunt truth is that it was rotten to be poor in 1979 and it remains rotten to be poor in 2012. If anything, it's become slightly less rotten—or rather, it was slightly less rotten until the aughts. Average income for families in the bottom 20 percent crept up a bit after 1979 (though not as rapidly as it did from 1950 to 1970), and during the 1990s the ratio between the fiftieth and twentieth percentiles was roughly stable.[24] Low-income people got some help through expansion of the Earned Income Tax Credit, and demand picked up a little for home health aides, fast-food workers, security guards, and some other low-wage job categories. Seven of the ten occupations identified by the Bureau of Labor Statistics as showing the fastest growth are for jobs it qualifies as "low wage" or "very low wage."[25]

The Great Divergence is about the difference between how people lived during the half century preceding 1979 and how they lived during the three decades after 1979. The most dramatic difference didn't involve the poor; it involved the middle class and the rich. And immigration's impact on the middle class (as distinct from its impact on high school dropouts) was fairly minor. For native-born high school graduates, Borjas calculated that from 1980 to 2000, immigration drove annual income down 2.1 percent on average, or 0.1 percent annually. For native-born workers with "some college," immigration drove annual income down 2.3 percent, or 0.12 percent annually. For *all* workers, annual income went down 3.7 percent due to all immigration, or 0.19 percent annually. To put these numbers into perspective, during this period the difference between after-tax income growth for the middle fifth of the income distribution and after-tax income growth for the top fifth of the income distribution was seventy percentage points.

The difference in growth between the middle fifth and the top 1 percent was 256 percentage points.[26]

Another obstacle to blaming the Great Divergence on immigration is that one of Borjas's findings runs in the wrong direction. From 1980 to 2000, immigration depressed wages for college graduates by 3.6 percent. That's because a significant minority of those immigrants were highly skilled. But the Great Divergence sent college graduates' wages *up*, not *down*. To reverse that trend would require importing *a lot* more highly skilled workers.

Gary Burtless, an economist at the Brookings Institution in Washington, proposes a different way to think about immigration. Noting that immigrants "accounted for one-third of the U.S. population growth between 1980 and 2007," Burtless argued in a 2009 paper that even if they failed to exert heavy downward pressure on the incomes of most native-born Americans, the million or so immigrants who arrive in the United States each year were sufficient in number and different enough in characteristics to skew the national income distribution *by their mere presence*. But while Burtless's methodology was more expansive than Borjas's, his calculation of immigration's effect was more modest. Had there been no immigration after 1979, he calculated, average annual wages for all workers "may have risen by an additional 2.3 percent" (compared to Borjas's 3.7 percent), or 0.08 percent per year.[27]

Before we leave this subject, a caveat: Economists work from available data, which at the national level are often five to ten years old. It's possible that immigration is currently having a greater impact on the wages of the native-born than past data indicate. It's also possible that the immigration most responsible for pushing down wages for the unskilled is beginning to ebb. It's even possible that *both* things are true.

Undocumented immigrants are currently believed to constitute 20 to 36 percent of construction workers in low-skill trades. Construction work is a significant step up from unskilled labor, and until recently a unionized construction worker could reasonably expect to inhabit the middle class. That's a lot less true today, and one likely reason is immigration. A 2008 doctoral dissertation by Sabrina Kay Golden found that in the Washington metropolitan area, undocumented immigrants constituted a 55 percent majority of construction workers in low-skill trades.[28] Was that finding accurate? If so, did it reflect a local anomaly? Or were the national numbers too low? It could be years before we know. Chuck

Gilligan, a labor lawyer in Washington, D.C., has estimated that in the D.C. metropolitan area the construction industry typically pays undocumented workers about $13 an hour to avoid paying native-born and legal-immigrant workers about $30 an hour. "In the past year," he wrote in 2010, "I have negotiated wages cuts of $2, $4, and $12—yes, $12—an hour for various groups with whom I work."[29] This may signal—and I emphasize *may*—that immigrants are starting to lower wages for middle-class workers.

On the other hand, what if illegal migration from Mexico to the United States, which is disproportionately responsible for the downward pressure on unskilled wages, were to recede? "No one wants to hear it, but the flow has already stopped," the Princeton sociologist Douglas Massey told the *New York Times* in July 2011. "For the first time in 60 years, the net traffic has gone to zero and is probably a little bit negative." It may be that this decline, too, was a blip related to the 2007–09 recession. A 2010 report by the Pew Hispanic Center estimated that the total number of undocumented immigrants in the United States had peaked in 2007 at 12 million and subsequently declined to about 11 million in 2009 and 2010. Pew called it "the first significant reversal in a two-decade pattern of growth." During the previous two decades there were three recessions, but only the 2007–09 recession—granted, by far the worst of the three—saw such a decline. The Pew report attributed the decline mainly to a reduction in the number of undocumented immigrants from Mexico; the number of undocumented immigrants from other parts of Latin America was unchanged.[30]

What besides the recession might have caused the change? Tougher border enforcement might be one reason; deportations doubled during the aughts.[31] But in the *New York Times* story, the reporter Damien Cave suggested another intriguing possibility: changes in Mexico itself. The country's fertility rate has fallen to two children per woman. Secondary school attendance is up. Per capita gross domestic product has increased more than 45 percent since 2000. Family income has increased by a comparable amount. During that same decade, family income in the United States *declined* slightly. In other words, more Mexicans may be choosing to seek a better life in their own country.

It would be rash to conclude that immigration's impact on low-wage workers in the United States is a problem in the process of solving itself. It would also be rash to conclude that immigration is poised to do to more skilled workers what it has already done to high school dropouts. For the moment, all we can conclude with certainty is that although immigration has helped create income inequality during the past three decades, it isn't the star of the show. "If you were to list the five or six main things" that caused the Great Divergence, Borjas told me, "what I would say is [that immigration is] a contributor. Is it the most important contributor? No."[32]

5

Kudoka and
the College Premium

THE CITY OF WELCH, A COUNTY SEAT DEEP in West Virginia coal country, lost three quarters of its population between 1950 and 2000. Since then it has lost an additional 10 percent.[1] Much of the city is a blighted landscape of shuttered buildings. The writer Jeannette Walls, who lived there as a child in the 1970s, recalled in her memoir *The Glass Castle* that "the stores, the signs, the sidewalks, the cars were all covered with a film of black coal dust." But though "shabby and worn out," Welch had once been "a place on its way up. On a hill stood a grand limestone courthouse with a big clock tower. Across from it was a handsome bank with arched windows and a wrought-iron door."

A local historian told the journalist Bill Bishop that six decades ago Welch was "a little San Francisco" where Glenn Miller's band came to play and Packards lined the streets. But as mining methods changed and steel industry demand slackened, the city entered a steep decline that never really stopped. Today the population is below three thousand. "Rational people leave, if they can," said the president of a nearby college.[2]

Welch would seem to have nothing in common with affluent neighborhoods like Venice, California, or Park Slope, Brooklyn. Yet all three are places where middle-class neighborhoods have disappeared. The demographic character of neighborhoods and cities has, of course, always been subject to change over time as various groups migrated and local industries rose and fell. But a 2006 Brookings study by Jason Booza, Jackie Cutsinger, and George Galster (a political scientist, sociologist, and economist, respectively, at Wayne State University) found something new. Between 1970 and 2000 the proportion of metropolitan neighborhoods in the United States that were predominantly middle-income (neighborhoods where the median income was within 20 percent of the metropolitan-area median) fell from 58 percent to 41 percent. About half of the vanishing 17 percent became upper-income neighborhoods, and about half became lower-income neighborhoods. Fewer middle-class neighborhoods remained in city centers than in the suburbs, but in the suburbs the changeover proceeded at about the same pace.[3]

In chapter 3 we saw that median income stagnated during the Great Divergence in comparison both to income growth for the wealthiest Americans and to earlier median income growth during the postwar Great Compression. We also considered how large expenses like housing, medical care, and higher education pinched middle-class incomes more during the Great Divergence than they did during the Great Compression. The Brookings study suggests something else is happening to the battered American middle class. It's shrinking.

The term "middle class" is maddeningly vague, but one reasonable definition can be arrived at by dividing the range of U.S. annual incomes evenly into seven categories and labeling as "middle class" people who fall into the middle three (households earning incomes between $25,000 and $74,999; these and all following figures are in 2008 dollars). If the population were distributed *evenly* across *all seven* income categories, a little less than half (three sevenths) would inhabit the middle three. In 1980 the distribution wasn't too far off from that target; about half of all U.S. households were in this midzone. By 2008, though, only 43 percent were. During the Great Divergence, then, the middle class has (at least by this definition) shrunk by about 14 percent. Most of the shrinkage occurred in the 1980s and the 1990s. It began not in 1979 but at the start of the 1970s, and was even more pronounced during that decade.[4]

Georgetown's Stephen J. Rose argued that the shrinking middle class was good news because it was offset by a near-equivalent increase in the proportion of households at higher incomes (roughly between $95,000 and $250,000), while the proportion of households that were poor and near-poor remained about the same.[5] That suggests that during the Great Divergence more middle-class people have been moving up the income scale than down it. The rate of upward mobility may not match its nineteenth-century heyday, nor even its rate during the 1950s, and compared to other industrialized democracies the U.S. rate is sluggish, as we saw in chapter 1. But upward mobility does continue to exist, and going up certainly beats going down or staying put.

Still, a thriving middle class is rightly judged an important indicator of a society's overall health. The alternative is extremes of wealth and poverty, mutual alienation, and, at some point, political instability. In the oft-repeated formulation of the late Harvard sociologist Barrington Moore Jr., "No bourgeois, no democracy."

When we talk about people being middle-class, what we really mean is that they have a job whose salary puts them in the middle of the nation's income distribution. Are middle-class jobs disappearing? Yes, although the extent to which it's occurring depends on how you pose the question. Certainly a great many of the better-paying jobs that the middle class previously depended on are gone forever. There's more than one explanation as to why that occurred, but right now let's consider the disruptions brought about by technological change.

Our story begins at the dawn of the computer age in the 1950s, when long-standing worries that automation would create mass unemployment entered an acute phase. Economic theory dating back to the nineteenth century said that technological advances wouldn't reduce net employment because the number of jobs wasn't fixed; a new machine might eliminate jobs in one part of the economy, but it would also create jobs in another part.[6] For example, someone had to be employed to make these new machines. But as the economists Frank Levy of MIT and Richard J. Murnane of Harvard point out in their 2004 book *The New Division of Labor*, computers represented an entirely different sort of new machine. Previously, technology had performed physical tasks. (Think of John Henry's nemesis, the steam-powered hammer.) Computers were designed to perform cognitive tasks. (Think of *Jeopardy* champion Ken Jennings's nemesis, IBM's Watson.) Theoretically, there was no limit to the kinds of work computers might eventually perform. In 1964 several eminent intellectuals, including the past and future Nobel laureates Linus Pauling and Gunnar Myrdal, wrote President Lyndon Johnson to warn him about "a system of almost unlimited productive capacity which requires progressively less human labor."

Such a dystopia may yet one day emerge. But thus far traditional economic theory is holding up reasonably well.[7] Computers are eliminating jobs, but they're also creating jobs. The trouble is that the kinds of jobs computers eliminate tend to be the ones previously occupied by moderately skilled middle-class workers, while the kinds of jobs computers create tend to be ones for highly skilled, affluent workers.

"Computers' comparative advantage over people," write Levy and Murnane, "lies in tasks that can be described using rules-based logic: step-by-step procedures with an action specified for every contingency." Where rule-based logic breaks down, they point out, is whenever an unforeseen contingency arises. They cite the example of an auto mechanic using computerized diagnostics to figure out what's wrong with a minivan whose front seat won't move forward or backward at the touch of an electric switch. The diagnostics can look for specific problems anticipated by the automakers—a broken wire, a faulty motor underneath the seat—but often the problem involves an interaction between two electronic components. When that's the case, the technician has to figure out the problem by eliminating possibilities through trial and error. Something else that can't easily be achieved through rule-based logic is pattern recognition, which depends on an understanding of context as well as an ability to recognize analogies that lie outside the immediate context. Perhaps the technician has never seen a seat in this particular minivan model that wouldn't move forward or back, but he has seen power windows that won't go up or down. If so, he might follow a hunch that whatever electronic component interfered with the power windows is here interfering with the power seats. Computers' difficulty with pattern recognition explains why, when you order concert tickets online, you are required to look at a random assembly of letters bent weirdly out of shape and type them into your keyboard. The ticket sellers want to make sure that these tickets are bought by a person, not a computer, and computers don't know how to decipher deliberately distorted letters of the alphabet.

Rule-based logic isn't the exclusive province of middle-income jobs. Levy and Murnane write that when the London International Financial Futures and Options Exchange substituted computers for trading pits in 1999, the pit traders whose jobs it eliminated could make $450,000 in a good year. In a September 2011 five-part series for *Slate*, the technology writer Farhad Manjoo describes incursions that robots have made into a number of high-paid professions, including medicine and the law. "If you do a single thing—and especially if there's a lot of money in that single thing," Manjoo writes, "you should put a *Welcome, Robots!* doormat outside your office."

Nor is pattern recognition the exclusive province of people in high-income jobs. A truck driver making a left turn on a busy city street, Levy and Murhane note, has to process visual and aural information about what's happening on the street; tactile information about the truck's probable speed once he hits the accelerator; and split-second calculations about probable trajectories for people and other vehicles. All this is well beyond the ability of a computer.[8]

Or so it seemed when Levy and Murnane wrote their book. In 2011 their MIT colleagues Erik Brynjolfsson and Andrew McAfee of the Sloan School of Management wrote that this conclusion had become obsolete by the end of 2010. In October of that year Google automated a fleet of Toyota Priuses and put them on the road (with human drivers behind the wheel as safety backups). The robocars navigated from Google's Mountain View, California, headquarters to its Santa Monica office, taking a detour along the way to wind down San Francisco's Lombard Street ("the crookedest street in the world"). The cars made the 350-mile trip with only a few minor human interventions. "Levy and Murnane were correct that automatic driving on populated roads is an enormously difficult task," Brynjolfsson and McAfee conclude, "and it's not easy to build a computer that can substitute for human perception and pattern matching in this domain. Not easy, but not impossible either."[9]

Levy and Murnane's larger point, however, is reinforced by Brynjolfsson and McAfee's caveat. The elimination of rule-based jobs tends to fall heavily on middle incomes—*including*, conceivably, truck drivers. Higher-income jobs seldom involve, in Manjoo's formulation, doing "a single thing."

In 1969 the two broad categories encompassing the occupations of the largest proportion of American workers were blue-collar work and administrative support. Together, Levy and Murnane calculate, these categories described 56 percent of the workforce. By 1999, they described only 39 percent. The decline occurred because many of these jobs were sufficiently rule-based that industrial robots and desktop computers could do them. During that same period, sales-related occupations increased from 8 to 12 percent; professional occupations increased from 10 to 13 percent; and managers and administrators increased from 8 percent to 14 percent. The first category encompasses employees at a variety of income levels, but chiefly at the top and bottom. The second and third encompass employees at the top. Shortly before becoming President Bill Clinton's first labor secretary, Robert Reich, in his 1991 book *The Work of Nations*, labeled people in the latter two categories "symbolic analysts." These were people who "simplify reality into abstract images that can be rearranged, juggled, or experimented with" using "mathematical algorithms, legal arguments, financial gimmicks, scientific principles, psychological insights," and other tools seldom acquired without a college or graduate degree. At the opposite end of the income distribution, Reich writes, were providers of "in-person services" like waitressing, home health care, and security. The middle, once occupied by factory workers, stenographers, and other moderately skilled laborers, was disappearing fast.

Consider the sad tale of the bank teller. When is the last time you saw one? In the 1970s, the number of bank tellers grew by 85 percent. It was one of the nation's fastest-growing occupations, and it required only a high school degree. In 1970, bank tellers averaged the equivalent of about $28,000 in 2010 dollars. But the writing was already on the wall. In September 1969 a Chemical Bank branch in Rockville Centre, New York, installed a Docuteller, the world's first automated teller machine. Dreamed up by a Dallas businessman while he stood in a bank line, the Docuteller initially cost the equivalent of seven bank tellers. But unlike a bank teller, the Docuteller worked twenty-four hours a day, every day. "On Sept. 2," a Chemical Bank ad announced, "our bank will open at 9:00 and never close again!"[10]

Karen Akers started working as a teller at Jefferson National Bank in 1987. Although ATMs were commonplace by then, they had not yet reached her branch in rural Stafford County, Virginia. Akers was one of five or six tellers at the branch. "You hand-wrote a cash-in," she recalls. "You hand-wrote a cash-out." At the end of the day you added it all up, using an adding machine. A runner would take the deposits and withdrawals to the main branch in the area, and from there someone would take them to the headquarters in Charlottesville.

A year or two in, the branch acquired an ATM. "You didn't have as many people coming in," she said, though "we were the ones that still had to open all those envelopes up." (Also, "it took awhile before people trusted their deposits in that machine.") The branch continued to employ the same number of tellers, but since Stafford County was growing rapidly at that time the bank probably would have had to build more teller windows and hire more tellers (or open more branches) if ATMs hadn't materialized. Not that the tellers were idle; quite the opposite. Computerization allowed them to do more of the work previously restricted to the customer service employees one step up in the bank hierarchy—the people who sat behind desks. For example, the tellers were able to see whether and when a check had been cashed, or print out a bank statement, or do some loan research—duties that previously tellers had been unable to perform. That meant the bank didn't need as many customer service employees. After Jefferson National was taken over in 1998 by Wachovia (itself taken over in 2008 by Wells Fargo), the tellers started doubling as salespeople, too. "They would run you through all kinds of sales classes," Akers recalls. Customers weren't supposed to leave the teller window "without you trying to sell them something else." Periodically a regional manager would come by and literally stand behind each teller in turn to make sure he or she was making the right pitch.

The job's stress level climbed steadily upward. "You have quotas to meet," Akers told me, "you have surveys done constantly that rate you." You were expected to score a seven. If you scored a six, that was "not good," and if you scored a five, you were "in trouble." It was not uncommon to see tellers in tears after they received their ratings. Originally Akers had taken the job in part because she was a working mother and a teller job allowed her to leave at two P.M. But now tellers work till at least five P.M.; "bankers' hours" are a thing of the past. The one thing that didn't change was the pay; her raises were pretty much limited to cost-of-living increases. "It's a low-paid job when you go in," Akers said, "and it's a low-paid job when you leave." Eventually she quit and went to work at a small community bank for slightly less pay because it was much less stressful.[11]

Today, the job category "bank teller" is one of the nation's slowest-growing occupations. The Bureau of Labor Statistics projects a paltry 6 percent growth rate during the next decade. The job now pays, discounting for inflation, 14 percent less than it did in 1970, averaging about $25,000 a year.[12] Akers makes a little more than $28,000. That's 12 percent *higher* than the current average and about what the average was in 1970, discounting for inflation. "They let us look at the money," Akers likes to joke. "They just don't give us any."

As this story plays out in similar occupations—cashiers, typists, welders, farmers, appliance repairmen (this last already so obsolete that no one bothers to substitute a plausible ungendered noun)—the moderately skilled workforce is hollowing out. This trend isn't unique to the United States. The Japanese have a word for it: *kudoka*. MIT's David Autor calls it "job polarization," and in his view it's driven by the substitution of jobs like the ones described above with lower-wage service jobs: "food service workers, security guards, janitors and gardeners, cleaners, home health aides, child care workers, hairdressers and beauticians, and recreation occupations." Between 1980 and 2005, service jobs' share of U.S. labor hours increased by 30 percent, according to a 2011 paper by Autor and David Dorn, an assistant professor of economics at the Center for Monetary and Financial Studies in Madrid. Among workers with no more than a high school education, service jobs' share of U.S. labor hours increased by more than half. During the three decades prior to the Great Divergence, these lower-wage service jobs' share of labor hours had either declined or stayed flat. Autor and Dorn's bottom line is that as moderately skilled workers' jobs were wiped out by automation they were pushed into lower-paid service jobs that computers can't perform but that people can.[13]

Autor and Dorn's bleak view of middle-class decline is challenged in *Where Are All the Good Jobs Going?*, a 2011 book by the Georgetown economist Harry Holzer in collaboration with Julia Lane, David Rosenblum, and Fredrik Andersson (economists at, respectively, the National Science Foundation, the University of Chicago's National Opinion Research Center, and the U.S. Office of the Comptroller of the Currency). Holzer et al. argue in effect that many of the service jobs that Autor, Dorn, Reich, and others have written off as low-skilled are actually medium-skilled, and that these medium-skilled jobs pay reasonably well (though not as well as the unionized manufacturing jobs that were the bedrock of middle-class prosperity during the Great Compression). For example, although some health aides do little more than bathe and feed the infirm, many others perform tasks that require some technical training to operate machinery and carry out rudimentary nursing functions. A phlebotomist, for instance, travels to people's homes to take blood samples. The catch is that whereas in earlier eras medium-skilled jobs were readily available to high school graduates who lacked college degrees, this newer type of medium-skilled job typically requires a bachelor's degree or at least an associate's degree from a community college. Phlebotomists must receive training at a hospital or community college, which usually takes a year or less, prior to receiving certification. "Autor is absolutely correct that there has been some shrinkage in middle-skill jobs requiring only the performance of routine tasks," Holzer writes in a 2010 paper, "especially production jobs for equipment operators and laborers and office jobs for clerical workers." But "the notion that we are developing an 'hourglass economy' with large top and bottom layers but a vastly shrinking middle, while not without basis, has been overblown."[14]

Even Autor concedes that computer-driven job polarization can't possibly explain why income inequality is so much worse in the United States than it is in other advanced industrialized democracies. That's because his research has found that *kudoka* is happening to roughly the same extent within the European Union. Another problem is that the Great Divergence began in 1979, well before most people had ever seen a personal computer. By the late 1990s, as businesses stampeded to the Internet, inequality slackened a bit. If computers were the principal factor driving inequality, the opposite should have happened. A final problem is that the economic returns to computer use for people with college or graduate-level education taper off at higher incomes, even as income inequality intensifies. If computers required ever-higher levels of education to manipulate ever-growing quantities of information in ever-more rococo ways, we'd expect the very richest people to be the biggest nerds. They aren't.[15]

Here, then, is a dilemma. We know that computers put a premium on more highly educated workers, but we can't really demonstrate that computers caused the Great Divergence. What is it that's so special about computers? The Harvard economists Claudia Goldin and Lawrence Katz think that's the wrong question to ask.

Yes, Goldin and Katz argue, computer technology had a big impact on the economy. But that impact was no larger than that of other technologies introduced throughout the twentieth century, starting in 1900 with the dynamo (electrical generator) that Henry Adams memorably contemplated as an object of religious worship at the Paris Exposition.[16] The first long-distance electric power transmission line appeared in the United States in 1889 (it used direct current and linked the Oregon cities of Willamette Falls and Portland, which stood a dozen miles apart), and the first electric streetlights appeared a decade before that. But it wasn't until the first two decades of the twentieth century that the full potential of electric power began to be realized in the United States. In his 1952 book *The Big Change: America Transforms Itself: 1900–1950*, the popular historian Frederick Lewis Allen, who was born in 1890, describes vividly the scarcity of "electrical services and devices" as of 1900.

The houses of the great majority were still lighted by gas (in the cities and towns) or oil lamps (in the country). Millions of Americans of the older generation still remember what it was like to go upstairs of an evening and then be consumed with worry as to whether they had really turned off completely the downstairs gas jets. A regular chore for the rural housewife was filling the lamps . . . For a good many years there had been refrigerator cars on the railroads, but the great national long-distance traffic in fresh fruits and vegetables was still in its infancy . . . In most parts of the United States people were virtually without fresh fruit and green vegetables from late autumn to late spring. During this time they consumed quantities of starches, in the form of pies, doughnuts, potatoes, and hot bread, which few would venture to absorb today. The result was that innumerable Americans were in sluggish health during the months of late winter and early spring, when [their] diet was short of vitamins.

This way of life would vanish within one generation. Between 1909 and 1929, Katz and Goldin report in their 2008 book *The Race Between Education and Technology,* the percentage of manufacturing horsepower acquired through the purchase of electricity rose sixfold. From 1917 to 1930, the proportion of U.S. homes with electricity increased from 24 percent to 80 percent. By contrast, from 1984 to 2003, the proportion of U.S. workers using computers increased from 25 percent to 57 percent.[17] Computer use has spread quickly, but not as quickly as electric power did during the early part of the twentieth century. Indeed, Allen reminds us that more than one technology-driven industry was created or transformed in life-altering ways within a handful of years after 1900. In 1901 J. P. Morgan and Andrew Carnegie created U.S. Steel, the world's first billion-dollar corporation. In 1903 the Wright Brothers took flight at Kitty Hawk. That same year Edwin S. Porter filmed *The Great Train Robbery,* thereby creating a U.S. industry in narrative motion pictures. In 1908 Henry Ford produced the first Model T. In 1909 Leo Baekeland introduced Bakelite, thereby inventing an industry in synthetic plastics. Around 1915 David Sarnoff dreamed up the "radio music box." Allen might also have mentioned that in 1915 Alexander Graham Bell (who of course had invented the telephone four decades earlier) participated in a public demonstration of the first transcontinental telephone line— telecommunications' equivalent of the golden spike.

Contemporary culture is so fixated on the computer revolution that the very word "technology" has become an informal synonym for "computers." But during the twentieth century's first half we witnessed not only the technological revolutions just noted but also the advent of the washing machine, antibiotics, television, air conditioning, petrochemicals . . . need one go on? Most of the new products had much the same effect as the computer—that is, they increased demand for progressively higher-skilled workers.[18] But (with the possible exception of radio) none of these consumer innovations coincided with an increase in inequality. Why not? In answering this question, Goldin and Katz invite us to turn our attention away from the *demand* for better-skilled workers and to focus instead on the *supply* of such workers.

Few things in American life seem as timeless as high school, but in important ways high school was itself an invention of the early twentieth century. To be sure, the nation's first public high school, Boston's English Classical School, dates all the way back to 1821. But it wasn't until 1910 that a movement began to build high schools outside major cities, and it wasn't until the 1930s that the majority of high-school-age kids in the United States actually attended high school. In general, universal education in the United States was established more gradually than is usually remembered. During the first half of the nineteenth century government only partly funded public schools in many states; the remainder was paid for by parents. The states didn't start making school attendance compulsory until the 1870s. For many years these laws were widely ignored, and high school attendance was exempt. In Michigan, a dispute arose as to whether public funding for high schools (as opposed to elementary schools) was even *allowed*. (It was, the Michigan Supreme Court ruled in 1874.) Before 1910, attending a secondary school usually meant going to a private school, or "academy," whose specific purpose was either to prepare students for college (these so-called classical academies included the still-extant Phillips academies, Andover and Exeter) or to provide specialized vocational or conservatory training. Vocational training was also available through apprenticeships.[19]

High schools differed from the academies in two ways. They were (eventually) funded entirely by government. And they were meant to serve not just teenagers who would go on to college, or teenagers who would bypass college and go to work at eighteen, but both groups. By the 1920s, Goldin and Katz report, high schools across the country had established a fairly uniform curriculum not too different from what you'd find in a public high school today, a mix of "college preparation, general education, vocational instruction, and commercial training."[20] You could learn the basics of chemistry or English literature; you could also learn how to type, or how to cook, or how to build things out of wood.

States felt compelled to build high schools because the public was demanding them. The public was demanding them because employers were starting to require high school diplomas. In the technology-driven economy of the early twentieth century, office workers had to know how to operate typewriters and adding machines. They had to master bookkeeping, billing procedures, and stenography. Farmers had to master elementary genetics to grow hybrid corn. Factory workers often had to know algebra and geometry, how to read mechanical drawings or mix chemicals, and grasp at least the basics of how electricity worked. As early as 1902, the personnel chief at National Cash Register Company in Dayton, Ohio, said, "In the factory we like the boys to have a high school education if possible."[21]

Goldin and Katz calculate that the more any given industry relied on purchased electricity and the more capital it amassed per employee, the better educated its blue-collar workforce was. Even salespeople were often required to hold high school diplomas. "It may be hard to believe that purchasing a radio once took skilled sales personnel," Goldin and Katz write, "but it did." The earliest radios required home installation, and purchasers needed to be shown how to use them. Radio sales clerks doubled as yesterday's equivalent to the Geek Squad, competing with radio hobbyists who hired themselves out for installation and repair work. As a boy growing up in Far Rockaway, Queens, the Nobel physicist Richard Feynman earned money during the Depression by fixing radios—tinkering with vacuum tubes, removing a burned-out resister, climbing onto neighbors' roofs and fixing their antennae.[22] Simple work for a budding genius, it required from mere mortals a high school education.

High school education was better than vocational training because the general knowledge it imparted allowed for more flexibility. Goldin and Katz cite the example of telegraphy. During the mid-nineteenth century, the job of telegrapher required a variety of skills and was therefore a valuable step on the occupational ladder; the young Andrew Carnegie and Thomas Edison were telegraphers. By the late nineteenth century, though, the job was routinized and became an occupational dead end, giving any telegrapher who'd been vocationally trained good reason to wish he'd finished high school instead. High school was also a way to escape an unskilled labor pool that from 1890 to 1920 was flooded by a wave of immigration never matched before or since. Immigrants constituted 42 percent of all manufacturing workers in the northeastern states. They were even more prevalent in certain artisanal trades. Fully 80 percent of all bakers in the Northeast were foreign-born. A high school education was a ticket to bypass immigrant-dominated workplaces and earn higher pay in higher-end manufacturing jobs such as typesetting, which required some familiarity with English grammar and spelling; in more technically oriented trades like those of electrician or plumber; or in white-collar jobs like that of office clerk.

High school also prepared you for college, which sometime around the mid-twentieth century displaced high school as a threshold requirement for skilled labor as technology advances drove the workplace's education needs still higher. Only 10 percent of those born in 1900 attended college, and fewer than 5 percent graduated. At the turn of the century college was often deemed unnecessary even if you wanted to enter one of the professions; medical schools and law schools frequently admitted students with only a high school diploma.[23] Colleges were for the ukulele-playing elite, a place where knowledge frequently took a backseat to clubbability. But in 1914 the theologian Albert Parker Fitch told students at Williams College that in the fourteen years since he'd graduated from Harvard, the place had been transformed. "Formerly," he wrote,

> if a man attended his lectures with decent regularity, and did some hard work in the weeks preceding his midyear and final examinations, he might spend the better part of his year in elegant leisure, and still make his degree, even make it with distinction. But now, by means of the frequent conferences and quizzes set in the elementary courses, and the large number of theses required in more advanced work, this is no longer true. The minimum of intellectual labor which a student must perform to maintain his undergraduate standing is much larger than it used to be, and it is steadily increasing.[24]

The infusion of new students bent on making themselves marketable in the twentieth-century economy accounted for the difference.

Between 1900 and 1933 the number of students attending public and private universities nearly quintupled. Much of the increase came from growth in existing public universities. (At the turn of the century, Goldin and Katz note, Harvard and Yale had more undergraduates—*each*—than the University of Michigan, and as late as 1933 nearly half of the twenty-five colleges and universities with the greatest number of undergraduates were still private ones.) During the 1940s the price of attending college relative to family income dropped precipitously and then remained stable from the 1950s until the start of the Great Divergence. The percentage of U.S. males who graduated from college grew from 5 percent for the cohort born in 1900 to 10 percent for the cohort born in 1920 to nearly 20 percent for the cohort born in 1940 and nearly 30 percent for the cohort born in 1950. In that year about 8 percent of all full-time workers were college graduates. By 2005, about 32 percent were, and an additional 29 percent possessed some college education.[25]

America's ever-growing commitment to mass education was not shared by the older and more "cultured" European nations. Europeans thought that educational egalitarianism was softhearted and wasteful. They preferred a system that selected only the most promising adolescents for further schooling, and even then the child's parents usually had to pay for it. As late as the 1930s, Katz and Goldin note, "America was virtually alone in providing universally free and accessible secondary schools." But while Continental sophisticates scoffed, America's better-educated masses became a vital component to its superior performance in a world economy that could no longer easily accommodate anyone whose education stopped at age twelve or thirteen.

Americans' educational level rose steadily with the growing technological sophistication of the workplace. The 1944 G.I. Bill, which paid tuition for returning servicemen, played an important role; so did the Sputnik-inspired National Defense Education Act of 1958, which increased federal spending on schools at all levels and created (at the suggestion of Milton Friedman!) a student-loan program for colleges. With the passing of each decade, the years of schooling achieved by twenty-four-year-olds increased on average by close to one year.

These gains virtually halted starting with 1976's cohort of twenty-four-year-olds. Educational attainment started growing again in the 1990s, but at a much slower rate. Here's another way to put it: The average person born in 1945 received two more years of schooling than his parents. The average person born in 1975 received only half a year more of schooling than his parents. In 1970 the high school graduation rate stopped climbing for the first time since 1890.[26] From 1970 to 1980 the high school graduation rate fell; after that it leveled off at about 75 percent.[27]

Unlike the computerization trend, the slowdown of educational attainment gains is not occurring in all industrialized nations; it is uniquely American. Remember those Europeans who scoffed at the Yanks' misty-eyed commitment to universal education? Around the middle of the twentieth century they started to wise up and expand educational opportunities in their own countries. By the end of the century Europe had caught up with or exceeded average educational attainment in the United States. According to the Organisation for Economic Co-operation and Development, the United States has proportionally fewer high school graduates (measured as the percentage of young people at the typical graduation age) than Germany, Greece, the United Kingdom, Ireland, and Italy. And while the college *attendance* rate in the United States has continued to rise, growth in the college *completion* rate has slowed sufficiently to put twenty-five- to thirty-four-year-olds in the United States behind Australia, Belgium, Denmark, Ireland, Norway, New Zealand, Canada, Japan, and Korea. "We have the most-educated fifty-five-year-olds in the world," Katz told me. "But we're in the middle of the pack for twenty-five-year-olds."[28]

The run-up during the Great Divergence in the "wage premium" for high school and college graduates in the United States—that is, the wage differences between people who held high school diplomas and those who didn't, and between people who held college diplomas and those who didn't—reflects the simple fact that America's production of high school and college graduates is no longer keeping pace with technological change. From 1915 to 1950 the high school premium declined, because the rapid increase in high school graduates outraced demand. But subsequently the pattern shifted. From 1950 to 1980, according to Goldin and Katz's calculations, the high school premium initially rose slightly, then leveled off, because the supply of high school graduates met demand. With the start of the Great Divergence, however, the high school premium began to climb, because the demand for high school graduates now exceeded the supply. The high school premium peaked in 2000 and declined slightly thereafter—a probable sign that by the twenty-first century employers no longer deemed the difference between a high school dropout and a high school graduate who failed to go on to college as great as they once did. During the Great Divergence the median compensation for a thirty-five- to forty-four-year-old male high school graduate who did not go on to college declined by 10 percent.[29]

For college graduates, the wage premium followed a similar pattern. The college premium declined from 1915 to 1950, bounced up and down from 1950 until the start of the Great Divergence, then climbed sharply from 1980 to 1990 and a bit more gradually after 1990, by which time it approximated its 1915 level. The Georgetown economists Anthony Carnevale and Stephen J. Rose calculate that demand for college graduates started exceeding supply around 1985. Since 1980, the college premium has nearly doubled.[30]

The post-1990 slowdown in the college premium's growth likely reflects the new reality that employers increasingly demand a *graduate* degree. The number of master's degrees more than doubled after 1990, driven largely by an increase among women. During the Great Divergence the median compensation for a male college graduate age thirty-five to forty-four who didn't go on to graduate school increased by 32 percent. Although that was far better than the high school graduate's 10 percent decline, 32 percent was less than half that era's productivity growth of 78 percent. Males in this age group with *graduate* degrees saw their incomes increase 49 percent—better, but also shy of the productivity increase. Only women in this age group possessing college and graduate degrees saw their incomes rise in tandem with productivity increases. Richard Vedder, an economist at Ohio University and the American Enterprise Institute, a conservative Washington think tank, quipped in 2011 to the *New York Times*, "In 20 years, you'll need a Ph.D. to be a janitor."[31]

The growth in the college premium after 1980 was kicked off by the end of the Vietnam draft in 1973. College students had received deferments, and until 1968 graduate students received them, too. The deferments had the effect of inflating college and grad-school enrollment, already enlarged by the baby boom, thereby lowering the market price for college graduates. By one estimate, draft avoidance raised college enrollment in the late 1960s by four to six percentage points.[32] In 1976 the Harvard economist Richard B. Freeman noted with concern, "For the graduates of the mid-1970s, falling salaries, scarce job opportunities, and dwindling career prospects are the new reality." This hadn't happened

Supply and Demand for College-Educated Workers Relative to 1970, 1915–2010

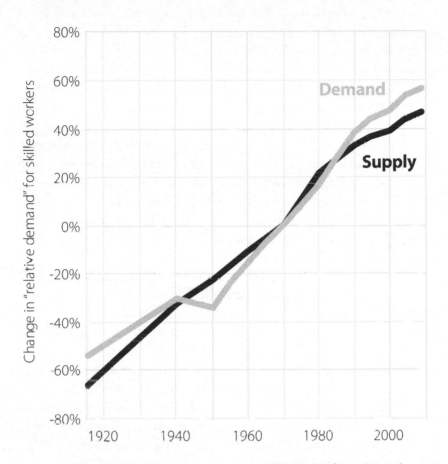

Source: Anthony P. Carnevale and Stephen J. Rose, "The Undereducated American" report (Washington: Georgetown University, Center on Education and the Workforce, June 2011), 19. Carnevale and Rose used data in Claudia Goldin and Lawrence F. Katz, *The Race Between Education and Technology* (Cambridge, MA: Harvard University Press, 2008), and applied a supply-demand model from David Autor, Lawrence F. Katz, and Melissa Kearney, "Trends in U.S. Wage Inequality: Revising the Revisionists," *Review of Economics and Statistics* 90, no. 2 (May 2008): 300–23.

since the Great Depression.[33] But with the Vietnam draft gone and the last of the baby boomers graduating from college, that trend began to reverse itself. It was no longer necessary to enroll in college if you wanted to stay out of Khe Sanh, and as the baby-boom cohort dwindled fewer kids were reaching college age. The college premium began to grow. The education premium has been growing ever since (see figure, p. 91). Goldin and Katz calculate that the increase in economic returns to education is responsible for about 60 percent of the increase in wage inequality between 1973 and 2005.[34]

Why did educational attainment slow down? Goldin and Katz are somewhat tentative on this point, but clearly the slowdown represents a failure by elementary and secondary schools to provide education relevant to the economy's growing demands, a task they performed much better during the first half of the twentieth century. Many of the qualities of K–12 education in the United States that helped the high school movement grow during the first half of the twentieth century—decentralization, for instance, and a forgiving approach to students who initially fail—became, Katz and Goldin argue, liabilities during the century's second half.

Goldin and Katz blame America's colleges and universities, too—not for any educational failing (the United States is a global leader in higher education) but rather for raising tuition, which since the 1980s has priced many families out of the market. College tuition fell (discounting for inflation) or remained stable from the 1940s through the 1970s—a significant benefit to the middle class during the Great Compression. From the 1950s to the 1970s, annual tuition at public and private universities averaged, respectively, 4 percent and 20 percent of annual median family income. Compared to tuition levels before 1950 and after 1980, these two university professors observe, "college was a real bargain." But tuition surged ahead of the already-high inflation rate during the 1970s, and has done so ever since. By 2005 college tuition at public and private universities averaged, respectively, 10 percent and 45 percent of median family income.

Goldin and Katz don't offer an explanation for why college tuition spiked, but the fact that it happened at the same time the education premium spiked suggests it was a simple matter of unquenchable demand. A college education is so inarguably necessary to thrive in today's economy that parents will pay whatever they can scrape together, even if it means dipping into retirement funds. Financial aid and student loans make up the difference for many families, and others pay sticker price. The rest do without. When the journalist Andrew Ferguson recently asked Richard Vedder why colleges charged so much for tuition and fees, Vedder replied, "Because they can!" He elaborated: "I mean, who's going to stop them? Parents? The government? There's nothing stopping them—literally nothing." William Massy, a former finance officer at Stanford, said much the same to *Time* in 2001. "Basically," he said, "we will raise the tuition as much as the market will bear." Increasing tuition can even be its own marketing strategy. In 1988 a dean at Mount Holyoke told *New England Monthly* that tuition was jacked up to lure applicants who equated price with prestige. This was known, he explained, as the Chivas Regal strategy.[35]

During the Great Divergence, the American education system has not been able to increase the supply of better-educated workers sufficiently to meet demand, and so the price of those workers (i.e., their incomes) has risen faster relative to the general population. At a time when the workforce needed to be smarter, Americans got dumber. Or rather: Americans got smarter at a much slower rate than they did during previous periods of technological change (and also at a much slower rate than people in many other industrialized democracies did). That was excellent news for people with college diplomas or advanced degrees, whose limited supply bid up their salaries. It was terrible news for everyone else.

<u>6</u>

Offshore

I TYPED THIS BOOK ON A LAPTOP THAT was made in China. Just about everything I own was made in China. Just about everything you own was made in China, too. In 1979, when the Great Divergence began, you and I didn't own anything made in China. With Mao only three years in the grave, China still had a sluggish, centrally planned economy. In that year, the new Chinese leader, Deng Xiaoping, decided enough was enough and inaugurated various market reforms. "Black cat, white cat," he famously said. "What does it matter what color the cat is as long as it catches mice?"

China ended up catching quite a lot of mice. In 1979, China was a net importer, with a trade deficit of $2 billion. Its total exports were about $14 billion. But by 2010, through aggressive capital investment and stunning productivity growth, China managed to achieve a trade surplus of $185 billion and total exports of $1.6 trillion. Since 1979, China's gross domestic product has increased by about 10 percent per year—nearly three times the average annual increase the United States enjoyed during the postwar golden years, 1950–73. Remember the 2007–9 recession? In the United States, the GDP shrank. In China, the recession merely meant that GDP growth dropped from 13 percent in 2007 to 9 percent in 2009. By 2010, China's GDP growth was back up to 10 percent. China displaced the United States as the world's second-biggest exporter in 2007, then displaced Germany as the world's biggest exporter in 2010. With a GDP of $10 trillion in 2010, China is today the world's second-largest economy, after the United States.[1]

You might be forgiven for concluding from all these impressive statistics that China is a rich country. But in many important ways, China is a poor country. In 2010, China's per capita gross national income was $4,260. That's lower than in Algeria, Jamaica, Cuba, and Bulgaria. These are all poor countries. Meanwhile, the United States, whose trade deficit with China in 2010 was $273 billion, in 2010 had a per capita gross national income of $47,140. Granted, that's not as high as in Sweden, Luxembourg, or Monaco (ranked number one at $197,460).[2] Let's further grant the United States' public debt level matches, roughly, its GDP. If you've gotten this far in this book you're also well aware that in America income is distributed more unequally than in any other advanced industrial democracy. Even so, a per capita income of $47,140 makes the United States a very rich nation—nearly ten times as rich as China (to whom the largest portion of U.S. public debt is owed). How can a manufacturing colossus like China, preeminent banker to the world's biggest economy and itself the world's second-biggest, have such a tiny per capita gross national income? Because China is the most populous nation on the planet. It is home to 1.3 billion people. Some of these people are quite prosperous, thanks to Deng's economic miracle, but most are very poor. The average monthly wage is $449, or about one tenth the average in the United States.[3]

When a manufacturing nation with an aggressively mercantilist trade policy and a preposterously huge pool of cheap labor (that's China) sells a lot of stuff to a manufacturing nation with a much smaller, more prosperous labor pool (that's the United States), the outcome will be lower wages for workers in the more prosperous nation. Or so established economic theory tells us. The theory in question is the Stolper-Samuelson theorem, first elaborated in a 1941 paper by two young economists, Wolfgang Stolper (of Swarthmore and later the University of Michigan) and Paul Samuelson (of MIT). Samuelson, who considered himself "the midwife, helping to deliver Wolfie's brainchild," would go on to write the twentieth century's bestselling economics textbook and to win the Nobel Prize. Fifty years after the theorem's debut, the Columbia economist Jagdish Bhagwati wrote, "I know of no major international economic theorist today who would not trade an arm and a leg" for its authorship.[4]

The Stolper-Samuelson theorem challenged the notion dating back to David Ricardo that everybody benefited when trade between nations proceeded unimpeded. According to classical economics, even higher-wage workers benefited when their country traded with a lower-wage nation. That was because the resulting drop in prices would so exceed their

reduced wages that the workers would net out with the practical equivalent of a raise. In their 1941 paper, Stolper and Samuelson showed that
the opposite was true. When a prosperous nation traded with a lower-
wage nation, its higher-wage workers' reduction in wages would exceed whatever benefit they received from the resulting drop in prices.
The workers would therefore net out with the practical equivalent of . . .
lower wages. Before Stolper and Samuelson came along, the economics
profession thought you had to be an ignoramus to believe that a tariff
could protect *any* workers' standard of living. In their paper Stolper and
Samuelson quoted, with apparent relish, the Harvard economists F. W.
Taussig and Gottfried von Haberler saying as much. Taussig scoffed that
it was "perhaps [the] most familiar and most unfounded of all" beliefs
about prices and wages, while von Haberler sneered that such notions "do
not merit serious discussion."[5] After Stolper and Samuelson, anyone who
believed that tariffs were a good idea was *still* deemed by any self-
respecting economist to be an ignoramus, because free trade was still
understood to be highly beneficial to most of the parties involved. But on
the narrower point of whether lower-wage workers became richer or
poorer when their country traded with even-lower-wage countries, the
economics profession finally conceded that the intuitive answer—the
comparatively higher-wage workers would become poorer—was the correct one. Mathematical models had finally caught up with common sense.

Paradoxically, though, economists experienced initial difficulty applying Stolper-Samuelson to the Great Divergence.

Adrian Wood, a British economist, argued a decade and a half after the
Great Divergence began that trade with low-wage countries was lowering
wages for unskilled workers in developed countries. "There is a clear in-
verse association," Wood wrote in a 1995 paper. "Countries with larger
increases in import penetration experienced larger falls in manufacturing employment." But in the United States, Wood had to concede, imports
of manufactured goods from low-wage countries still totaled less than
3 percent of gross domestic product. By itself, that wasn't enough to displace many workers. Wood answered by arguing that the effects were
subtle and indirect. For example, he wrote that imports from low-wage
countries required more labor than other goods, and therefore displaced
more U.S. workers than did imports from high-wage countries.[6]

Most leading economists in the United States didn't buy it. Paul Krugman (then at Stanford, now at Princeton) and Robert Lawrence (at Har-

vard) argued in a *Scientific American* article published in 1994 that international trade had played a much smaller role in the United States' manufacturing decline than had domestic considerations. Among these, ironically, was the U.S. manufacturing sector's own efficiency, which had lowered prices on consumer products and therefore on the proportion of U.S. spending on goods (TVs, refrigerators, groceries) as opposed to services (CT scans, legal advice, college tuition). From 1970 to 1990, the prices of U.S. goods relative to services had fallen by nearly one quarter. "Although the effect of foreign competition is measurable," Krugman and Lawrence concluded, "it can by no means account for the stagnation of U.S. earnings."[7]

The two economists accepted the validity of the Stolper-Samuelson theorem but found that its applicability was limited because the average manufacturing wage in countries that traded with the United States was fully 88 percent of the U.S. average.[8] The United States wasn't trading all that much with low-wage nations. Prior to the late 1970s, very few less-developed nations had exported *any* manufactured goods; exports from such places were still mostly raw materials.[9] And the few low-wage countries that did trade manufactured goods extensively with the United States prospered so much that they became high-wage countries. Krugman and Lawrence cited the example of Japan, which as recently as 1960 had been a low-wage country. "Goddamn cheap Japanese flying packs," Woody Allen muttered in his 1973 futuristic comedy, *Sleeper*, as he struggled to gain altitude while being chased by security forces. A decade later the joke was already a puzzling anachronism because Japanese exports were famous not for cheapness but for superior quality. Krugman and Lawrence calculated that U.S. trade with low-wage countries had increased the wage gap between skilled and unskilled by a mere three percentage points. Around the same time, the Harvard economists Richard Freeman, George Borjas, and Lawrence Katz put out an even lower estimate of 1.4 percent.[10]

In the mid-aughts, Krugman decided his earlier analysis no longer held up. "My argument was always yes, in principle" imports from low-wage countries could affect income inequality, Krugman told me. But in the 1990s there weren't enough of them. That changed after the century turned. In a December 2007 *New York Times* column and a 2008 paper for the Brookings Institution, Krugman observed that the United States had in 2006 reached "an important watershed: in that year, for the first time, the United States began doing more overall trade in manufactured goods with developing [low-wage] countries than with other developed countries." Imports of manufactured goods that came from less-developed nations had more than doubled as a percentage of gross domestic product, from 2.5 percent in 1990 to 6 percent in 2006.

As recently as 1975, America's top ten trading partners had included Italy, the Netherlands, and Belgium, all high-wage nations. China didn't make the cut. By 1990, China made the top ten, but just barely; it ranked tenth. By 2005, the three European nations had all been displaced by Asian nations, of which the biggest player by far was China. China placed third in the 2005 rankings, after Canada (then as now the United States' top trading partner) and Mexico, which since 1975 had moved up from fifth place to second.[11] The two countries ramping up U.S. trade the fastest—China and Mexico—were both increasing GDP substantially, but they were increasing their U.S. trade even more rapidly. Krugman attributed this, in Mexico's case, partly to the 1994 North American Free Trade Agreement. Experts disagree about the extent of NAFTA's impact on Mexican exports, but surely it isn't entirely coincidental that since the law took effect exports from Mexico to the United States have quadrupled.[12] In China's case Krugman speculated that two major factors were declines in the cost of international communications and of shipping.

Meanwhile, wages in both countries were considerably lower not only than wages in the European countries they displaced after 1975 but also than wages in the countries whose increased U.S. trade created the greatest alarm in the 1990s: South Korea, Taiwan, Hong Kong, Singapore. The Southeast Asian nations had, in 1990, paid workers about 25 percent of what U.S. workers received. By 1995, they paid 39 percent. But as of 2005, Mexico and China paid 11 percent and 3 percent, respectively. This was enough to lower the average manufacturing wage in countries that traded with the United States to 65 percent of the U.S. average. By the logic of Stolper-Samuelson, that drove up the U.S. wage gap between skilled and unskilled workers by much more than Krugman's previous estimate of 3 percent. Krugman didn't calculate a new estimate, but he concluded: "It is likely that the rapid growth of trade since the early 1990s has had significant distributional effects." Borrowing a mathematical model from Krugman's earlier paper, Josh Bivens of the liberal Economic Policy Institute plugged in new data and concluded that trade accounted for 12.5 percent of the growth in income inequality between 1980 and 1995.[13]

Lawrence, looking at the same new data, continued to believe that trade did not affect U.S. income inequality to any great extent. Lawrence focused on the fact that China was increasingly exporting computers and other sophisticated electronics. To depress the wages of lower-skilled workers in the United States, Lawrence reasoned, China would have to compete with American firms that employed lower-skilled workers. But the U.S. tech sector doesn't, for the most part, employ lower-skilled workers. It employs higher-skilled workers. If trade with China were throwing anybody out of work, Lawrence concluded, "it is likely to be . . . workers with relatively high wages." And in fact, Lawrence wrote, during the first decade of the twenty-first century there was comparatively little measured increase in income inequality "by skill, education, unionization or occupation." Income inequality did increase through the aughts, but that was largely because incomes soared at the top of the income-distribution scale. (More on this in chapter 10.) It didn't increase because less-skilled workers got squeezed—or, rather, it didn't increase because less-skilled workers got squeezed much more than they did during the previous two decades. At the very bottom, incomes actually edged up slightly.[14]

Krugman wasn't convinced by his former collaborator's argument. "There is good reason to believe that the apparent sophistication of developing country exports is, in reality, largely a statistical illusion," he answered in his Brookings paper. Unskilled laborers who were paid a pittance in China weren't really doing high-tech work, Krugman reasoned. They were (as Lawrence acknowledged) grabbing sophisticated components manufactured in more advanced and higher-paid economies like Japan, Ireland, and—yes—the United States, and they were slapping them together on an assembly line. That couldn't be good news for less-skilled workers in the United States. Krugman said he couldn't quantify the effect without "a much better understanding of the increasingly fine-grained nature of international specialization and trade."

Globalization's effects were much easier to keep track of in bygone days when trade was conducted *between* countries but the manufacturing of a particular item took place *within* a *single* country. Now that both trade and manufacturing are international, economists are struggling to come up with a clear understanding of precisely who exports what.[15]

That was a challenge even in the 1990s, when Rone Tempest of the *Los Angeles Times* reported that Mattel's "Made in China" Barbie doll was actually made in Saudi Arabia (which produced the oil refined into ethylene); Taiwan (which turned the ethylene into plastic pellets); Japan (which supplied Barbie's mane of nylon hair); the United States (which supplied molds, pigments, and cardboard packaging); China, Indonesia, and Malaysia (which poured Taiwan's plastic pellets into America's mold to make Barbie's body and attached Japan's nylon to the top of Barbie's head); China again (it supplied the cotton cloth used to make Barbie's dress); and Hong Kong (which managed the whole process and arranged shipping). Of the $9.99 list price, thirty-five cents stayed in China.

The same pattern persists today, but the volume and technological sophistication of today's "Made in China" products are much greater. The Personal Computing Industry Center at the University of California, Irvine, has produced a fascinating series of papers describing the supply chains for Apple's most popular consumer products. Although electronic components assembled in China are more sophisticated than molds and plastic pellets, it remains true that the money mostly stays in the United States while the production jobs mostly go abroad. PCIC calculated that in 2006 the business of making and selling Apple's iPod employed 41,170 people worldwide, of whom 13,920—not quite one third—were located in the United States. The good news for the United States was that nearly $750 million of the roughly $1 billion generated worldwide by iPod sales stayed in this country, even though the iPods were assembled in China. The U.S.-based production workers—all computer-chip fabricators—were paid reasonably well: $47,640 on average. (For production jobs in all U.S. business sectors, the average wage that year was $30,480.) The bad news was that these chip fabricators numbered exactly thirty. You could invite all the U.S.-based iPod production workers to dinner and feed them with a single pot of chili! Among the other Americans who made or sold iPods in 2006, more than half worked in retail and distribution (average income: $25,580), and the rest were highly skilled professionals of various kinds—engineers, managers, and so on—most of whom worked at Apple's headquarters in Cupertino, California. They were paid, on average, $85,000.

About two thirds of all the people who made or sold iPods in 2006 were located overseas, most of them in production jobs. Close to half the overseas workers—12,270—were in China, where the iPods were assembled. The production workers in China averaged $1,540, or about 3 percent—that isn't a typo—of what their (better-skilled) U.S. counterparts made. Production workers in the Philippines, who numbered 4,500, averaged slightly more: $2,140. They manufactured hard drives and hard-drive inputs, though some of the Chinese production workers made these as well. Production workers in Japan made the iPod's display panels and modules and were paid a lot more: $40,400 on average. Production workers in Singapore, Japan, Korea, and Taiwan built various other technologically complex inputs and received wages that averaged somewhere in between, though all in the five figures.

These higher-skilled offshore production workers, in competing with higher-skilled American production workers, may conceivably narrow the U.S. wage gap between skilled and unskilled workers. (That might be the type of "fine-grained" detail that kept Krugman from calculating trade's impact on the Great Divergence.) Then again, if these jobs were performed stateside—these are, after all, the manufacturing jobs we most hate to lose to foreign competition—mightn't that narrow the U.S. wage gap between skilled production workers and more affluent workers? There's probably little point in puzzling out such questions, because even if one could force Apple to move all these high-skilled production jobs to the United States, the impact would be extremely modest: In 2006 they numbered only 2,195. The vast majority of production labor involved in manufacturing even a cutting-edge high-tech consumer product like the iPod—cutting-edge as of 2006, anyway—is low-skilled assembly work.

Less-detailed PCIC studies suggest the story is pretty much the same for the more recent iPhone and the iPad. The jobs go overseas, to China, Korea, Taiwan, and Japan. The money does not. In 2010 total labor costs represented a mere 5.3 percent of the sales price for an iPhone and 7 percent for an iPad. Meanwhile, Apple's profit represented 59 percent of the sales price for an iPhone and 30 percent for an iPad.[16]

Apple is, by the reckoning of *Fortune* magazine, the twentieth-most-profitable company in the world, but even worldwide it doesn't come close to making *Fortune*'s list of the fifty biggest employers. With a total headcount of 60,400 in 2011, Apple had less than one quarter as many employees as *Fortune*'s fiftieth-biggest employer, AT&T. At the time of Apple founder Steve Jobs's death in 2011, many commentators compared him to Henry Ford. As innovators and creators of shareholder value the two men were indeed comparable. But as employers they were not. During the

1930s Ford employed more than one hundred thousand people at a *single plant*—Michigan's River Rouge complex. And the Rouge was only one of many Ford plants in the United States and abroad.[17]

Foreign trade enriches the United States, but it also changes employees' relationship with their employers. One of the ways that the real-world economy differs from theoretical models is that bosses tend not to think about employee salaries as they relate to the labor market. Or rather, the boss doesn't typically compare an individual employee's salary to the labor market after he hires him. Instead, the boss thinks about how good a job the employee is doing, how much cash the company has on hand this year (or doesn't have) for raises and bonuses, what the company's internal (perhaps union-negotiated) compensation policies are, and so on. The moment when the boss *does* compare an employee's salary to the labor market typically occurs when he makes the hire. *I need a guy to do X*, the boss thinks. *How much do guys like that get paid?* After that, the employee ceases to be an economic abstraction and is judged based on his own performance (perceived or genuine) and, if the performance is good, on the company's ability (perceived or genuine) to reward him. If the employee gets laid off, it won't likely be because the boss has been poring over Bureau of Labor Statistics data. It will be because the employee's performance was judged unsatisfactory and/or because the boss thinks the company needs to tighten its belt. In a unionized firm, seniority may also come into play. (An important caveat is that this description bears almost no relationship to the hiring of top executives. In that instance, the formalities of labor market research may be observed at the outset, but only in the same way the Geneva Conventions were observed at Abu Ghraib. Afterward the governing principle typically becomes "For God's sake, give him whatever he wants." More on this in chapter 9.)

The pattern described here, wherein an employee is evaluated as a unit of labor when hired but subsequently gets evaluated as an actual human being, was termed a "shielding agreement" by Marianne Bertrand, an economist at the University of Chicago's business school, in a 2004 paper. (Another term might be "common decency.") Bertrand found that between 1976 and 1992 such shielding agreements were eroded by foreign trade. The more foreign competition a company faced, the more responsive its wages became to the current unemployment rate. Similarly, a 2006 paper by Mine Zeynep Senses, an economist and assistant professor at the Nitze School of Advanced International Studies at Johns Hopkins, looked at plant-level data for U.S. manufacturers in industries that outsourced heavily. She found that employment levels there had become more responsive to changes in prevailing wage levels, thereby decreasing workers' bargaining power. This increased responsiveness made both employment and wages become much more volatile.[18]

So far we've reviewed how trade and offshoring in the manufacturing sector might have affected the Great Divergence. But during the past few years many economists have become preoccupied by a more recent trend: offshoring in the *service* sector. The Princeton economist Alan Blinder estimated that more than one quarter of all existing U.S. jobs may become threatened by offshoring.[19] This is where globalization's impact on U.S. income distribution gets murky.

"The service sector" is a vague term that describes, in effect, how most people in the world's more prosperous economies make their living nowadays: not through the sale of tangible goods but through the sale of services. Jobs in the service sector run the gamut from low to high incomes. A janitor inhabits the service sector. So does a hamburger flipper at McDonald's, or a masseuse, or an auto mechanic. But so, too, does an internist or a divorce lawyer. Estimates of the number of U.S. service-sector jobs lost to offshoring thus far range from about sixteen thousand annually to somewhere south of one million.[20] But we're still in the early innings. If you have a job that you can perform from home, it's worth asking yourself whether an English speaker could perform the job tolerably well from halfway around the world at one thirtieth the pay. (The answer for all the service occupations mentioned earlier in this paragraph is "No.")

Service-sector offshoring is far likelier than manufacturing-sector offshoring to affect highly skilled workers. Consequently, its impact on income distribution may turn out to be neutral. It may even serve to promote income *equality*. In the past, Blinder wrote in a 2007 paper, the crucial distinction was "between jobs that require high levels of education and jobs that do not." Measure the wage gap between the two and you got a decent snapshot of one common form of income inequality. But as service jobs migrate offshore, the more relevant distinction is between what

Blinder calls "personally-delivered services" and "impersonally-delivered services." Only impersonally delivered services can be moved offshore.[21]

Impersonally delivered services bear some similarity to, but are not exactly the same as, jobs requiring "rule-based logic," which, as noted in the previous chapter, are the jobs that the MIT economist Frank Levy and the Harvard economist Richard Murnane deem most vulnerable to automation. But impersonally delivered services include a lot more high-skill jobs (though they include lots of low-skill jobs, too). Securities analysis (high-skill) can be delivered remotely; so can keyboard entry (low-skill), radiology (high-skill), and customer complaint centers. Governments have become enthusiastic exporters of service jobs, though in the United States it's typically done through private-sector subcontractors. In Albert Brooks's 2006 film *Looking for Comedy in the Muslim World*, Brooks is seen repeatedly walking past a call center in Delhi, allowing us to hear a sequence of increasingly outlandish salutations capped finally by "This is the White House. How may I direct your call?" A 2006 report by the U.S. Government Accountability Office found that much administration of state government programs had been shifted offshore, including—in what seemed like a cruel joke—the processing of unemployment insurance claims.[22]

"Twenty or thirty years from now," Blinder mused, "will Economics 101 lectures at Princeton University be delivered by a life-like hologram of a well-educated and well-spoken professor who is actually in Mumbai, but who can see and hear the Princeton students via video and audio hookups—and who earns one-fifth of what I do?"[23] Blinder predicted that "tens of millions" of U.S. service jobs will be moved offshore, creating enormous disruptions to the U.S. economy. Here the country to watch is not China but India, whose edge is its population's easy familiarity with the English language. By one 2005 estimate India was performing nearly half the world's offshored business service functions and fully 65 percent of the world's offshored services in information technology.[24] India has the world's fourth-largest GDP ($4 trillion). But as the world's second-most-populous nation (1.2 billion), India is, like China, a rich country whose people are poor, with a per capita annual income of $1,340.

How the offshoring of service jobs affects income inequality depends on how many of Robert Reich's "symbolic analysts" end up delivering services impersonally from Bangalore or someplace like it. In a 2009 paper, Blinder took a closer look at the skill question and concluded that slightly more high-skill jobs than low-skill jobs were vulnerable to getting shipped offshore in the future. Managers and lawyers, he found, will be harder to offshore than employees and paralegals, but in the sciences and engineering higher skills will make workers *more* offshorable. Computer operators (low) are difficult to offshore; computer engineers (high) are less difficult; and computer scientists (high) aren't difficult at all. The two most offshorable jobs, Blinder calculated, were computer programming (high) and data entry (low). The seven occupations that Blinder judged least offshorable included architects (high), but they also included postal service mail sorters (low).[25]

One factor we should perhaps bear in mind is politics. The people holding high-skill jobs may be slightly more likely than low- and medium-skilled workers to see their jobs moved offshore, but they are *a lot* more likely to have their worries about that danger heeded in Washington, in state governments, and in professional societies. Blue-collar calls for protectionist policies have fallen on deaf ears. Similar demands from the affluent might not. Indeed, to some extent they've already been heeded. American radiologists, MIT's Frank Levy and Kyoung-Hee Yu of the Australian School of Business note in a 2006 paper, have managed to keep a pretty tight regulatory lid on the offshoring of their services, which are nothing if not impersonally delivered. I have done business with perhaps half a dozen radiologists in my life, but I have never met one face-to-face, nor even spoken to one by phone; their job is to read and interpret scans, not to interact with the people who've been scanned, and the task of explaining what the interpretations mean falls to a third party—the patient's physician. At the moment, though, the offshoring of radiology is limited mainly to "nighthawk services" in which U.S. board-certified offshore radiologists perform mainly preliminary reads in the middle of the night, mostly for smaller hospitals that don't want to pay to keep a radiologist on the premises overnight.[26]

Will this continue to be the case as qualified radiologists proliferate in India and other low-wage countries? Dean Baker, codirector of the Center for Economic and Policy Research, a liberal think tank in Washington, D.C., noted tartly that free-trade-supporting economists (virtually the entire mainstream) haven't spent a lot of time bemoaning the barriers to free trade—typically, visa restrictions—that benefit doctors,

lawyers, and other professionals. In 1997, U.S. doctors' associations successfully lobbied to cut back on the number of doctors entering the
country—not because the foreigners were unqualified, but because they
were depressing wages. Yet there were, Baker wrote,

> no prominent economists involved in this debate making the obvious
> economic argument, that foreign doctors are depressing the wages of
> U.S. born doctors, *and this is good*. Lower wages for doctors means
> lower health care costs, which will increase the money that consumers
> have available for other spending and lead to more economic growth.
> The model is exactly the same whether the X axis is labeled "steel" or
> "physicians' services."[27]

The same logic applies to complaints likely to be heard in coming
years about the offshoring of professional services. Will professionals
enjoy greater success than lower-income workers at collecting meaningful levels of compensatory government subsidies? Back in 1941, Stolper
and Samuelson said that the logical way to deal with workers harmed by
free trade was to compensate them, and that remains the solution embraced by most economists. But it's easier to legislate in a college lecture
hall than on Capitol Hill.

The federal Trade Adjustment Assistance program, which provides
wage subsidies, job retraining, and other benefits to workers displaced
by foreign competition, has been around since the Kennedy administration, but it's never done much to ease the painful dislocations felt in the
Rust Belt. In 2006 the Labor Department ruled that software engineers,
whose pleas for eligibility had previously gone unheeded on the grounds
that software was not an imported "article" as defined in the law, could
apply for Trade Adjustment Assistance. In 2009 the job-stimulus
bill extended Trade Adjustment Assistance to the service sector. The
provision expired early in 2011 but was renewed later that year.[28] It will be
interesting to see whether future displaced doctors and Wall Street analysts manage to invigorate this perpetually underfunded and marginally
beneficial federal program.

To review: Trade with low-wage nations, which was negligible until
the twenty-first century, is responsible for 12 to 13 percent of the Great
Divergence, and perhaps more. The complexities of offshoring make it

difficult to know with much certainty, but in manufacturing, trade's impact is likely increasing. Overall, though, future offshoring of service jobs is likely to occur on a much larger scale then offshoring of manufacturing jobs (if only because there are fewer and fewer manufacturing jobs left to offshore). The growing importance of service offshoring could blunt trade's impact on U.S. income inequality or even start to reverse it. But if the more affluent parties whose jobs are threatened succeed in securing government protection, all bets are off.

7

Unequal Government

When business really tries, when it is fully unified and raring to go,
it never loses a big battle in Washington.

—Former Procter & Gamble lobbyist Bryce Harlow, in a 1984
essay describing the business of corporate representation

LEFT-OF-CENTER POLITICIANS AND ACTIVISTS have long argued that the
federal government caused the Great Divergence. And by "federal government," they generally mean Republicans, who have controlled the
White House for most of the past thirty years. According to this narrative, the policy changes initiated by President Ronald Reagan and carried forward by the Bush presidencies, *père et fils,* effected a long-term
shift in American demographics. The leftist intellectual Michael Harrington, author of *The Other America*, once summarized these policies
as "a bizarre anti-welfare-state Keynesianism for the rich."

There can be no question that Reagan and his Republican White House
successors, in attempting to reduce government's size, made it less beneficial to people at lower income levels and more accommodating to
people at higher income levels. When Reagan publicly embraced supply-
side theory (a since-discredited[1] notion that lowering marginal income-
tax rates would stimulate sufficient economic growth that the tax cut
would pay for itself), his critics characterized it as "trickle-down economics," a Marie Antoinetteish fantasy that tax cuts for the rich would

somehow benefit everybody else. Reagan's budget chief, David Stockman, later conceded the point when he stated, in a controversial 1981
Atlantic Monthly profile by William Greider, that the president's bill
phasing in across-the-board cuts in income tax rates was really "a Trojan
horse to bring down the top rate." Stockman elaborated: "It's kind of
hard to sell 'trickle down,' so the supply-side formula was the only way to
get a tax policy that was really 'trickle down.' Supply-side is 'trickle-
down' theory."[2] That same year, when congressional leaders asked President Reagan how he intended to make good on his promise to cut federal
spending, he repeated a cherished, highly exaggerated, and racially in-
flammatory campaign chestnut about a "Chicago welfare queen" with
"eighty names, thirty addresses, twelve Social Security cards," and "four
nonexisting deceased husbands" (on whom she collected veterans benefits)
who amassed a tax-free income of more than $150,000. The woman, an
African American named Linda Taylor, whose case had been unusual
enough to attract substantial attention in the Chicago press, had long
since been convicted of defrauding the government (not of $150,000 but
of $8,000, using two aliases, not eighty).[3]

Reagan's Republican White House successors similarly advocated
government policies more favorable to people of higher incomes. Did
these efforts contribute significantly to the Great Divergence? Until recently, the consensus among academics—even most liberal ones—was
that they didn't. Economists argued that the Great Divergence was the
result not of Washington policymaking but of larger "exogenous" (exter-
nal) and "secular" (long-term) forces. In 2009 government spending
reached 24 percent of GDP, the highest it had been since World War II.[4]
But even with federal spending at this unusually high level (necessitated
by a severe recession),Washington's nut remained less than one quarter
the size of the economy. Most of that nut was automatic "entitlement"
spending over which Washington policymakers seldom exert much control. Brad DeLong, a liberal economist at Berkeley, expressed the prevailing view in 2006: "The shifts in income inequality seem to me to be too
big to be associated with anything the government does or did."[5]

The journalist Mickey Kaus took this argument one step further in
his 1992 book, *The End of Equality*, positing that income inequality was
the inevitable outgrowth of ever-more-ruthlessly efficient markets, and
that government attempts to reverse it were certain to fail. "You cannot
decide to keep all the nice parts of capitalism," he wrote, "and get rid of

all the nasty ones." Instead, Kaus urged liberals to combat *social* inequality by nurturing egalitarian civic institutions (parks, schools, libraries, museums) and by creating some new ones (national health care,
national service, a jobs program), thereby removing many of life's most
important activities from the "money sphere" altogether.

Finding ways to increase social equality is an important goal, and
Kaus's book remains a powerfully argued and informative read. But the
academic consensus that underlay Kaus's argument (and DeLong's more
modest one) has lately started to crumble.

Economists and political scientists previously resisted blaming the
Great Divergence on government mainly because it didn't show up when
they looked at the changing distribution of income taxes. The income tax
is the most logical government activity to focus on, because it is directly
redistributive. The government takes money from one group of people
(through taxes) and then hands it over to another group (through government benefits and appropriations).

Another compelling reason to focus on the income tax is that its structure has changed very dramatically during the last thirty years. Before
Ronald Reagan's election in 1980, the top income-tax bracket stood at or
above 70 percent, where it had been since the Great Depression. In the
1950s and early 1960s, the top bracket exceeded 90 percent. Throughout
the Great Compression, as the economy boomed and income inequality
dwindled, the top bracket remained at a level that even most Democrats
would today call confiscatory. Reagan dropped the top bracket from 70 to
50 percent, and eventually pushed it all the way down to 28 percent.
Since then, it has hovered between 30 and 40 percent. In 2010, when
President Barack Obama wanted to let income-tax cuts enacted by Bush
II expire for families earning more than $250,000, congressional Re-
publicans maneuvered him into extending them through 2012 by holding hostage an extension in unemployment benefits. (The unemployment
rate was then 9.4 percent.) Had Obama gotten his way, the top bracket
would have risen from 35 percent to a whisker under 40 percent, which
still would have been thirty to fifty percentage points below what it was
under Presidents Eisenhower, Nixon, and Ford. That's how much Reagan changed the debate.

But tax brackets, including the top one, tell you only the *marginal* tax
rate, that is, the rate on that portion of earnings exceeding a given
threshold. The percentage of total income that you actually pay in taxes is

known as the *effective* tax rate. And the effective income-tax rate on top incomes, you might be surprised to learn, didn't change all that much.

In 1979, when the top marginal rate was 70 percent, the effective income-tax rate on households in the top 0.01 percent (a group that today encompasses everyone making $9.1 million or more) was 21 percent. In 1988, President Reagan's last year in office, the effective income-tax rate on this very wealthy cohort was slightly higher, at 21.5 percent. (Some Trojan horse!) President George H. W. Bush raised the top marginal rate from 28 to 31 percent, thereby enraging antitax conservatives to whom he'd pledged, while accepting his party's nomination, "Read my lips: No new taxes." Then President Bill Clinton enraged these antitax conservatives even more by raising the top marginal rate much higher, to 39.6 percent. But the combined effect of these two controversial increases was to raise the effective income-tax rate on the top 0.01 percent from 20.1 percent in 1990 to 24.4 percent in 1995. By the end of Clinton's second term it had dropped down to 22.1 percent. After President George W. Bush dropped the top marginal rate down to the current 35 percent, the effective income-tax rate on the top 0.01 percent dropped to 17 percent in 2005—a more dramatic change than any effected in either direction by Reagan, the elder Bush, or Clinton, but still a matter of only 5.1 percentage points. Between 1979 and 2005 the effective income-tax rate on the top 0.01 percent dropped a mere 4 percentage points.[6]

In a 2007 paper, the economists Thomas Piketty and Emmanuel Saez, of the Paris School of Economics and Berkeley, respectively, concluded that the reduction in marginal income-tax rates "contributed only marginally to the decline of progressivity of the federal tax system." Various deductions, exemptions, and other forms of special treatment blunted the impact of the marginal rate changes.

As their phrasing suggests, Piketty and Saez *do* believe that U.S. federal taxes have become more regressive—"dramatically" so, they wrote in their paper. Moreover, they attributed this principally to changes made during the Reagan and Bush II presidencies. They just don't believe that the decline had much to do with the halving of the top marginal income-tax rate. Much more important, they argued, was a drop in corporate income taxes and ("to a lesser extent") a drop in estate and gift taxes, combined with a proportional shift in the composition of top incomes away from capital-derived income (dividends, interest, and rents) and toward labor-derived income (wages and salaries, including stock options, as

well as business income derived from partnerships, sole proprietor-
ships, and S-corporations, this last a legal tax dodge for individuals and
families who work as independent contractors and want to pay less in
Social Security and Medicare taxes). When you factor in *all* federal taxes
(and also the federal payroll tax, which started out regressive and has
become even more so), the effective tax rate on the top 0.01 percent fell
from 59.3 percent in 1979 to 34.7 percent in 2004—a drop of nearly
twenty-five percentage points.[7] In their 2010 book *Winner-Take-All Politics,* the political scientists Jacob Hacker of Yale and Paul Pierson of
Berkeley note Piketty and Saez's calculation that between 1970 and 2000
the top 0.1 percent (a group that today encompasses everyone making
$1.7 million or more each year) increased its share of the nation's after-
tax income from 1.2 to 7.3 percent. Hacker and Pierson then extrapolate
that if in 2000 this group had been taxed at its (much higher) 1970 effective level, then instead of rising to 7.3 percent, its share of the nation's
after-tax income would have risen to 4.5 percent. That's a significant
difference in income inequality.[8]

But to say that *maintaining* prior tax levels would have helped *mitigate*
income inequality is not to say that *dropping* tax levels *caused* it. Let's
imagine that 1970's effective tax rates had remained unchanged. The
after-tax income share for the top 0.1 percent would *not* have remained
the same (1.2 percent) thirty years later. It would, as Hacker and Pierson
observed, have risen to 4.5 percent. That's because the top 0.1 percent's
share of the nation's pretax income increased nearly *ten times* faster than
its effective tax fell. Another consideration is that Piketty and Saez, because they wanted to focus exclusively on taxes, excluded from their calculations government cash and in-kind payments (such as Social
Security, Medicare, welfare payments, and food stamps) and employer-
provided health insurance (which doesn't get taxed). A 2008 Congressional Budget Office memo that included these factors in its calculation
of the effective combined federal tax rate—in other words, that looked at
the federal government's direct income redistribution in its totality—
found a decline, for the top 0.01 percent, from an effective combined tax
rate of 42.9 percent in 1979 to 32.3 percent in 2004. (It bottomed out at
25.9 percent toward the end of the Reagan presidency; peaked at 40.9
percent midway through the Clinton presidency, then fell to 32 percent
by its end; and went up, then down under Bush II.) Instead of the drop
of nearly twenty-five percentage points calculated by Piketty and Saez,

the CBO mapped for the same demographic in the same time span a nearly eleven-percentage-point drop. Another way to say this is that the effective federal tax rate on the top 0.01 percent fell by about a quarter. That's a big drop. But during that same period pretax income share for the top 0.01 percent grew by 217 percent.[9]

The Congressional Budget Office calculates that in 1979 the combined effect of federal taxes and government benefits on income inequality (as measured by the Gini index) was to reduce inequality by 23 percent. By 2007 the combined effect remained progressive. The federal government was still distributing money downward. But it was reducing it by 17 percent. That means that during the Great Divergence the federal government has reduced its direct redistribution—through collecting taxes and awarding benefits—by about a quarter. So the effect of all federal taxes and benefits is significant—much more so than the effect of income taxes alone.[10]

But what about that stunning increase in pretax income share for the wealthiest Americans? During the Great Divergence it doubled for the top 1 percent and more than tripled for the top 0.01 percent before you factored in any direct government redistribution.[11] For years, academics concluded that this change in how the market distributed income couldn't have much to do with the government. But recently a few prominent economists and political scientists have suggested looking at the question differently. Rather than consider only taxes and benefits, they recommend looking at what MIT's Frank Levy and Peter Temin call "institutions and norms." It's a vague phrase, but in practice what it mostly means is "stuff the government did, or *didn't* do, in more ways than we can count." In Levy and Temin's view, the Great Divergence was the product of "a shift in the political environment." Great income inequality, they wrote, would be impossible to achieve "without government intervention and changes in private sector behavior." The two were mutually reinforcing.[12]

In his 2007 book *The Conscience of a Liberal*, Paul Krugman concluded that there is "a strong circumstantial case for believing that institutions and norms ... are the big sources of rising inequality in the United States." Krugman elaborated in his *New York Times* blog.

The great reduction of inequality that created middle-class America between 1935 and 1945 was driven by political change; I believe that politics has also played an important role in rising inequality since the 1970s. It's important to know that no other advanced economy has seen a comparable surge in inequality.[13]

Proponents of the institutions and norms theory tend to make their case not by measuring the precise impact of each thing government has done, but rather by charting strong correlations between economic trends and political or partisan ones. The most damning partisan findings (for the GOP) appeared in the 2008 book *Unequal Democracy,* by the political scientist Larry Bartels, then at Princeton and now at Vanderbilt. Indeed, they were *so* damning that Bartels felt compelled to assure readers in his book's preface that when he began the project he was "an unusually apolitical political scientist" who hadn't voted since 1984—when he pulled the lever for Ronald Reagan. During the two election cycles that followed his book's publication, Bartels did not, records indicate, donate to any candidate for federal office. Yet his conclusion boiled down to a bluntly partisan message. You don't like income inequality? Then don't vote Republican. "My projections," Bartels wrote,

> based on the historical performance of Democratic and Republican presidents suggest that income inequality would actually have *declined* slightly over the past 50 years . . . had the patterns of income growth characteristic of Democratic administrations been in effect throughout that period. Conversely, continuous application of the patterns of income growth observed during periods of Republican control would have produced a much greater divergence in the economic fortunes of rich and poor people than we have actually experienced—a Platinum-Gilded Age.

Bartels came to this conclusion by looking at average annual pretax income growth (corrected for inflation) for the years 1948 to 2005, a period encompassing much of the egalitarian Great Compression and most of the inegalitarian Great Divergence. The White House during this period was occupied by five Democrats (Truman, Kennedy, Johnson, Carter, Clinton) and six Republicans (Eisenhower, Nixon, Ford, Reagan, Bush I, Bush II). Bartels broke down the data according to income percentile and whether the president was a Democrat or a Republican. Figuring the effects of White House policies were best measured on a one-year lag,

Income Growth Rates 1948-2005

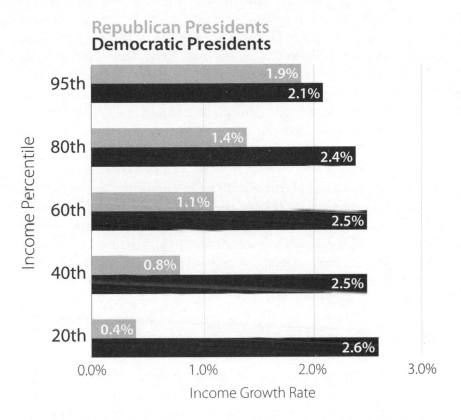

Source: Larry Bartels, *Unequal Democracy: The Political Economy of the New Gilded Age* (Princeton, NJ: Princeton University Press, 2008), 32.

Bartels eliminated each president's first year in office and substituted the year following departure. Here is what he found:

Under Democratic presidents, the biggest income gains went to people in the bottom twentieth income percentile (2.6 percent), then tapered off as you traveled up the income scale (2.5 percent for the fortieth and sixtieth percentiles, 2.4 percent for the eightieth percentile, and so on). Under Republican presidencies, the pattern was precisely opposite. The biggest income gains went to people in the ninety-fifth percentile (1.9 percent), then tapered off as you traveled further *down* the income scale (1.4 percent for the eightieth percentile, 1.1 for the sixtieth percentile, etc.).

Another point worth noting is that during Democratic presidencies pretax income increased much faster than during Republican presidencies, not just for the twentieth percentile but also for the fortieth, sixtieth, and eightieth. Americans were richer *and* more equal. During Republican presidencies pretax income increased more slowly than during Democratic presidencies not just for the twentieth percentile but also for the fortieth, sixtieth, and eightieth. Americans were poorer *and* less equal. At the ninety-fifth percentile Democrats produced marginally faster income growth than Republicans, but the difference was trivial. The lesson here was that once you reached the top 5 percent in incomes (who today make about $150,000 or more) these partisan differences began to break down. The richest cohort received favorable treatment from both Democratic presidencies *and* Republican ones. (More about that in chapter 9.)

Bartels also measured income distribution patterns more directly by looking at the ratio of incomes at the eightieth and twentieth percentiles—a fairly standard income-distribution metric—during these same eleven presidencies. He found that the ratio *increased* during all six Republican presidencies and *decreased* during four of the five Democratic presidencies. The Democratic exception was the Carter presidency. That's not particularly surprising, because that the Great Divergence began on Carter's watch.[14]

What did Democrats do right? What did Republicans do wrong? Bartels doesn't know; in *Unequal Democracy* he writes that it would take "a small army of economists" to find out. But since his partisan comparisons are based on pretax numbers, the difference obviously doesn't involve either levying taxes or distributing government benefits. How does the government influence pretax income distribution? Partly through macroeconomic policy. Republicans, Bartels notes, are more willing to risk high unemployment to keep inflation down, while Democrats are more willing to risk high inflation to keep unemployment down. Neither party, of course, can afford to be indifferent to either unemployment or inflation, and too much of either tends to worsen income inequality. But Republicans generally fear inflation more than unemployment because financiers and corporate chiefs *really* hate inflation, while Democrats generally fear unemployment more than inflation because labor unions and working people *really* hate unemployment.

But what about that top 5 percent—the privileged group that gets pampered by Democrats and Republicans alike? Hacker and Pierson are especially interested in this group, because since the mid-1990s the Great Divergence has been driven largely by the growing income share for these wealthiest of all Americans. Like Bartels and Krugman, they believe that government action (and inaction) at the federal level played a leading role in creating the Great Divergence. But the culprit, they say, is not so much partisan politics as it is institutional changes in Washington. Which brings us to Bryce Harlow, whose frank description of business interests' superior power in Washington policymaking provides this chapter's epigraph.

A founding father of the modern corporate-lobbying industry, Harlow was much more forthright than his latter-day successors in naming the enemy. "The Achilles heel of every democracy," he said in a 1962 speech to the Merchants and Manufacturers Association (delivered in Palm Springs),

> has been the drive of the enfranchised to use the mighty weapon of political equality to enforce economic equality. The days of a democracy are numbered, say the philosophers, when the belly of the system takes charge of its head—when the vagrant on the street corner, resentfully eyeing the passing limousines of the privileged, the talented, and the influential, sets about using his equal vote as he would use a pistol in a bank.

"Our principal occasion for alarm," he concluded, "if alarm be warranted in the developing situation, is the role of our Federal Government in accelerating the drive for equality."[15]

When a grand old Washington figure reaches old age and starts to think about the legacy he'll leave behind, usually he wants to be remembered as a wise and trusted tribune of democratic governance. Clark Clifford spent half a dozen years working for Democratic presidents and four decades working as a Washington fixer for corporate clients. But when the time came to write his memoirs, Clifford titled them *Counsel to the President*. Bryce Harlow was different. Much admired in Washington for his probity, his political wisdom, and his gentlemanly manner, Harlow served as a high-ranking aide to two Republican presidents—Eisenhower and Nixon—and when he died in 1987, the *New York Times* obituary duly identified him as "a Presidential counselor and speechwriter." But the foundation that bears Harlow's name, established while he was still alive, is dedicated to "enhancing the quality of professional advocacy and increasing the understanding of its role in the development of sound public policy," that is, legitimizing corporate lobbying as a profession worthy of the public's respect.[16] Harlow was dean of the Washington lobbyists. Henry Kissinger, in the introduction to an authorized Harlow biography published in 2000, wrote that Harlow "virtually single-handedly created the entire modern advocacy industry."[17] (Kissinger, of course, has hired himself out for years as a "consultant" to private companies and foreign nations; though not exactly a lobbyist, he has marketed his prestige and connections.)

The son of a politically active textbook publisher in Oklahoma, Harlow came to Washington in 1938 to work at the House of Representatives library while he conducted research for a master's thesis about the Ways and Means Committee. During World War II Harlow was a speechwriter and congressional liaison under the U.S. Army chief of staff George Marshall. After the war he moved back and forth between Oklahoma, where he worked in the family publishing business, and Washington, where he served first on the House Armed Services Committee staff and subsequently at the White House as a speechwriter and congressional liaison for President Dwight Eisenhower (in the process switching his party allegiance from Democrat to Republican). After the GOP lost the White House in 1960, Harlow accepted an offer from Eisenhower's former defense secretary, Neil McElroy, to create a government relations office in Washington for Procter & Gamble, where McElroy was now chairman.

Joel Jankowsky, an aide to Democratic House Speaker Carl Albert during the early part of the 1970s (and subsequently a lawyer-lobbyist for the law firm Akin Gump Strauss Hauer & Feld), recalls that prior to the mid-1970s the only industries with notable Washington presence or clout were oil and gas, steel, and agriculture. Defense contractors had Washington offices, but their purpose wasn't to lobby so much as to sell products to the Pentagon. "By and large," Jankoswky told me, "the Democratic Congress was thinking about the middle class and those who hadn't reached the middle class." When Harlow opened P&G's K Street office in 1961, that thoroughfare was not yet synonymous with corporate influence. Only about a dozen corporations bothered to maintain full-time lobbyists in Washington. "My tiny outpost was charged with keeping close tabs on events unfolding in Congress and the executive branch," Harlow later recalled, "and with helping Procter's top people decide which matters required their attention and presence." In time, however, "we began to do as well as look—to become players as well as observers."[18]

One of Harlow's first assignments was to forestall a congressional ban on alkylbenzene sulfonate (ABS), an ingredient in Tide and other P&G cleaning products that didn't break down in sewage treatment and left trails of foam in rivers and streams. Harlow succeeded, but the company later bowed to public pressure and stopped using ABS. George Koch, then a Washington lobbyist for Sears Roebuck and Company, remembers teaming up with Harlow to defeat an amendment introduced by Democratic senators Albert Gore Sr. and Eugene McCarthy that would have denied capital gains (i.e., favorable) treatment to lump-sum payments from corporate profit-sharing plans. Sears and P&G, Koch later recalled, "had more money in profit-sharing than all the rest of the profit-sharing plans in the world, so it just immediately brought us together like magnets."[19] Gore and McCarthy introduced their amendment on a Friday; by Saturday, Koch was in Chicago urging all rank-and-file employees to phone Washington to complain. "McCarthy's phone fell off the hook, mail poured in," Koch told me. Then Koch found a Sears tire changer with more money in his profit-sharing plan than the company chairman (whose capital-gains tax break had generated bad publicity in the press and brought the issue to Capitol Hill's attention). Koch arranged for the tire changer to testify at a Senate hearing to demonstrate that raising taxes on profit-sharing wouldn't just harm the swells; it would harm proles, too. The capital-gains proposal died.[20]

By the mid-1960s, though, corporations were winning fewer such fights. A July 1962 exposé by the *Washington Post*'s Morton Mintz about the dangers that the sedative thalidomide posed to unborn children prompted Congress to pass a bill tightening safety standards for drugs. Harlow, in his speech to the Merchants and Manufacturers Association that year, warned darkly that the new law would "close the Federal fist not only around prescription drugs, but also around proprietary drugs, foods, and cosmetics." Between 1966 and 1969 Congress passed significant new laws increasing regulation of automobiles (previously unregulated at the federal level), supermarket product labels, meat safety (previously regulated only when meat products crossed state lines), gas pipelines, the information that banks provided their customers, flammable fabrics, and coal-mine safety. This consumer-protection trend, Harlow warned in a 1966 speech to a Chicago meeting of the Better

Business Bureau's Research and Education Foundation, would "interdict the business-customer ties which are at the heart of healthy private enterprise" unless "the business community bestirs itself more powerfully, more unitedly, and more skillfully than it has been of a mind to do." But even this would not be enough: "Business urgently needs to devise new ways to re-demonstrate convincingly and dramatically to the public the dependability of American business and the mutuality of the business-consumer interest."[21]

Richard Nixon's election in 1968 brought Harlow into the White House, where he ran the legislative affairs office until he was squeezed out in 1970 by Chief of Staff Bob Haldeman. In 1973 Nixon would bring Harlow back as counselor to the president after the Watergate scandal forced Haldeman's resignation. (Harlow stayed a year, leaving a few months before Nixon's own resignation, and thereafter provided frequent outside advice to President Gerald Ford.) But neither the Republicans' recapture of the White House nor Harlow's intermittent presence inside it halted the liberal trend in domestic policymaking. Nixon's first term alone saw the establishment of the Environmental Protection Agency, the Occupational Safety and Health Administration, and the Consumer Product Safety Commission; passage, under Nixon's signature, of a tax bill that raised the maximum capital gains rate, eliminated an investment tax credit, reduced the oil-depletion allowance, and limited depreciation of real estate; and a congressional cutoff, over Nixon's protests, in funding for Boeing's supersonic transport plane.

Business, which had prospered since the end of World War II, hit a rough patch. Corporate profits as a share of national income peaked in the mid-1960s and fell sharply in the late 1960s and early 1970s; they wouldn't really resume their upward climb until the start of the Great Divergence. In 1975, President Gerald Ford's treasury secretary, William Simon, complained that since 1960 capital formation in the United States had been "the lowest of any major industrialized country in the free world." That same year a survey of its readers by the *Harvard Business Review* found that a large majority held serious doubts that America would maintain its commitment to private property and limited government. The business community increasingly blamed its problems on government but remained flat-footed in exercising its power in Washington. Ford was more pro-business than Nixon had been, but when he signed into law a bill setting minimum standards for consumer product warranties it took corporate America by surprise. "We started getting calls from major businesses around the country," Jeffrey Joseph, the U.S. Chamber of Commerce's chief lobbyist, would later recall, "saying, we just heard that this bill passed, what is it?" The businesses "weren't that sophisticated," Joseph said. "They weren't well organized."[22]

But the tide was already turning. In 1971 Lewis Powell, a Richmond, Virginia, lawyer in private practice who within weeks would be nominated to the Supreme Court, wrote a memo for a friend at the U.S. Chamber of Commerce that repeated, in shriller tones, the alarm Harlow had been sounding for years. "No thoughtful person," the Powell memo began, "can question that the American economic system is under broad attack." This assault was coming not only from "Communists, New Leftists and other revolutionaries" but also from "perfectly respectable elements of society: from the college campus, the pulpit, the media, the intellectual and literary journals, the arts and sciences, and from politicians." Yet "the painfully sad truth is that business, including the boards of directors and the top executives of corporations great and small and business organizations at all levels, often have responded—if at all—by appeasement, ineptitude and ignoring the problem." The business world, Powell wrote, needed to learn a lesson "long ago learned by labor" that "political power is necessary; that such power must be assiduously cultivated; and that when necessary, it must be used aggressively and with determination—without embarrassment and without the reluctance which has been so characteristic of American business."[23]

A year after Powell wrote the memo it was leaked to the Washington columnist Jack Anderson, who faulted Powell for not disclosing it at the time of his Senate confirmation. That prompted the Chamber to publish the entire text in its newsletter, where it received a warm reception from the business community. Harlow, back at P&G, took to quoting Powell's memo in his speeches around the country.

In response to Powell's memo, the Chamber launched a "concerted program to increase public understanding of the American economic system and to answer attacks on the private sector."[24] By 1980 the Chamber had tripled its budget and doubled its membership. The National Federation of Independent Business, which would play a more direct role fighting regulation, expanded its membership from three hundred in 1970 to six hundred *thousand* in 1979. In 1966 Koch had left Sears to become president of the Grocery Manufacturers of America, which he promptly moved from New York to Washington, D.C.; in 1973 the National Association of Manufacturers followed suit. The number of corporations with lobbying offices in Washington grew from the dozen when Harlow opened P&G's shop in 1961 to one hundred in 1968 to five hundred in 1978. The size of the lobbying operations grew as well. Between 1968 and 1977 General Motors expanded its Washington staff from three to twenty-eight. "My job used to be booze, broads and golf," one veteran lobbyist told *Business Week* in 1979. "Now it is organizing coalitions and keeping information flowing."

Harlow himself served on the governing board of the Business-Government Relations Council, a nonprofit founded in 1966 that grew in influence over the years. He also met regularly with the Carlton Group, a gathering of lobbyists that met weekly at the Carlton Hotel. But Harlow's most significant contribution was his participation in the 1972 creation of the Business Roundtable, an organization that he was himself ineligible to join because its membership was limited to chief executive officers. "What our real friends in Washington have long yearned for, and keep pleading for," Harlow told the new group in 1974, "is some business equivalent to COPE, Common Cause, or even Nader's Raiders."[25] The Roundtable quickly became, Thomas Byrne Edsall wrote in his 1984 book, *The New Politics of Inequality*, "in effect, the political arm of big business."

By the late 1970s, all this business organizing was producing results. Harlow himself played a lead role in getting Congress to defeat a proposed federal agency for consumer advocacy ("as harmful a bill as I have seen in 34 Washington years") that Nader had been trying to establish for years.[26] Also at the business lobby's instigation, Congress derailed the Federal Trade Commission's attempt to impose strict limits on advertising to children. A labor law reform bill increasing penalties imposed on companies that violated laws protecting labor organizers—a crucial weapon if labor was to succeed in its push to organize workers in the South—was defeated in Congress, and a drop in the top capital gains rate from 49 to 28 percent got pushed through. In his book *Fluctuating Fortunes: The Political Power of Business in America*, the Berkeley political scientist David Vogel notes that the 1978 capital gains cut was a "major milestone in federal tax policy" that "laid the groundwork for the even more sweeping changes" in Reagan's 1981 tax bill, portions of which were literally written by members of the Carlton Group. Harlow had already reviewed, at candidate Reagan's request, the Republican presidential nominee's package of proposed tax and spending cuts prior to its release in September 1980. He'd found it much to his liking.

Every one of these changes elevated the financial interests of business owners and stockholders above the well-being, financial or otherwise, of ordinary citizens. Consumer-oriented laws and regulations were seen by business as a particular threat to corporate bottom lines because they typically increased Americans' ability to sue companies for financial damages. It may not seem obvious, in retrospect, that expansion of the regulatory state had much to do with income distribution, because government regulations don't usually put money into the pockets of the poor and the middle class. But they took money *out* of the pockets of Americans who occupied the upper reaches of business. They saw themselves as victims of an angry, anticapitalist mob. "At one time or another every consumer has had an unhappy experience with a particular product or appliance or serviceman or merchant," Harlow said in 1966. "In almost every citizen, therefore, there is an unspoken resentment that makes him or her responsive to demands for rectitude and fair play in a marketplace described as exploitative and deceitful."[27]

It wasn't just Harlow who feared that the government was "accelerating the drive for equality." In his 1971 memo, Lewis Powell complained that America had "moved very far indeed toward some aspects of state socialism." Powell's anxiety is palpable in the margin scribblings he made before writing it. On a clipping of a June 1971 column by William Raspberry of the *Washington Post* criticizing a proposal by President Nixon to liberalize depreciation for manufacturing equipment, Powell underlined the words "its direct benefits would accrue only to the rich, the owners of big companies." On a torn-out *New York* magazine piece by Jack Newfield titled "A Populist Manifesto: The Making of a New Majority," Powell underlined the words "the root need to redistribute wealth and the commitment to broaden democratic participation."[28]

The threat was still felt seven years later by former treasury secretary Simon, who was by then president of the militantly pro-business Olin Foundation. In his bestselling 1978 jeremiad *A Time for Truth*, Simon expounded at length on the new levelers.

> The egalitarian . . . wishes to wrest the rewards away from those who have earned them and give them to those who have not . . . The more one achieves, the more one is punished; the less one achieves, the

more one is rewarded. Egalitarianism is a morbid assault on both ability and justice . . . Since men of achievement will not—and should
not—freely consent to being hacked down, in order not to tower above
those less able, they must be forced to do so. Accordingly, egalitarians
seek to use the police powers of the state to accomplish their goals.

The ramping-up of business influence in Washington never ended.
Where back in 1977 a lobbyist's strategy session might include only two
people (you and your client), today, Akin Gump's Jankowsky says, it will
more likely include a dozen: you, your client, representatives of and lobbyists for other companies with whom you're working as a team, grass-
roots experts, media experts, and so on.[29] More than $3 billion annually
is spent on lobbying, according to official records cited by Hacker and
Pierson (which, they note, understate true expenditures). That's nearly
twice what was spent a decade ago. In 2010 the groups that spent the
greatest sums on lobbying, according to the Center for Responsive Politics, a Washington-based nonprofit, were the Chamber of Commerce
($132 million); PG&E ($45 million); General Electric ($39 million); Fed-
eral Express ($26 million); and the American Medical Association ($23
million). Not a single labor union was to be found in the top twenty, and
the only lobby group in the top twenty that was unaffiliated with business
was the American Association of Retired Persons. (And in some ways
even the AARP, as it prefers to be known today, is a business lobby because it sells health insurance.)

How did the Republicans and the resurgent business lobby alter income distribution? Thus far I've only been able to mention a few mechanisms in passing. The scholarship on this question, alas, tends to be more
impressionistic than comprehensive. But the impact of government action (and inaction) in three particular areas—labor, finance, and corporate compensation—is relatively clear and well documented. I'll explore
that impact in the next two chapters.

8

The Fall of Detroit

WITH A DOMESTIC PAYROLL OF ROUGHLY 1.4 million, Walmart is the largest private employer in the United States. Not one of those 1.4 million employees belongs to a union. Only once has anybody successfully unionized a Walmart store lying within U.S. borders. That occurred in the winter of 2000, when ten meat cutters in a Jacksonville, Texas, Walmart Supercenter voted 7–3 to affiliate with Local 540 of the United Food and Commercial Workers International Union. Within days of the vote Walmart announced that it was phasing out meat cutting at all its Supercenters, starting with 180 stores that just happened to include the one in Jacksonville. The Supercenters would instead sell meat that was prewrapped, precut, and prelabeled. No meat cutters, no meat cutters union. "This decision was in no way related to the Jacksonville situation," a Walmart spokeswoman explained.[1]

Four years later, Josh Noble, a young employee in the tire and lube department of a Walmart in Loveland, Colorado, decided to give it another try. "We got fed up," he told Human Rights Watch. Workers in the tire and lube shop were "not getting lunches or breaks on time" and were being "asked to do jobs that are not part of our job description," he said. And, of course, the pay was lousy. Alicia Sylvia, a single mother of ten-year-old twins who worked with Noble, told the *New York Times* she earned nine dollars an hour (the average for other large general merchandisers was more like twelve dollars) and couldn't afford the company's health insurance (which enrolled fewer than half its employees). Noble contacted the UFCW and invited co-workers to an organizing meeting at a local restaurant. Six people showed up, including Sylvia, and turned in signed union cards calling for a vote on affiliation.

That meeting was held on a Sunday evening in November. The next day three members of Walmart's "labor relations team" arrived from the company's headquarters in Bentonville, Arkansas, and called a store-wide meeting (even though Noble was trying only to organize the tire and lube department). Company videos and PowerPoint presentations were shown. As Noble later recalled, one message was that "wages could be cut drastically" in collective bargaining. "People were giving me dirty looks," Sylvia remembered. "I'm the only [union supporter] there, and they're all staring at me like I'm the demon person from hell." The labor relations team continued to hold similar meetings until the union vote took place in February. Meanwhile Noble, Sylvia, and the other pro-union employees weren't permitted to discuss the union at all while they were on company property.

Noble noticed that store managers were spending more time, in greater numbers, at the tire and lube department, presumably to keep a close watch on the employees there. "They were constantly on your back to try to catch you doing something wrong," Sylvia told Human Rights Watch. "They make you nervous so you mess up." At one point Sylvia was disciplined for swearing—not exactly a noteworthy occurrence in any auto parts shop. A co-worker who was against the union (and wouldn't permit Human Rights Watch to identify him by name) said the flying wedge from Bentonville let him know they were aware he'd applied to the company's management-training program. "I felt I'd be taken care of," he said, "because, without being asked, I'd give them information" about the labor organizers committing petty company infractions like speaking on a cell phone during working hours. "They had everybody going about it with one another, not just me."

Six new employees were brought into the tire and lube department. A Walmart spokesman told the *New York Times* it was to replace three workers who had left—one of them (a union supporter) was fired, according to Noble—and to improve the department's efficiency. But of course it was a tactic to alter the odds in management's favor. Another favored tactic is to let workers know that all raises must be put on hold for the duration of a union campaign. That never fails to infuriate rank and file, who are told that it's necessitated by the union drive: Any raise given during this period might be construed as a bribe.

Sylvia started to get cold feet. "She's just kind of a hard-to-read-type person," Noble can be heard saying in *Wal-Mart: The High Cost of Low*

Price, a 2005 documentary that includes footage from the Loveland organizing campaign. "She's definitely into it. She's real strong." We next see
Sylvia telling the filmmakers, "I . . . don't really want to vote, but then I
kinda have to." Then we see Noble on the phone with Sylvia: "You're getting freaked out because of what they're saying. They're not gonna know
how you voted."

At one point in the union campaign Noble thought he was pretty
close to the majority he needed. But when the election was finally held
on February 25, 2005, his was the only vote in favor. Seventeen voted
against and two didn't vote. Alicia Sylvia was one of the abstainers. "It
was my day off," she told Human Rights Watch.

> I went in, and Dave [from the UFCW] calls me to make sure I was
> going in to vote. Josh [who is epileptic] was in the hospital with a sei-
> zure, so he couldn't vote. Demetre had moved. Cody had gone to school.
> Justine had moved. Brooks had been given a temporary manager
> position. Rob got scared. I knew that me and Josh were the only ones.
> Ryan had changed his mind, too . . . I walked around the store for an
> hour. I was so scared. "Should I do it?" I walked around the store.
>
> I chickened out. I felt so bad. They wheeled Josh in, and he voted
> for the union. I felt like I let him down. I was scared of being the only
> one, so I didn't vote . . . But if they're all there and they see you go in,
> they know you voted. I thought they'd fire me.

Most (possibly all) of the bullying tactics described here are legal. For
the UFCW to prove any of them illegal would probably have taken years
of litigation, with only the remotest likelihood of a satisfying outcome.
The union didn't file suit.[2]

That's what labor organizing is like three decades into the Great Divergence.

The age of inequality has coincided with a dramatic decline in the
power of organized labor. Union membership in the United States
reached its historic peak in 1979 at about 21 million, representing about
21 percent of the workforce. Today membership stands at about 15 million and represents about 12 percent. When you exclude public-employee
unions (more than half of all union members today work not for a private company but for the government), union membership has dropped
to about 7 percent of the private-sector workforce. Draw one line on a

graph charting the decline in union membership, then superimpose a second line charting the decline in middle-class income share (with "middle class" defined broadly as the middle 60 percent), and you will find that the two lines are nearly identical.[3]

The chief purpose of a union is to maximize the income of its members. Since union workers earn, on average, 10 to 30 percent more than nonunion workers, and since union members in higher-paying occupations tend to exercise more clout than union members in lower-paying ones, you might think higher union membership would *increase* income inequality. That was, in fact, the consensus among economists before the Great Divergence. But Harvard's Richard Freeman demonstrated in a 1980 paper that at the national level unions' ability to reduce income disparities *among* members outweighed other factors, and therefore their net effect was to *reduce* income inequality.[4] A logical conclusion was that as union membership declined, income inequality would likely grow. And that's what happened.

The number of union members started falling in 1979, but as a percentage of the workforce the decline actually began a generation earlier. What labor economists call "union density" peaked in 1954 at 28 percent. If you eliminate from this calculation government workers (who were not yet widely unionized) and if you add to the "union members" category nonunion members who were nonetheless covered by union contracts, the union-density peak was closer to 40 percent. After 1954, union density began a slow downward slide that picked up speed in the 1980s as the absolute number of union members began to drop. The Berkeley economist David Card calculated in a 2001 paper that the decline in union membership among men explained about 15 to 20 percent of the growth in male income inequality between 1973 and 1993. (Among women—whose incomes, as noted in chapter 3, have been largely unaffected by the Great Divergence—union membership declined much less precipitously, and its impact, Card concluded, was minimal.) In 2007 Freeman calculated that the decline of unions explained about 20 percent of the Great Divergence among *all* workers. In 2011 the sociologists Bruce Western of Harvard and Jake Rosenfeld of the University of Washington added in such indirect effects as the threat of unionization on nonunion workers and concluded that one third of the Great Divergence among men could be attributed to the drop in union membership. "By this measure," they concluded, "the decline of the

American labor movement has added as much to men's wage inequality as the relative increase in pay for college graduates."[5]

A precise estimate is hard to calculate because labor's decline was as much cultural as it was quantifiably economic. In their 2007 paper "Inequality and Institutions in 20th Century America," MIT's Levy and Temin describe unions not merely as organizations that strike wage bargains but more broadly as institutions that, before the Great Divergence, played a large role in shaping societal attitudes (a theme later elaborated by Princeton's Paul Krugman and Larry Bartels). A telling example they give arose from a labor-management conference convened by President Harry Truman in November 1945, three months after World War II ended. The conference was intended to hammer out an agreement governing postwar industrial conversion from armaments back to civilian goods. It failed to do so. But looking back on the conference today, Levy and Temin are struck less by its lack of results than by its very existence. Business leaders were sitting down with labor leaders to discuss ways to manage not just individual companies but the entire economy. They didn't do it because they wanted to. They did it because they *had* to, a circumstance wholly unimaginable today. The following year, Eric Johnston, president of the U.S. Chamber of Commerce, made a statement whose spirit of conciliation would likely get any current Chamber president fired: "Labor unions are woven into our economic pattern of American life, and collective bargaining is a part of the democratic process. I say recognize this fact not only with our lips but with our hearts." No smelling salts were needed to revive any who heard it.[6] After a century of struggle, unions had won acceptance as an inevitable component to the modern industrial economy. America's labor movement stood at the summit of its power.

Walter Reuther was a living embodiment of labor's ascendancy. Had the decades that followed gone a bit differently, his name might be as familiar to today's schoolchildren as that of Martin Luther King Jr. (with whom Reuther stood as King gave his "I Have A Dream" speech). Reuther was the greatest American labor leader of his era, and arguably the greatest of any era. A major force in the United Auto Workers union throughout the war, Reuther in 1946 became its president, a position he held until 1970, when he died at sixty-three in a private plane crash.

Reuther was born in Wheeling, West Virginia. His father, Valentine Reuther, was a beer wagon driver who was an active trade unionist and

Socialist, and he raised all five of his children to share those values. After his hero, Eugene V. Debs, was convicted of sedition (for giving a speech criticizing U.S. participation in World War I), Valentine took Walter (age twelve) and Walter's younger brother Victor (age seven) to the nearby Moundsville Penitentiary to pay their respects. Later Victor recalled it was the only time he ever saw his father weep. Walter dropped out of high school at sixteen and apprenticed as a tool and die worker. He lost his big right toe at seventeen when a four-hundred-pound die that he and two co-workers were trying to move slipped and crashed down on his foot. At nineteen, Walter heard that Henry Ford—then phasing out the Model T and preparing to introduce the Model A—was paying tool and die workers a princely $1.25 an hour. He made a beeline for Detroit. Victor joined him three years later.

Thriving at Ford, Walter was able, at night, to acquire his high school diploma and to enroll in college. He even considered law school. But with the advent of the Great Depression, Walter was drawn deeper into the Socialist Party. With Victor he left Ford to make a political tour of Europe and ended up spending nearly two years in the Soviet Union, where the two brothers took jobs at the Gorky Auto Works and rhapsodized (in naive tones characteristic of many Socialists during that period) about "the atmosphere of freedom and security." Returning to Detroit in 1935, Walter got himself elected to the executive board of the newly consolidated United Auto Workers and threw himself into the contentious, often violently resisted struggle to unionize the country's three largest automakers: General Motors, Ford, and Chrysler.

Looking back a decade later at a series of sitdown strikes that the UAW staged during the late 1930s, the leftist writer Irving Howe and the labor activist B. J. Widick wrote that "not even the bloodiest strikes in the late nineteenth century posed the issue of 'property rights' versus 'labor rights' so sharply." Management pushed back hard, but in 1937 General Motors and Chrysler let the UAW in. The lone holdout was Henry Ford. In 1937 Reuther himself, while attempting to distribute UAW leaflets at Ford's River Rouge complex, was punched, thrown on his back, kicked, and hurled down a flight of stairs by Ford-hired thugs. Later dubbed the Battle of the Overpass, the attack on Reuther and another UAW official occurred in the presence of news photographers and reporters, some of whom had the film ripped out of their cameras and their notebooks grabbed out of their hands.

The emergence of strong industrial unions during the 1930s, of which the UAW was but one example, didn't happen by chance. Pressure from below had been building for decades, and the Great Depression stirred additional labor unrest. Then, in 1933, the National Industrial Recovery Act guaranteed the right of employees to join unions. Even though there was little the government could do to protect that right, the law's passage stirred the rank and file to action. In 1935 the Wagner Act, often described as labor's Magna Carta, established unions' right to engage in collective bargaining and created the National Labor Relations Board (NLRB) to protect that right. Reuther's beating two years later received prominent attention at an NLRB hearing on Henry Ford's union-busting tactics, and the NLRB ordered Ford to desist. After Ford resisted the NLRB ruling in the courts, a UAW-organized strike at the Ford plant in 1941 persuaded the company to surrender. In an NLRB-supervised election Ford workers voted in the UAW, and the union's organization of the big three automakers was complete.

Even before he was elected UAW president in 1946, Reuther became its most powerful voice and the labor movement's most creative thinker. He broke with his union's Communist faction (whose muddled, Moscow-dictated agenda was as much a practical hindrance as the 1939 Nazi-Soviet pact was an ideological affront); more quietly distanced himself from the Socialists; and allied himself with Franklin Roosevelt's Democratic Party. Within the labor movement, that pegged him a right-winger. But at the same time, Reuther pressed for greater union involvement in management decisions not only about what happened on the shop floor but also about how companies positioned themselves in the marketplace. This caused business leaders, jealous of their management prerogatives, to label him a dangerous left-winger.

In retrospect, Reuther looks—at least in the context of a U.S. economy dominated far more than it is today by a few very large industrial corporations—like a pragmatist eager to align his union's interests with those of the larger public. "The working class and the employing class have nothing in common," the Industrial Workers of the World ("the Wobblies") had declared at the time of their founding in 1905. Reuther believed that the working class and the employing class had plenty in common, if only the mulish bosses could be made to listen. Anticipating by several months Roosevelt's December 1940 call for an "arsenal of democracy," Reuther put forth a plan to pool resources from the entire auto industry into a single production unit to manufacture "500 planes a day." It was a scheme premised, in the words of the Reuther biographer Nelson Lichtenstein, on the idea that "veteran machinists and tool and die men had a better overall understanding of industry technics than did any individual corporate manager," which was almost certainly true. Reuther's plan had only one drawback, observed Treasury Secretary Henry Morgenthau: It came "from the 'wrong' source." That was enough to scuttle it. General Motors president "Engine" Charlie Wilson was bracingly honest about the reason that Detroit rejected it. "Everyone admits that Reuther is smart," he said, "but this is none of his business . . . he has no right to talk as if he were Vice-President of a company."[7]

Reuther offered a similarly bold proposal after V-J Day in August 1945. The government's wartime price controls had decreased take-home pay for autoworkers even as the cost of living had risen 30 percent. Reuther proposed a 30 percent wage increase to allow autoworkers to catch up with prices, but to prevent a wage-price inflationary spiral he said the automakers should do this *without raising automobile prices*. Reuther had been kicking this idea around since June, but it acquired greater urgency after the Japanese surrender when President Harry Truman issued an executive order permitting wage increases only if they didn't lead to price increases.

Once again, the response from management to Reuther's pragmatic bid was that the proposal might have merit (one GM board member circulated a letter saying circumstances justified it) but that the precedent was unacceptable. General Motors, which quickly became Reuther's principal adversary in this fight, took out an ad in the *New York Times* stating, "The idea of ability to pay, *whatever its validity may be* [italics mine], is not applicable to an individual business within an industry as a basis for raising its wages beyond the going rate." George Romney, chief spokesman for the Automobile Manufacturers Association (also future chairman of American Motors, Michigan governor, presidential aspirant, and father of the Massachusetts governor and presidential candidate Mitt Romney) used the occasion to pronounce Reuther "the most dangerous man in Detroit."

When the time came for Reuther to negotiate the pay hike/price freeze with GM, he asked that reporters be present. GM vetoed that, so Reuther had transcripts made of the talks and gave them out to anyone who asked. More than sixty years later, they stand as a vivid record of a

moment when America briefly debated elevating labor unions to a collaborative role in industrial management, as would occur in western
Europe after the war.

> REUTHER: But don't you think it is constructive for us to relate our
> wage question to prices?
>
> HARRY COEN (GM): Nobody is doing that but you. You are the fel-
> low that wants to get the publicity out of this whole thing. You want
> to enhance your personal political position. That is what the whole
> show is about . . .
>
> REUTHER: If I came in here and said we want 30 percent and we
> don't care about prices, we don't care about profits, that is your bus-
> iness . . . then you would say Reuther is being a trade unionist and
> not trying to build himself up politically. But when Reuther comes
> and there is what you say is an attempt to be a statesman [i.e., advo-
> cating positions of greater benefit to the company and the nation
> than to the union, per se] you think that is bad. I think if I didn't do
> it that way, it would be bad. I think if we came in here on a selfish
> basis and said, "We want ours and the world be damned," then you
> should take our pants off.
>
> COEN: You put a lot of things in my mouth that I haven't said, and
> you shade the things I have said in the direction of your thinking.
> None of the other labor leaders have taken the position you are tak-
> ing. I am on sound ground there.
>
> REUTHER: What do you mean when you say that?
>
> COEN: They are asking for a $2 a day increase. That is what the oth-
> ers are asking.
>
> REUTHER: They don't care what happens to prices?
>
> COEN: I don't know whether they care or not. They haven't coupled
> it up with their demand. And I think they are a damn sight smarter
> than you in this instance.

Failing to reach any resolution, the UAW launched a 113-day strike
against GM. *Time* put Reuther on its cover, and *Life* praised the "smart
young strategist" (he wasn't even UAW president yet) as someone "who
can rise above the bear-pit level of wage-and-hour battling to attack the
great problems of the national economy." In the end, UAW workers won
a small, symbolic increase but no pledge from GM on prices, and during

the three months after the strike's conclusion automakers raised prices three times. An entirely predictable wage-price spiral ensued.

The solution finally hammered out between Reuther and GM's Wilson in May 1950 was a five-year contract that included cost-of-living adjustments, productivity-based wage increases, health insurance, and guaranteed-benefit pensions that, in combination, were estimated to raise workers' compensation by 35 percent in inflation-adjusted dollars. Daniel Bell (then a writer for *Fortune* magazine, later a prominent sociologist at Columbia and Harvard) named the agreement, versions of which would be adopted not only by the other automakers but also by Big Steel and other industries (not all of them unionized), the Treaty of Detroit.

Cost-of-living adjustments were still a relative novelty in 1950, and health insurance and pensions had previously been mainly a management perk. But in writing about the agreement, Bell focused on the 2 percent annual productivity increases, or "annual improvement factor." Reuther had failed in his bid to give labor a voice in issues nominally unrelated to the union, but now Detroit was aligning labor and management in another way. When workers increased their productivity, they would have a share in the results. It was, Bell explained, "the most resounding declaration yet made by any big union that the U.S. can grow more prosperous only by producing more."

Labor productivity is the lifeblood of economies, but it's a concept more discussed than understood. Many people believe, erroneously, that it measures the output per dollar invested in man- (or woman-) hours worked. In fact, dollars don't enter into it. It is merely the output per man- (or woman-) hours worked. If one country's productivity rises faster than other countries', it can pay its workers more in salary and benefits and still remain competitive because its workers are, in effect, more valuable. That's what happened under the Treaty of Detroit. For the UAW, the treaty's benefits were obvious. For GM, which was expanding its postwar production, the benefit was predictability. For five years, Reuther was pledging not to direct UAW workers to strike. It wasn't European-style industrial democracy, not by a long shot. But it was as close as the United States would ever get. The Treaty of Detroit ushered in, observe MIT's Levy and Temin, "a stable period of industrial relations." From 1950 until 1973, labor and management shared in America's postwar prosperity.

The federal government, though not a signatory to the Treaty of

Detroit, played a significant role in enforcing it, Levy and Temin emphasize, and not only through the National Labor Relations Board. Between
1948 and 1964, the historian Judith Stein points out, every Democratic
presidential nominee began his general election campaign with a Labor
Day rally in Detroit's Cadillac Square. When President John Kennedy
proposed a tax cut on investment and income, he worried that higher
inflation might result. So his Council of Economic Advisers publicized
"guideposts" on wages and prices that were followed to some degree;
the feared inflation did not occur. Writing about the guideposts a few
years later, Kennedy's CEA chairman, Walter Heller, expressed satisfaction that industry was coming to recognize that keeping wages in line
with productivity increases still left "ample rewards to capital, as is vividly demonstrated by the doubling of corporate profits after taxes" from
1961 to 1966.

Kennedy persuaded steelworkers to limit wage demands in their
1962 contract with U.S. Steel in order to minimize the risk of inflation.
But when U.S. Steel followed up with a 3.5 percent price increase, Kennedy felt betrayed. "My father told me businessmen were all pricks," he
told Labor Secretary Arthur Goldberg, "but I didn't really believe he was
right until now." Kennedy readied legislation to freeze steel prices and
called a press conference to denounce the company. "At a time when restraint and sacrifice are being asked of every citizen," he said, "the
American people will find it hard, as I do, to accept a situation in which
a tiny handful of steel executives, whose pursuit of private power and
profit exceeds their sense of public responsibility, can show such utter
contempt for the interest of 185 million Americans." The White House
phoned reporters to suggest hostile questions they should pose to U.S.
Steel's chairman; Defense Secretary Robert McNamara redirected a
multi-million-dollar steel-plate order to build Polaris submarines from
U.S. Steel to one of its a smaller competitors; and Attorney General Robert Kennedy dispatched the FBI to investigate whether U.S. Steel was
colluding with Bethlehem Steel to fix prices (an allegation for which
there was precious little evidence).

In the face of all this pressure, U.S. Steel backed down, and so did
other steel companies that had decided to match its price increase. According to Levy and Temin, Kennedy's display of muscle "helps to explain why the reduced top tax rate" enacted two years later (it fell from
91 to 77 percent) "produced no surge in either executive compensation

or high incomes per se." Fear of attracting comparable attention from President Lyndon Johnson kept corporations from showering the bosses with obscene pay hikes.

Already, though, the White House's appetite for such a fight was diminishing. In 1964 Reuther, under pressure from the CEA to stay within its inflation guideposts, told the White House that he would moderate the UAW's wage demands if President Lyndon Johnson would tell the automakers to keep a lid on prices. Heller thought a bargain was possible, but Johnson, who was busily soliciting campaign contributions from auto executives for that year's presidential election, refused. Reuther went on strike instead and won a contract that, he told the president defiantly, "bent the hell out of" the CEA guideposts. A tight labor market emboldened other unions to wage similar strikes in other industries, and this, combined with deficit financing of the Vietnam War, created an inflation surge that worsened considerably when oil and food prices spiked in the early 1970s.[8] The tripartite agreement among management, labor, and the government to maintain a balance between wages and prices was breaking down.

"The formula wasn't really designed to handle the kind of inflation that broke out in the 1970s," Levy explained to me. "It was a terrible setup for an increasingly globalized world."[9] Foreign competitors were pricing U.S.-made automobiles and steel out of the market. Unemployment rose and incomes began to stagnate. Most calamitously, productivity, the bedrock on which the Treaty of Detroit had been built, fell. Productivity had grown by 3 percent annually between 1947 and 1973. Between 1973 and 1995 it was half that, for reasons economists still can't really explain.[10] Productivity growth in the United States would resume its upward climb in the 1980s and especially during the 1990s and the aughts. Between 1995 and 2008 average annual productivity growth was just a whisker short of the post–World War II rate. A major reason for this climb was a technology-driven surge in output per worker in the retail industry, which to a great extent reflected Walmart's pioneering use of computer technology. The consulting firm McKinsey and Company called it "the Walmart effect." But during this recent era of rising productivity, average hourly income did not resume growing in tandem. A gap between the two opened up starting in the 1980s and has been growing ever since. The sad story of Josh Noble's failed union drive in

Loveland, Colorado, suggests that this was (at least in part) another "Walmart effect".[11]

The structure of the economy has changed since the late 1970s, with manufacturing jobs giving way to service jobs. Obviously that contributed to labor's decline, since manufacturers are more likely to be unionized. But it didn't contribute as much as is often supposed. The Trinity University economist Barry Hirsch calculated in a 2007 paper that if the *only* change between 1983 and 2002 had been the shift in where the jobs were, private-sector union density would have fallen by less than two percentage points. Instead, it fell by eight.[12]

Many of the calamitous economic conditions of the 1970s were not unique to the United States. The oil shocks affected all industrialized nations, similar productivity declines were observed elsewhere, and the very nature of global competition is that it's, well, global. But in other industrialized nations, the effects were quite different. Union density actually increased in most industrialized countries during the 1970s even as it was decreasing in the United States. (Since then union density has tended to decrease in other industrialized countries, but not nearly so dramatically as in the United States.) And in these other countries, once productivity resumed its upward climb, real wages resumed climbing at about the same rate. Richard Freeman estimated that if real wages had followed the same pattern in the United States, average earnings for industrial workers would, in 2005, have been twenty-five dollars per hour. But they didn't, and hourly earnings were instead sixteen dollars per hour.[13]

In other countries, the unfavorable economic conditions of the 1970s caused pain, but labor unions rode them out. Only in the United States did these conditions bring down big labor like a house of cards. Part of the reason was that management and labor were more adversarial in the United States than elsewhere. Mechanisms for compromise, either public or private, were few, and there was little tradition of joint economic stewardship. The resultant conflict made old-line industrial unions appear, to much of the public, maddeningly intransigent as the Rust Belt fell into steep decline. Some unions, like the Teamsters, were blatantly corrupt, with extensive ties to organized crime. That didn't help labor's image either.

But an underlying reason for labor intransigence was that Reuther was never able to build on the Treaty of Detroit sufficiently to establish a partnership between labor, management, and government comparable to what western Europe achieved after the war. American management wouldn't allow it. It was too socialistic, too impertinent. When a corporate leader believed that Reuther had an excellent idea about how to run his business, he still felt compelled to reject it, on principle.

Another reason unions fell fast and hard was that the Treaty of Detroit, formidable though it was when constructed in 1950, lay atop the fault line of an antilabor law whose passage big labor had been unable to prevent three years earlier. If the 1935 Wagner Act was labor's Magna Carta, the Taft-Hartley Act was its Little Bighorn. In 1946 the war's end, Roosevelt's death, Truman's unpopularity as his successor, and runaway postwar inflation allowed the Republicans to regain the House and Senate for the first time since 1930. The new Congress wasted little time passing a bill to rein in what the Republicans (and more than a few southern Democrats) judged an out-of-control labor movement. Declaring Taft-Hartley "a shocking piece of legislation" that was "deliberately designed to weaken labor unions," Truman vetoed it. But Congress promptly overrode the veto, and Taft-Hartley became law in June 1947.

The momentum enjoyed by the labor movement and the remarkable job-creating postwar prosperity that would emerge within a few years (and on which big labor would come to depend) obscured for a couple of decades what a powerful weapon Taft-Hartley placed in management's hands. "After ten years of experience" with the law, the University of Buffalo economist Joseph Shister wrote in 1958, "this controversial piece of legislation can be viewed with considerably less emotion." Shister concluded that while the law had made it somewhat more difficult for unions to organize, the power relationship between management and labor was essentially unchanged. That judgment was correct for 1958, but it didn't remain so. The law almost immediately halted the phenomenal increase since the advent of the New Deal in the proportion of U.S. workers who belonged to unions. Between 1933 and 1954 union density rose from 7 to 28 percent, but between 1954 to 1973 it declined very gradually to 21 percent. By 1983 it stood at 18 percent, and today it's 12 percent—and remember, these calculations include public-sector union members who were virtually nonexistent in 1931 but represent the majority of all union workers today.[14] Remove those, and private-sector union membership is right back where it was, proportionally, the year Franklin Roosevelt became president. It's as if the New Deal never happened.[15]

What did Taft-Hartley do? For starters, it immediately reduced the proportion of civilian workers protected by the Wagner Act from 56 to 50 percent. This was achieved mainly by eliminating Wagner Act coverage for any workers who performed a supervisory role over other workers (as had, for instance, Reuther when he worked at Ford). This provision acquired greater reach over the years as courts and the NLRB expanded the definition of "supervisor" to encompass a greater number of workers.[16]

Taft-Hartley also gave management much greater control over the NLRB certification process. Previously, only unions had the power to initiate an NLRB-supervised union election, but under Taft-Hartley employers could, too. Why would an employer petition the NLRB for a union election? Purely for strategic reasons: Management could improve its chances of defeating the union by scheduling an election well before the union had won sufficient support among the rank and file. Taft-Hartley also required any union that lost an NLRB-supervised election to wait a full year before petitioning NLRB for a second election. Under the Wagner Act, the union could petition for the second election within a few months, and if it could demonstrate that membership had increased in the interval, the NLRB would likely allow that election to proceed. Steven Abraham, an industrial relations expert at the State University of New York at Oswego and a former law professor at the University of Northern Iowa, explained in a 1994 article for the *Hofstra Labor Law Journal* that a union's best chance of succeeding in a follow-up election was to hold the second election sooner rather than later, while memories were still fresh of an employer's broken promise to shower benefits on workers if they would only (please God!) vote against unionization.

Taft-Hartley also eliminated so-called card check certification, an alternative to secret-ballot elections that involved the quiet collection of authorization cards from a majority of employees. The disadvantage to unionizing via card check (a method that labor tried and failed to get Congress to revive after President Barack Obama's election in 2008) is that it risks subjecting wavering rank-and-file members to unseemly and perhaps thuggish pressure from union organizers. But the *absence* of card check (as an alternative to an NLRB-supervised election; the method remains legal as a step to *initiate* a union election, as we saw with Josh

Noble's organizing effort) has allowed employers to engage in fear-
mongering campaigns (and some thuggery of their own against employees who campaign visibly for unionization) prior to union elections.[17]
The formal union elections required under Taft-Hartley can also drown
organizing drives in procedure. In his 1991 book *Which Side Are You On?*
Thomas Geoghegan, a Chicago-based labor lawyer, complains that Taft-
Hartley "required hearings, campaign periods, secret-ballot elections,
and sometimes more hearings, before a union could be officially recognized." Taft-Hartley also created the "decertification" election, in which a
unionized workforce could choose no longer to belong to its union. (Previously, the workforce could only reject one union in favor of another
union.) Decertification elections remained rare for a while, but their
number increased steadily over the decades.[18] In the overwhelming majority of these elections, workers voted to scuttle their union.

Under the Wagner Act, unions could engage in "secondary boycotts"
aimed not at the employer but at another company that did business
with the employer. The Teamsters, for example, often exerted leverage
by having truckers refuse to transport products made by the employer's
more highly valued clients. Taft-Hartley outlawed secondary boycotts.[19]
Sit-down strikes of the type that won the UAW recognition from Detroit automakers during the 1930s had already been ruled illegal by
the Supreme Court, but Taft-Hartley made it easier for employers to
fire workers who engaged in such practices. Under the Wagner Act the
UAW and many other unions were able to make their workplaces a
"closed shop," meaning you couldn't get hired unless you already belonged to the union. Taft-Hartley banned the "closed shop." Taft-Hartley
also outlawed strikes whose purpose was to pressure management into
joining employer's associations that bargained with labor unions on an
industry-wide basis. And it outlawed "mass picketing," in which the
sheer size of a picket line was used to block or intimidate workers from
crossing it. This, too, had been a technique widely used in the organizing drives of the 1930s.

Unsurprisingly, after Taft-Hartley's enactment the labor movement
won unionization votes less frequently. In 1946 and 1947, the two years
prior to the law's taking effect, unions won victories in 80 and 75 percent of NLRB-supervised elections. That dropped to 73 percent in 1948
and 71 percent in 1949. Election victories bumped up to 83 percent in
1950, the year the Treaty of Detroit was signed, but through the rest of

the 1950s the percentages dropped steadily downward to 62 percent. By the late 1970s labor was losing more votes to unionize than it won.[20]

In *Which Side Are You On?* Geoghegan argues that Taft-Hartley

> encouraged employers to threaten workers who want to organize. Employers could hold "captive meetings," bring workers into the office and chew them out for thinking about the union. And Taft-Hartley led to the "union-busting" that started in the late 1960s and continues today. It started when a new "profession" of labor consultants began to convince employers that they could violate the [pro-labor 1935] Wagner Act, fire workers at will, fire them deliberately for exercising their legal rights, and *nothing would happen.*

If the Wagner Act had never had real sanctions, why did managers wait until the passage of Taft-Hartley to violate it with impunity? According to Geoghegan, when they tried to in the 1930s and 1940s labor retaliated by using various strong-arm tactics later banned under Taft-Hartley: "mass picketing, secondary strikes, etc." The provisions banning these practices *did* have real sanctions, including hefty fines and possible jail sentences. The best measure of management's impunity in violating labor laws, Harvard's Freeman argues, is the ratio of persons fired (illegally) for union activity divided by the total number of people who vote for union representation. At the time of the Treaty of Detroit it was about 0.5 percent. By the early 1980s it was 4.5 percent.[21] No wonder Alicia Sylvia was too scared to vote for the union in Loveland.

In 1993 Martin Jay Levitt, a "labor relations management consultant" who'd grown disgusted with his trade, published a book titled *Confessions of a Union Buster.* His testimony was eye-opening. Levitt wrote that to discredit a "pusher" (what anti-unionists called a union activist) he had "routinely pried into workers' police records, personnel files, credit histories, medical records, and family lives in search of a weakness." If the worker was "impeccable," Levitt would start a false rumor that the activist was gay or cheating on his wife ("a very effective technique, particularly in blue-collar towns"). During one particularly contentious anti-union campaign Levitt "dispatched a contingent of commandos to scratch up the cars of high-profile pro-company workers." Why *pro-*company workers? So he could blame it on the union.

In the two decades since Levitt published his book the union-busting industry has stepped out of the shadows. Type www.preventunion.com into your computer, for instance, and you're whisked to Russ Brown Associates ("When You Must Prevail"), a consulting firm run by a former NLRB official. RBA promises any client company "a significant discount" in the unlikely event that Brown and his crack team fail to bust whatever union is troubling management's sleep. "The vast majority of our work force was determined to bring in the union," reads a testimonial from an unnamed "major" oil company. "One week before the election the union withdrew thanks to RBA."

The presidency of Ronald Reagan was the first to adopt a public stance that was openly and unapologetically anti-union.[22] In 1981, when the air-traffic controllers' union defied a legal prohibition against going on strike, Reagan fired the entire workforce and replaced it with scab labor. Rather than revile him for it, Congress eventually renamed Washington's National Airport in his honor. Reagan lent enthusiastic support to Paul Volcker, the Carter-appointed chairman of the Federal Reserve Board, when the Fed's inflation-fighting policies brought on a brutal recession in 1981–82. This recession—until the most recent one the worst since the Great Depression—eliminated so many Rust Belt manufacturing jobs that the proportion of private-sector workers who belonged to unions dropped to 16 percent in 1985, down from 23 percent in 1979. Volcker's actions were necessary to eliminate the inflationary spiral that plagued the United States throughout the 1970s, but Ron Blackwell, chief economist for the AFL-CIO, believes that they ushered in a new era in which the Fed became relatively indifferent to the unemployment rate.[23]

Reagan further clarified where his sympathies lay by appointing Donald Dotson to chair the National Labor Relations Board. Dotson had previously worked as a management-side labor adversary for Wheeling-Pittsburgh Steel, and he believed collective bargaining led to "the destruction of individual freedom." Dotson's NLRB issued a succession of rulings that gave management greater leeway to interrogate and fire union supporters and to make misleading statements during union elections. It also processed unfair labor practice claims against management so slowly that the agency ended up with its biggest backlog in history.[24] Reagan helped out by cutting the NLRB's budget, "making it difficult," according to the union buster Levitt, "for agents to carry out full, lengthy investigations."

Under Reagan's two terms, the federal minimum wage, which previously had been adjusted upward every year or two, would remain stuck at $3.35 an hour for close to a full decade. Similarly, President George W. Bush, another two-term Republican, later let the minimum wage remain at $5.15 (to which it had risen during the presidencies of his father and Bill Clinton) for a few weeks shy of ten years, by which time its buying power had reached a fifty-one-year low.[25]

Academics may argue about the significance of any one of these decisions. Raising the minimum wage, for instance, reduces income inequality to a degree that some experts judge negligible and others judge substantial.[26] Where Levy and Temin (who lean toward "negligible") and Bartels (who leans toward "substantial") agree is that policies like setting the minimum wage don't occur in a vacuum; they are linked to a host of other government policies likely to have similar effects. Bartels emphasizes partisan differences and Levy and Temin emphasize ideological ones that occur over time, but both constitute changes in the way Washington governs. Levy and Temin concede that the ideological shift was influenced by changing circumstance (inflation *did* rise, productivity *did* fall, Rust Belt manufacturers *did* face increased foreign competition, and the structure of the economy *did* change). But they argue that the policies embraced, and the increased income inequality that resulted, were not inevitable. The proof lies in the fact that other industrialized nations faced similar pressures but embraced different policies. Their unions lost members, but they survived. And their incomes never became as unequal as those in the United States.

9

Rise of the Stinking Rich

IN 2003 THOMAS PIKETTY AND EMMANUEL Saez noticed a dimension to the Great Divergence that had nothing to do with the gap between college graduates and high school graduates, or the decline of labor unions, or the differing political philosophies of Democrats and Republicans. The causes of this newly discovered trend were so fundamentally different from most of what's been discussed in this book thus far that it's best to think of it as a separate and distinct phenomenon: the Great Divergence, Part 2.

What Piketty and Saez saw was that the very richest Americans had, during the preceding two decades, swallowed up a lot more of the nation's collective income than had been previously understood. Prior to the publication of their groundbreaking paper "Income Inequality in the United States, 1913–1998," the data typically used to analyze U.S. income distribution came from monthly household income surveys conducted by the U.S. census. This data set, known to experts as the Current Population Survey, was very useful if you wanted to track income trends for households as divided into quintiles (five groups, richest to poorest). But it wasn't particularly useful if you wanted to break down the population into much smaller groups, especially at the top end of the income scale. There were two reasons for this. First, the Current Population Survey didn't distinguish among incomes of $1 million per year or more. Households that made that much money were "top-coded" as belonging to a single category. The second problem with the Current Population Survey was that it was based on sampling data. Sampling is very useful when you're measuring extremely large populations; that's why demographers are forever recommending that the Census Bureau's much better-known project, the decennial census, quit trying to count every last American—a method that's bound to miss some hard-to-find people—and instead conduct a scientifically rigorous sampling, which would be more accurate. But sampling becomes a lot less accurate when you're measuring trends within a very small subgroup of the larger population. And the proportion of households with annual incomes above $1 million is well under 1 percent.[1]

Rather than rely on the Current Population Survey for broad-brush data about the rich, Piketty and Saez did what Simon Kuznets had done prior to his groundbreaking 1954 analysis of U.S. income distribution. They looked at data from the Internal Revenue Service. Except perhaps for a very few criminals who possess a superhuman ability to hide enormous quantities of cash, *everyone* in the United States who makes $1 million or more files a yearly tax return, and the IRS keeps track of *precisely* how much each of these people rakes in. That solved the top-coding and sampling problems. The IRS data posed a different problem: Some people don't have to file income tax returns because they don't make enough money. Today that's a pretty small group of people at very low incomes, but prior to 1944 it was true of most people. Even so, Piketty and Saez found that anyone whose income put them in the top decile (the top 10 percent, which today would mean a combined family income of $109,000 or more) *always* had to file, going all the way back to 1916.[2] That enabled Piketty and Saez to create a field of study—you might call it "decile-ology"—examining America's top income decile over a longer period and slicing it into smaller and smaller subgroups ("fractiles")— the top 1 percent, the top 0.1 percent, the top 0.01 percent—than anyone had ever done before. Like Antonie van Leeuwenhoek peering into a droplet of lake water teeming with spirogyra and vorticella, Piketty and Saez put the top decile under their microscope and scrutinized various fractiles of rich Americans.

"If a $100,000-a-year household thinks itself to be middle class," the neoconservative writer Irving Kristol once wrote, "then it *is* middle class." This sentiment is widely held, but it makes no mathematical sense. Any family whose income exceeds that of 90 percent of all other families cannot sensibly be called anything but rich. To believe otherwise would oblige you to judge your child mediocre when his teacher gives him an A.[3] But within the top decile distinctions are nonetheless worth making.

- *Sort of Rich.* Let's call these everyone making between $109,000 and $153,000. That situates them today in the bottom half of the top 10 percent.
- *Basically Rich.* That's everyone making between $153,000 and $368,000 (the bottom threshold for the top 1 percent).
- *Undeniably Rich.* That's everyone making between $368,000 and $1.7 million (the bottom threshold for the top 0.1 percent).
- *Really Rich.* That's everyone making between $1.7 million and $9.1 million (the bottom threshold for the top 0.01 percent).
- *Stinking Rich.* That's everybody in the top 0.01 percent, making $9.1 million or more.[4]

You can be Stinking Rich and still get snubbed by a hedge-fund manager who pulls down $10 million or more, but now we're down to about 8,400 households in America and narrower distinctions start to seem fetishistic.[5]

Piketty and Saez didn't employ the blunt terminology used here, but they sliced their top-decile sampling along these lines, and in so doing made the following discoveries (all numbers that follow are updated through 2008, the last year for which data are available):

- The American aristocracy is in one respect more like the rest of us than it used to be. "Before World War II," Piketty and Saez wrote, "the richest Americans were overwhelmingly rentiers deriving most of their income from wealth holdings (mainly in the form of dividends)." (A rentier is someone who lives off income from fixed assets like stocks, bonds, or real estate.) But today, Piketty and Saez found, at least as many are job holders deriving most of their income from their wages (a category of compensation in which they included stock options offered to employees in lieu of wages). Does that mean it became posh to have a job? A better way to put it is that having a job—the right job, anyway—became the way to get posh. That's encouraging in one sense: To roll in the dough you don't have to inherit it. But it's discouraging in another sense: You can't blame enormous income disparities on coupon-clipping Bertie Woosters who exist outside the wage structure (and reality as most of us understand it). The wage structure *itself* is grossly misshapen.

- The rich, defined as the top 10 percent (which today means everyone making $109,000 or more), increased their share of national income during the Great Divergence from about one third (34 percent) to nearly one half (48 percent).
- The top 5 percent (Basically, Undeniably, Really, and Stinking Rich; today, everybody making at least $153,000) increased their share of national income during the Great Divergence from 23 to 37 percent.
- The top 1 percent (Undeniably, Really, and Stinking; today, everybody making at least $368,000) more than *doubled* their share of the national income during the Great Divergence, from 10 to 21 percent. A chart showing this found its way into President Obama's first budget, prompting the *Wall Street Journal* columnist Daniel Henninger to call it "the most politically potent squiggle along an axis since Arthur Laffer drew his famous curve on a napkin in the mid-1970s." But where Laffer's squiggle was an argument to *lower* taxes, Piketty and Saez's (the conservative Henninger noted with some dismay) was an argument to *raise* them on the rich.[6] It was also what later inspired 2011's Occupy Wall Street protest slogan, "We are the 99 percent."
- The top 0.1 percent (Really and Stinking; today, everybody making at least $1.7 million) *tripled* their share of the national income during the Great Divergence, from 3 to 10 percent.
- The top 0.01 percent (Stinking; today, everybody making at least $9.1 million) nearly *quadrupled* their share of the national income during the Great Divergence, from 1.4 to 5 percent.[7]

Notice a pattern? The richer you are, the faster you expand your slice of your country's income. Or as Saez put it to me, "The [inequality] phenomenon is more extreme the further you go up in the distribution," and it's "very strong once you pass that threshold of the top 1 percent."[8]

Perhaps you view "the rich get richer" as an inexorable fact of economic life, like compounding interest. But (as with the middle-income-based divergence that we've considered thus far) the top-incomes-based divergence is not typical of past American history. And while it's true that an upward pattern in top-income shares has since 1979 been fairly common in other developed countries, it isn't universal. Top-income shares in these other countries are lower and, where they are increasing,

do so less rapidly. An inequality trend driven by large and quickly growing income shares at the summit is not capitalism's norm.

Piketty and Saez found the top decile consumed about 45 percent of
the nation's income from the mid-1920s until 1940. That decreased to
about 34 percent during World War II and remained in that range through
the 1981–82 recession. In 1984—the year President Ronald Reagan ran
for reelection on the theme that it was "morning in America"—the top
decile's income share began to increase significantly, and it has increased
most years ever since. In 2008 the top decile's income share was 48 percent. For the top 10 percent, then, the income-share norm during the
twentieth century wasn't the current 48 percent, but rather the 34 percent
level that prevailed for about forty years after World War II.

A look at the fractiles demonstrates that the trend was driven by the
richest people within the top decile.

Income share for the top 1 percent—the Undeniably, Really, and
Stinking Rich, all with incomes today above $368,000—reached 24
percent in 1928, decreased to 13 percent by the end of World War II,
decreased more slowly in the postwar years, and by 1960 stood at 10 percent, which was about where it stayed until Reagan's morning in America.
Then it increased to 12 percent in 1984, 14 percent in 1994, 20 percent in
2004, and 21 percent in 2008. For the one-percenters, the forty-odd years
of relative stability after World War II suggest that the twentieth-century
norm was an income share about half what it is today. To the extent that
income share for the top 1 percent changed in the postwar years, it decreased rather than increased. The same pattern can be observed for the
top 0.1 percent (the Really and Stinking Rich) and the top 0.01 percent
(the Stinking Rich).

Not only, then, is it not a fact of economic life that the income share
of the very richest Americans must be as high as it is today; it is also not
a fact of economic life that the very richest Americans must increase
their income share over time or even maintain it at the same level. Their
income share can dwindle over a long period, as it did in the decades
after World War II, without hurting the economy. Dwindling income
share for the very rich may even help the economy. "None of the bad
consequences one might have expected from a drastic equalization of
incomes actually materialized after World War II," Paul Krugman
writes in The Conscience of a Liberal. "On the contrary, the Great Compression succeeded in equalizing incomes for a long period—more than

Income Share for the
Top 10%, 5%, 1%, 0.1% and 0.01%

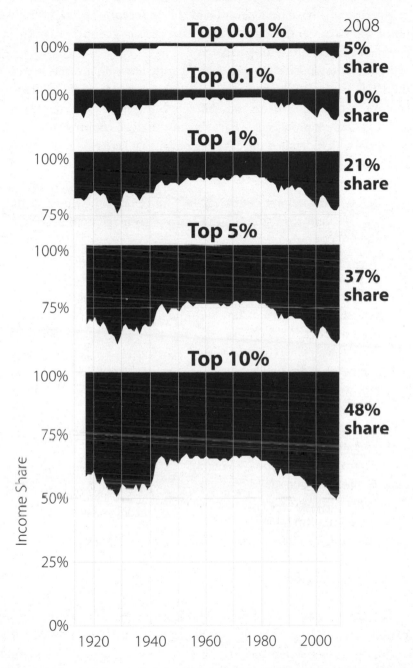

Top I percent income share includes capital gains. Source: Alvaredo et al., "The World Top Incomes Database."

thirty years. And the era of equality was also a time of unprecedented prosperity, which we have never been able to recapture." Trickle-up economics has a better track record over America's last century than trickle-down (see figure, preceding page).

In other developed countries, significantly growing income shares for the Undeniably, Really, and Stinking Rich are common, but hardly the rule. In 2011, Piketty, Saez, and Anthony B. Atkinson, a senior research fellow at Oxford, produced a chart showing sixteen countries around the world for which detailed tax data were available through 2005. You can separate these countries into three groups.

- In *four* (Singapore, Sweden, Japan, France), income share for the top 1 percent rose no more than two percentage points from its previous trough.
- In *three* (Netherlands, Germany, Switzerland), income share for the top 1 percent either remained flat or declined.[9]
- In *nine*, income share for the top 1 percent rose more than two percentage points, but nowhere did it rise as much as in the United States.

The nine countries where income share for the top 1 percent rose significantly were, in declining order:

1. The United States (up ten percentage points)
2. Norway (up eight)
3. The United Kingdom (up eight)
4. Canada (up six)
5. India (up five)
6. Argentina (up four)
7. Australia (up four)
8. New Zealand (up four)
9. Finland (up four)

The United States' top 1 percent ended up with a 17 percent income share, excluding capital gains.[10] Only Argentina matched it. Every other country's one-percenters had to make do with a smaller income share. In the United Kingdom it was 14 percent; in Canada, 14 percent; in India, 9 percent; in Finland, 7 percent; in Australia, 9 percent; in New Zealand, 9 percent; and in Norway, 12 percent. In the seven countries where the Undeniably, Really, and Stinking Rich experienced no significant increase in income share, the end percentages were all well below that of the United States.[11]

To summarize: The Great Divergence (Part 2) is a dramatic departure from the status quo that prevailed in the United States from the end of World War II through the early 1980s. Although top income shares are rising in many developed countries, nowhere are they rising as fast as in the United States. Also, nowhere (except Argentina) have top income shares reached the same high level as in the United States. Indeed, if you update income share for America's one-percenters to 2008, the United States pulls slightly ahead of Argentina—not that this is a competition any sensible country would want to win.

Who is it exactly who got rich?

A 2010 study by Jon Bakija, Adam Cole, and Bradley Heim, economists at Williams College, the U.S. Treasury, and Indiana University, respectively, looked at that question by examining income tax records for 2005. They found that among the Really and Stinking Rich—the top 0.1 percent, who currently make at least $1.7 million   43 percent were executives, managers, and supervisors at nonfinancial firms, and 18 percent were financiers. Together they accounted for the majority. The professions next in line were law (7 percent), medicine (6 percent), and real estate (4 percent).[12]

The skyrocketing increase in nonfinancial executive pay has been well documented. A *New York Times* survey of two hundred corporations with revenues of $10.78 billion or more found that in 2010 median compensation for chief executives was just under $11 million, a 23 percent increase over 2009. (The comparable median for all workers fell slightly during the same period.) The largest payout went to Philippe Dauman, president and chief executive of Viacom, the entertainment conglomerate that owns Paramount Pictures and Comedy Central. Dauman got $84.5 million, an amount that exceeds the entire 2011–12 town budget for North Haven, Connecticut. It takes a village to pay a corporate titan.[13]

Where does the money go? In 2007 the *Wall Street Journal* columnist Robert Frank published a sort of travelogue about the lives of America's out-of-sight wealthy on what turned out to be the eve of a financial meltdown. He titled it *Richistan*. One discovery he made was that there was an acute butler shortage. Carol Scudere, founder of a butler training school in Ohio, told Frank, "My biggest problem now is finding students. There are plenty of jobs for them." Most of her graduates, she said, earned a yearly salary of $75,000 or more. "[A butler] should be receiving an executive salary of in the range of $50–$150,000 a year," confirms Steven M. Ferry in *Butlers and Household Managers: 21st Century Professionals*, a primer the British-born ex-butler self-published in 2008. "The only difference between him and the slave of olden times is that the butler works for you because he wants to." If a willing slave isn't your cup of tea, how about a watch that will give time, day, date, and phase of the moon for a thousand years at the low, low price of $736,000? The manufacturer is Franck Muller, which Frank identifies as "one of a number of new brands known only to the rich."

American chief executives typically get paid two to three times what their European counterparts earn. Such pay levels were not the norm during most of the twentieth century. In 2005 Carola Frydman and Raven Saks, two young economists at Harvard (later MIT) and the Federal Reserve, respectively, surveyed pay records on file at the Securities and Exchange Commission dating back to 1936, two years after the SEC was created. They found that pay for top executives declined steeply during World War II, increased gradually from the mid-1940s to the mid-1970s, and then took off like a rocket during the 1980s and 1990s. In 1973, a survey of large companies in the United States found that chief executives were paid twenty-seven times more than the average worker. By 2005 that had risen to 262 times.[14]

Frydman and Saks were especially struck by the "considerable stability" during the 1950s and 1960s, a time when firms were growing rapidly and the economy was booming. They noted that changing tax policy had some influence on executive compensation, but otherwise they couldn't really account for the change. The Treaty of Detroit surely provides part of the answer. Back when union leaders were powerful, they trained a wary (and at least slightly inhibiting) eye on their bosses' pay packages.

Another likely factor is the growing tendency of corporations to hire chief executives from outside the company, often someone who has been chief executive or president somewhere else. In his 2002 book *Searching for a Corporate Savior*, the Harvard Business School professor

Rakesh Khurana argues that this is driven by corporate directors' desire to impress the financial markets, which crave leaders with established reputations and mediagenic personalities. Since the pool of such people is necessarily limited, the job candidate ends up "in an unusually strong position to bargain with the board about subsequent power and compensation arrangements." Khurana argues that if corporate directors paid greater attention to job candidates who possessed skills and experience relevant to their particular business, they would likely promote more new chairmen from within the company, thereby avoiding the premium paid to outsiders (and likely improving corporate performance as well).[15]

By 1991, the continuing run-up in top corporate salaries, which was accompanied by widespread recessionary layoffs, persuaded candidate Bill Clinton to make a political target of the tax deduction that corporations were permitted to claim on top salaries. In 1993, President Clinton pushed through Congress a bill limiting tax-deductible salaries to $1 million. But the bill exempted performance-based bonuses and stock options, on the theory that these tied chief executives' compensation to company profitability. Corporate compensation committees responded in three ways. First, "everybody got a raise to $1 million," Nell Minow, a corporate governance critic, told me.[16] Next, corporate compensation committees, which remained bent on showering chief executives indiscriminately with cash, started inventing make-believe performance metrics. For instance, AES Corp., a firm based in Arlington, Virginia, that operates power plants, made it one of chief executive Dennis Bakke's performance goals to ensure that AES remained a "fun" place to work. ("To some, it's soft," the fun-loving Bakke told *Businessweek*. "To me, it's a vision of the world.")

Third, and most important, corporations showered top executives with so many stock options that this form of compensation came to account, on average, for the majority of CEO pay. The growth in stock options exceeded whatever salary growth would likely have occurred had the $1 million limit not been imposed. That's because stock-option awards, unlike salaries, were *free* from a bookkeeping point of view. They didn't show up on the balance sheet because corporate accountants said the options' future value couldn't be known. "They'd say they're not worth *anything*," Minow told me, "and I'd say, 'Really? Then give *me* some.'" Between

1992 and 2000, average stock options granted to chief executives grew from $800,000 to $7 million. Total compensation to chief executives more than quadrupled.

The Financial Accounting Standards Board, a private group that the Securities and Exchange Commission relies on to set corporate accounting rules, tried to require corporations to put stock options on the books, but the business lobby fought back by getting Senator Joe Lieberman of Connecticut (then a Democrat, subsequently an independent) to sponsor a nonbinding resolution opposing it. The resolution passed a Democratic-controlled Senate by an overwhelming majority in May 1994, and SEC chairman Arthur Levitt (in a decision he'd later remember as "probably the single biggest mistake I made in my years at the SEC") persuaded the FASB to drop the matter lest Congress politicize accounting standards further. Only in 2005, after accounting scandals at Enron, Global Crossing, and other companies, was the FASB able to compel corporations to subtract stock option grants from profit calculations.[17]

In theory, paying a top executive in the form of stock options is a good way to reward or punish him according to how well (or poorly) he manages his company. But in practice the value of stock options was seldom "indexed" to measure the company's individual stock market performance against the overall rise (or fall) in the stock market. Unsurprisingly, corporate boards resisted indexing chief executives' stock options throughout the bull market of the 1990s, with the predictable result that the value of awarded stock options reflected mainly . . . the bull market of the 1990s.

Another cure that proved worse than the disease was the advent of compensation consultants. Under fire from stockholders for maintaining a too-cozy relationship with CEOs, corporate compensation committees turned to outside consultants to set pay levels for top executives. But a 2007 study by the Corporate Library, a corporate-governance watchdog that Minow cofounded, revealed that companies that hired such consultants actually paid their CEOs more than companies that didn't, and that these higher pay levels were not associated with greater returns to shareholders. Some of the consultants represented clients whose CEO base salaries averaged out to 15 to 19 percent above the "peer median." One reason was what SEC commissioner Roel C. Campos, in a 2007 speech, called the "real estate appraisal phenomenon." A real estate appraisal, he noted, almost never falls below purchase price, because any appraiser who routinely scotches sales with low estimates of houses' value won't likely win much business from people who make their living selling and financing real estate. "I think it's pretty similar with CEO salaries," Campos said. Even when they aren't hired directly by the CEO—as, amazingly, has sometimes occurred in the past (only recently was this made illegal)—consultants don't want to be the ones to screw up an important hire. Though tasked with calculating what individuals in comparable positions have been paid elsewhere, "consultants can pretty much find high comparable income data to support paying a high amount to the CEO," Campos explained. "No compensation consultant gets fired for saying 'you're underpaid,'" Minow told me. Indeed, the consultant may cast so wide a net that he discovers perks that the board might never have heard about otherwise. "CEO perks at one company are quickly copied elsewhere," the financier Warren Buffett, a frequent critic of CEO pay, wrote in his 2007 "chairman's letter" to shareholders in his company, Berkshire Hathaway. "'All the other kids have one' may seem a thought too juvenile to use as a rationale in the boardroom. But consultants employ precisely this argument, phrased more elegantly of course, when they make recommendations to comp committees."[18]

The 43 percent of the Really and Stinking Rich who run America's nonfinancial corporations were very significant players in the Great Divergence (Part 2). No other occupational group had a larger membership among the top 0.1 percent. But, incredibly, the quadrupling of chief executives' pay during the 1990s wasn't enough to *increase* this group's presence among the Really and Stinking Rich once the run-up in top income shares began. Proportionally, its membership actually diminished slightly, from 48 percent in 1979 to percent to 43 percent in 2005. The group to watch—the group that *expanded* its share of the top earners' pie—was the nation's financiers. Back in 1979, the financial sector represented only 11 percent of the Really and Stinking Rich. By 2005, financiers represented 18 percent.[19] That's because changes during this period in how nonfinancial corporations did business paled in comparison to changes in how Wall Street did business.

In their 2010 book *13 Bankers*, Simon Johnson, an economist at MIT's Sloan School of Management, and James Kwak, a former consultant at McKinsey and Company, describe the financial sector's astonishing growth over three decades through mergers and expansions into new businesses.

Between 1980 and 2000, the assets held by commercial banks, securities firms, and the securitizations they created grew from [the equivalent of] 55 percent of GDP to [the equivalent of] 95 percent. Financial
sector profits grew even faster, from an average of 13 percent of all domestic corporate profits from 1978 to 1987 to an average of 30 percent
from 1998 to 2007. The growth was faster still for the largest banks.
Between 1990 and 1999, the ten largest bank holding companies'
share of all bank assets grew from 26 percent to 45 percent, and their
share of all deposits doubled from 17 percent to 34 percent. And they
continued to grow. In 1998, the merged Travelers and Citibank had
$700 billion in assets; at the end of 2007, Citigroup had $2.2 trillion in
assets, not counting $1.1 trillion in off-balance-sheet assets, even after
the spinoff of the Travelers insurance businesses. Bank of America was
not far behind, growing from $570 billion after the NationsBank–Bank
of America merger to $1.7 trillion at the end of 2007.[20]

In effect, Wall Street ate the economy. *Take General Electric*: You probably think of it as a maker of lightbulbs and appliances, right? And in
1980, manufacturing did indeed account for 92 percent of its profits.
But by early 2008, GE's financial business accounted for 56 percent of
its profits. (Its GE Capital subsidiary happens to be the largest nonbank
lender in the United States.) Now consider General Motors: It makes
cars, doesn't it? But before its financial arm, GMAC, got caught up in
the subprime mortgage crisis of the late aughts, GMAC routinely accounted for 60 to 90 percent of the parent company's profits. (GM sold
off GMAC but has since replaced it with a new financial division, GM
Financial.) When the wildly leveraged U.S. economy crashed and
burned at the end of 2008, many predicted that Wall Street's era of economic dominance had ended. But by March 2011, the *Wall Street Journal*
could report that the financial sector once again was creating about 30
percent of corporate profits in the United States. While still short of the
2002 peak, when finance generated fully 44 percent of corporate profits, 30 percent was the financial sector's average during the subprime
bubble.[21]

Yves-André Istel, seventy-six, is a senior adviser and former vice
chairman at Rothschild's Global Financial Advisory, which provides
corporate advice to businesses, governments, and individuals but does
not itself underwrite securities. Istel emigrated from France at age four

and speaks in the accent of his adopted Manhattan. In 1958, fresh out of Princeton and the army, he enrolled in the trainee program at the white shoe investment bank White Weld & Co. His pay was $4,800 a year, the equivalent today of about $37,000. That's about half the current average starting salary;[22] in those days starting compensation at investment banks wasn't notably different from what it was at other private companies. "I was able," Istel told me, "to rent a nice apartment on the East Side for $120 a month."[23]

At that time, Istel recalls, Wall Street was structured more or less as it had been since the turn of the twentieth century. Morgan Stanley, Dillon Read, and Kuhn Loeb were the first tier, or "bulge bracket," that is, the banks that got top billing in any initial public offering deal they participated in. First Boston was "just below." The power of these firms was a vestige of history. Since none had brokerage divisions, they relied on a network of independent brokers to sell their securities to individual investors. "It was," says Istel, "a hugely antiquated structure." Brokerage commissions were fixed under a gentlemanly arrangement literally dating from the 1792 establishment of the trading body that evolved into the New York Stock Exchange. The NYSE blocked members from making stock transactions off the exchange floor, limiting competition. Both archaic practices would linger until late in the twentieth century, when they were swept away amid pressures to scale up and increase competition.

When Istel started out, Wall Street had not yet gone global. Only a handful of American firms specialized in international markets, which would become Istel's specialty. (In the early 1960s practically the only contemporary Istel knew who shared his interest in foreign securities was George Soros.) One such firm was Kuhn Loeb, which Istel joined in 1964. International finance "wasn't that profitable," Istel says, though it would become steadily more so through the 1960s. One index of that era's constraints on international commerce: In 1966 the maximum number of transatlantic phone calls that could occur simultaneously between North America and Europe was 138.[24] "The main ways that a Kuhn Loeb or a Dillon Read made money was more on the equity underwritings and on a merger and acquisition business that was not called that at the time," Istel says. "And even then it was no secret that Kuhn Loeb didn't make much money." In 1977 Kuhn Loeb was folded into the much more profitable Lehman Brothers, where Istel became managing director.

Three changes are typically mentioned in any discussion of Wall Street's transformation during the Great Divergence:

1. The principal activity within investment banks shifted from banking (corporate underwriting, mergers, and acquisitions) to trading (buying and selling financial products on behalf of wealthy institutions, very wealthy individuals, or the investment bank itself).
2. Investment banks abandoned or drastically modified their partnership structures to become publicly traded corporations.
3. The government greatly reduced the level of regulation under which Wall Street had operated since the New Deal.

Banking Versus Trading

Wall Street bankers' unsuccessful struggle to maintain dominance over Wall Street traders became the subject of a riveting narrative about Lehman by the journalist Ken Auletta that was published in the *New York Times Magazine* in 1985 and later expanded into the book *Greed and Glory on Wall Street*. Bankers, Auletta explained, "have a longer horizon. A banker often invests several years in cultivating a relationship before it turns into a client." Traders, on the other hand, made "quick, firm decisions" in the service not of clients but of individual transactions. Pete Peterson, Lehman's chairman (former commerce secretary under President Nixon and before that chairman of Bell & Howell, which manufactured movie projectors), belonged to the traditional banking culture and described what traders did as "de-clienting the business," that is, replacing long-standing institutional relationships with short-term transactional ones. But by the early 1980s, trading *was* the business, accounting for two thirds of Lehman's profits, and Peterson (who admitted to Auletta that he lacked "a detailed grasp" of the firm's trading activities) was pushed out by his co–chief executive, Lew Glucksman, who had come up on the trading side. It was a watershed moment. Trading became Wall Street's principal activity.[25] And with the aid of high-speed computers, trades could be done on a scale never previously imagined.

In moving from banking to trading, investment banks exchanged (relative) stability and (relatively) modest profits for high risk and (when they didn't go bust) high return on capital. As managing director and board member at Lehman, Istel had a ringside view (and, being a banker rather than a trader, had his own tense encounters with Glucksman; he left for First Boston in 1983). "When Pete Peterson joined Lehman" in 1973, Istel notes, "Lehman had almost gone under . . . because of its trading." Later, after it was sold in 1984 to a brokerage arm of American Express, "it almost happened again." Lehman's heavy investment in commercial real estate eventually brought an end to the firm in 2008. It was the largest bankruptcy in history.

Partnerships into Corporations

Until 1970, members of the NYSE were prohibited from "going public," that is, selling shares in their firms on the stock exchange as a public corporation.[26] This limited the amount of available capital, but it also limited risk. In an investment banking partnership, partners were loath to make risky bets with what was in effect their own money. The now-defunct Donaldson, Lufkin, & Jenrette led the way in 1970; the invest-ment bank Goldman Sachs became the last major Wall Street firm to go public, in 1999.

When Kuhn Loeb merged with Lehman Brothers in 1977, the com-bined assets of the new firm were a mere $70 million (the equivalent today of $262 million). Three decades later, when Merrill Lynch merged with Bank of America, the combined assets of the new firm were $2.7 trillion. Daniel Alpert, managing partner of the investment bank West-wood Capital, cites two reasons investment banks went public: "The most important [was] the opportunity to use OPM (other people's money) and be able to withdraw their own. The second reason [was] that if everyone else was going public and using public equity to grow total balance sheet, then anyone who wanted to stay in the bulge bracket had to do likewise."[27] Three decades ago, when managing partner John Gut-freund sold the privately held Salomon Brothers to the publicly traded Phibro Corporation, it earned Gutfreund a (then-impressive) $30 mil-lion payday. Before Goldman's partners voted to go public, its retired former co-chairman John Whitehead wrote them in a letter: "I don't find anyone who denies that the decision of many of the partners, particu-larly the younger men, was based more on the dazzling amounts to be deposited in their capital accounts than on what they felt would be good for the future of Goldman Sachs." The average windfall from the initial public offering for past and present Goldman partners was $63.6 million.[28]

Deregulation

For four decades after the 1929 crash, Washington kept a tight rein on what banks could and couldn't do. The best known post-crash regulation was Glass-Steagall, a 1933 prohibition against commercial banks participating in investment banking (and vice versa). But there were others. In 13 Bankers, Johnson and Kwak make note of a 1956 law limiting bank holding companies' ability to own banks in more than one state; a 1967 law regulating savings and loan deposit rates through the Fed; and consumer protections like the 1968 Truth in Lending Act and the 1970 Fair Credit Reporting Act.

Starting in the 1970s, though, political pressure began building to deregulate. In his 2011 book Age of Greed, Jeff Madrick says it began with Walter Wriston, chairman of First National City (now Citigroup) in the 1970s, who spent his career dreaming up ever-more-imaginative ways to circumvent or outright defy existing regulations. Washington regulators went along either because they were fearful that tightening the reins would worsen what was, during the 1970s, an already shaky economy or because (increasingly, as time passed) they got caught up in the antiregulatory ideology that was coming into vogue. Another factor was the business lobby's growing influence in Washington (as discussed in chapter 7). As the market evolved in new directions, an increasingly gridlocked Washington was unable to evolve with it by regulating newly important financial products like hedge funds and derivatives.

"The removal of Glass-Steagall," Istel says, was "largely meaningless." By the time it was formally repealed in 1999, "it was like the Maginot Line. It was there and in force but everybody was running around it to do whatever they needed to do with the Fed's approval." More important, Istel notes, was the Securities and Exchange Commission's easing of leverage restrictions. Before it went bust Bear Stearns's ratio of debt to assets reached 33 to 1.

In retrospect, the extent of Wall Street's leveraging prior to the 2008 crash seems insane, no matter how lucrative in the short term. According to Istel, not only did the trend reflect a generational change (Wall Street leaders were no longer children of the Depression who harbored an innate aversion to debt); it also reflected technological hubris. "Everybody thought that their risk control models were increasingly sophisticated and able to tell them what their real risks were," Istel says. Wall Street firms hired math wizards ("quants") to create elaborate computer programs calibrating downside risk with greater precision than proved possible. Sometimes the models were right but weren't understood or followed by everyone else. In a droll 2009 op-ed for the *New York Times*, the journalist Calvin Trillin recalled that when he'd gone to Yale in the 1950s it was the bottom third of the class that went on to careers in Wall Street. "Now we realize that by the standards that came later, they weren't really greedy," he wrote. "They just wanted a nice house in Greenwich and maybe a sailboat." What spoiled everything, Trillin argued, was "when you started reading about these geniuses from M.I.T. and Caltech who instead of going to graduate school in physics went to Wall Street" to craft derivatives. "Do you think *our* guys could have invented, say, credit default swaps? Give me a break! They couldn't have done the math." Warren Buffett would seem to agree that genius and finance are a lethal combination. He reportedly once proposed (presumably in jest) firing any financial manager found to have an IQ above 115.[29]

Trillin didn't know when he wrote his op-ed that his comical speculation was well grounded in the latest academic research. A 2009 paper by the economists Thomas Philippon of New York University and Ariell Reshef of the University of Virginia reported that the skills required to work in the financial industry and wages paid to those who did were quite high from 1909 to 1933, when banks were relatively free of regulation. They declined precipitously during the 1930s, when regulators imposed strict limits on banking, and more moderately from the 1950s through the 1970s, as those limits continued and some new ones were imposed. After 1980, as deregulation once again made finance a "high-skill, high-wage industry," skills and wages returned to the levels of the 1920s.[30]

Yet another inducement for Wall Street to place risky bets is the expectation that if the bets don't pan out the federal government will bail the banks out. In 2009 Karen Ho, an associate professor of anthropology at the University of Minnesota, published an "ethnography of Wall Street" titled *Liquidated.* Approaching Wall Street as if it were some peculiar

South Sea island culture, Ho asked: "How can investment bankers be arguably the most highly compensated workers in the world when their practices so often generate crisis and economic decline?" Partly, she concluded, the sky-high pay was compensation for job insecurity. Three years after the Internet bubble burst, one in ten securities-industry employees had lost his or her job (though it can be assumed a great many of these people moved from one firm to another). But another significant factor, she concluded, was the widespread expectation of government rescue in the event of catastrophe. Peter Felsenthal, a bond trader at Salomon Smith Barney (now Morgan Stanley Smith Barney) told Ho, "You have all of the upside when things go well. If you do poorly, you don't owe anybody money, so you might as well take as much risk as possible." That assumption proved fatal for Lehman Brothers when the government let it go under in 2008. But the more that investment banks consolidate after episodes like the subprime bubble, the greater the potential cost to the economy should any remaining bank fail. And the greater that cost to the economy, the greater the likelihood that Washington will fulfill the bankers' expectation of a government bailout next time the bottom falls out. That isn't a recipe for restraint.

NO DISCUSSION OF the Really and Stinking Rich is complete without some consideration of the phenomenal run-up in income for top entertainment figures and athletes. The 2010 study by Bakija, Cole, and Heim found that people in the arts, media, and sports represented only 3 percent of the Really and Stinking Rich, so you can't really blame the Great Divergence on Tiger Woods. But celebrities are hard to ignore. After Greta Garbo's runaway success in the 1926 silent film *Flesh and the Devil*, she refused to go back to work at MGM ("I think I go home," she said, and sailed for Sweden) until Louis B. Mayer gave her a raise to $5,000 per week (the equivalent today of $64,000). It was so extravagant that Cole Porter made "Garbo's salary" one of the witty superlatives in his classic song "You're the Top." But when Charlie Sheen got himself kicked off his top-rated sitcom *Two and a Half Men* in 2011 for bizarre anti-Semitic rants against a producer named Chuck Lorre ("I violently hate Chaim Levine," he told the celebrity gossip Web site TMZ), Sheen was making, after inflation, about *thirty times* what Mayer gave to Garbo.

Sheen is the beneficiary of what the University of Chicago economist

Sherwin Rosen called "The Economics of Superstars" (in a 1981 paper of that title), and that the economists Robert Frank and Philip Cook called *The Winner-Take-All-Society* (in a 1995 book of that title).[31] With improvements in communications technology and an ever-more-globalized marketplace, performers and athletes can scale up the size of their audience to a degree that wasn't possible before (even for silent movies, which posed no language barriers). This ought to make a thousand flowers bloom, but either the rarity of extraordinary talent, or perhaps the public's psychological need to focus on just a few popular personalities at a time, serves to narrow competition to a few winners who dominate a vastly expanded market. We've all heard that the best cellist in the world is Yo-Yo Ma, and for all I know he really is. But most of us who listen raptly to Ma's recordings couldn't name the second or third or tenth best cellist in the world. One cellist is all we need! Before the development of high-fidelity recording, when the only way to hear a really great cello soloist was to go to a concert hall, one cellist wasn't enough. Now it is.[32]

Why worry about the ever-fattening paycheck of the Really and Stinking Rich? Why obsess about distinctions measured in deciles and fractiles? Or, for that matter, about the gulf that we're likelier to live with on an everyday basis, between college grads and high school grads, professionals and working stiffs? Up to this point I've assumed the reader would instinctively believe that growing income inequality was inherently undesirable in a democratic society. In the next chapter, I'll stop assuming and address arguments that say income inequality isn't something we really need fret about.

10

Why It Matters

Clarence the Angel: We don't use money in heaven.
George Bailey: Comes in pretty handy down here, bub.

—Frank Capra's *It's a Wonderful Life* (1946)

THE DECLARATION OF INDEPENDENCE says that all men are created equal, but we know that isn't true. George Clooney was created better-looking than me. Stephen Hawking was born smarter, Evander Holyfield stronger, Jon Stewart funnier, and Warren Buffett savvier at playing the market. All these people have parlayed their exceptional gifts into very high incomes—much higher than mine. Is that so odd? Odder would be if Buffett or Clooney were forced to live on my income, adequate though it might be to a petit bourgeois journalist. Lest you conclude my equanimity is some sort of affectation, Barbara Ehrenreich, in her 2001 book *Nickel and Dimed*, quotes a woman named Colleen, a single mother of two, saying much the same thing about the wealthy families whose floors she scrubs on hands and knees. "I don't mind, really," she says, "because I guess I'm a simple person, and I don't want what they have. I mean, it's nothing to me." The prospect of wealth certainly isn't "nothing" to *me*—I'd love to have a lot more dough, and so, I suspect, would Colleen. But I accept (and I take from Colleen's comment she accepts) that even in a much more egalitarian society, popular comedians and Wall Street financiers would still make

considerably more money than housecleaners and journalists. They always have, and they always will.

But to accept that *some* inequality is a fact of life in a capitalist economy is not to accept that *ever-greater* inequality is either necessary or
desirable. Some commentators—most of them conservatives—have
made that leap. Others have argued that the Great Divergence matters
little because of other, more important changes in American society.
Their arguments need to be answered.

Inequality Is Good

Every year the American Economic Association invites a distinguished
economist to deliver at its annual conference the Richard T. Ely Lecture.
Ely, you'll recall from chapter 1, was mentor to Willford King, the University of Wisconsin economist who pioneered the study of income
distribution, and he was an important leader in the Progressive movement. Ely was also one of the AEA's founders. Judging from what we
know about Ely's beliefs, it seems fair to conclude that he would have been
horrified by the AEA lecture that Finis Welch, a professor of economics
(now emeritus) at Texas A&M, delivered in his name in 1999. Its title was
"In Defense of Inequality."

Welch began by stating that "all of economics results from inequality.
Without inequality of priorities and capabilities, there would be no
trade, no specialization, and no surpluses produced by cooperation." He
invited his audience to consider a world in which skill, effort, and sheer
chance played no role whatsoever in what you got paid. The only decision that would affect your wage level would be when to leave school.
"After that, the clock ticks, and wages follow the experience path. Nothing else matters. Can you imagine a more horrible, a more deadening
existence?" In October 2011 Richard Epstein, professor of law at New
York University, made a similar argument on the PBS *NewsHour* after
the Congressional Budget Office issued a much-discussed report on income inequality.

> If, in fact, it turns out that inequality creates an incentive for people to
> produce and to create wealth, it's a wonderful force for innovation. . . .
> You start changing the particular policies so that there [are] high

marginal rates on taxable income, two things happen simultaneously. People have less money to invest, and people will be less willing to invest it because they will get a lower rate of return.

Following a similar line of argument, Thomas Garrett, an economist at the Federal Reserve Bank of St. Louis, wrote in 2010: "Income inequality should not be vilified."[1]

Welch, Epstein, and Garrett are of course right that *some* degree of income inequality is necessary to reward effort and skill. Capitalism depends on it. But something close to the dystopia they envision where effort and skill don't matter already exists for those toiling in the economy's lower tiers. They should have a chat with their office receptionist. Or they could read *Nickel and Dimed*, or the 2010 book *Catching Out*, by Dick J. Reavis, a contributing editor at *Texas Monthly*, who went undercover as a day laborer. Waitresses, nonunion construction workers, dental assistants, call-center operators—people in these jobs are essentially replaceable, and usually have bosses who don't distinguish between individual initiative and insubordination. Even experience is of limited value, because it's often accompanied by diminishing physical vigor. A little further up the income scale, median income has declined during the past decade while productivity has increased. Where's the incentive for the middle class to perform a job well if there's no monetary reward for doing so? The only motivator is the fear of being fired. That's a pretty "deadening experience."

Welch said that he believed inequality was destructive only when "the low-wage citizenry views society as unfair, when it views effort as not worthwhile, when upward mobility is viewed as impossible or as so unlikely that its pursuit is not worthwhile." Colleen's comment "I don't want what they have" might at first appear to suggest that she views society as fair. But I omitted what she went on to say: "But what I would like is to be able to take a day off now and then . . . if I had to . . . and still be able to buy groceries the next day." Colleen may not begrudge the rich the material goods they've acquired through skill, effort, and sheer chance, but that doesn't mean she thinks her own labors secure her an adequate level of economic security. Clearly, they don't.

As for the prospect of upward mobility, we saw in chapter 2 that parental income is roughly as heritable as parental height. Climbing the ladder is not impossible, but neither is it as common as it was during the late nineteenth and early twentieth centuries, when Horatio Alger and James Truslow Adams formulated notions about American opportunity that persist today. In the national discussion about income inequality that grew out of the 2011 Occupy Wall Street protests, there were inklings that this message was starting to break through. It was even mentioned in the GOP presidential debates that the United States had become less upwardly mobile than Europe.[2] But when Welch gave his lecture, word of this development had not yet reached him. He claimed that "if there is a consensus" about intergenerational mobility in the United States, "it is that opportunities abound, much more than, say, three decades ago." Echoing this theme, Representative Paul Ryan (a Republican from Wisconsin) gave a speech in October 2011 that contrasted America's "ladder of opportunity" with a Europe in which "top heavy welfare states have replaced the traditional aristocracies, and masses of the long-term unemployed are locked into the new lower class." Welch and Ryan had it exactly backward. Opportunities in the United States are about the same as, or fewer than, they were prior to the Great Divergence, and they are definitely fewer than in most western European countries. Unlike America's industrial revolution, which increased both inequality and opportunity, the Great Divergence has increased only inequality.[3]

Welch judged the growing financial rewards accruing to those with higher levels of education a good thing insofar as they provided an incentive to go to college or graduate school. But for most of the twentieth century, smaller financial incentives attracted enough workers to meet the economy's growing demand for higher-skilled labor. That demand isn't being met today, as Harvard's Claudia Goldin and Lawrence Katz have shown, and as a consequence the rewards have gotten larger. Welch also said that both women and blacks made income gains during the Great Divergence (duly noted in chapter 3, though the gains by blacks were so tiny that it's more accurate to say they didn't lose ground). But that hardly constitutes evidence that the growth of income inequality unrelated to gender or race doesn't matter. Finally, Welch argued that the welfare state has made it too easy not to work at all. But since passage of the 1996 welfare-reform bill, the welfare state has made joblessness a good deal more difficult. Welfare assistance is now time-limited, and fewer than half as many people receive assistance. Since the 2007–9 recession, the most common criticism of Temporary Assistance for Needy

Families (the program that replaced Aid to Families with Dependent Children) has not been that TANF coddles the unemployed. Rather, it's been that TANF lacks the necessary flexibility to expand caseloads during periods of high unemployment.[4] And anyway, the group that's lost the most ground during the Great Divergence isn't the poor but the middle class, which is ineligible for welfare.

Income Doesn't Matter

In most contexts, libertarians have a very high regard for income. Tax it to even the slightest degree and they cry foul. If government assistance must be extended, they prefer a cash transaction to the provision of government services. The market is king, and what is the market if not a mighty river of cash?

Bring up the topic of growing income inequality, though, and you're likely to hear a different tune. Case in point: "Thinking Clearly About Economic Inequality," a 2009 Cato Institute paper by Will Wilkinson. Income isn't what matters, Wilkinson argued; consumption is, and "the weight of the evidence shows that the run-up in consumption inequality has been considerably less dramatic than the rise in income inequality." A similar theme was sounded in an October 2011 paper from the American Enterprise Institute by Bruce Meyer and James Sullivan, economists at the University of Chicago and the University of Notre Dame, respectively.[5] Wilkinson was honest enough to concede (as Meyer and Sullivan did not) that the available data on consumption were shakier than the available data on income. He might also have mentioned that consumption in excess of income usually means debt—as in, say, subprime mortgages. If the have-nots compensated for their lower incomes by putting themselves (and the country) in economically ruinous hock, clearly that wasn't sustainable. Indeed, if it weren't for a 2008 bank bailout that enraged Tea Party activists and Occupy Wall Street protesters alike, that year's debt-driven financial crisis could easily have caused a worldwide economic depression to rival that of the 1930s. Was it income inequality that drove the worldwide economy to the brink of ruin?

More than one economist believes that the Great Divergence played some role in the 2008 meltdown. David Moss of Harvard Business School produced an intriguing chart that shows bank failures tend to

Inequality and Debt

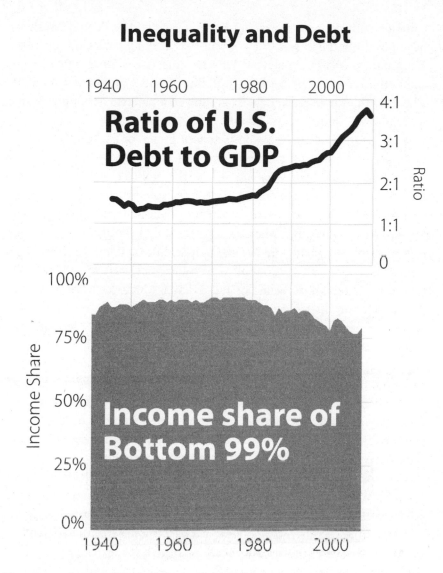

Top 1 percent income share includes capital gains. Sources: Based on Federal Reserve Board (flow of funds historical data); Bureau of Economic Analysis (GDP historical tables); and Alvaredo et al., "The World Top Incomes Database."

coincide with periods of growing income inequality. "I could hardly believe how tight the fit was," he told the *New York Times*. Princeton's Paul Krugman similarly considered whether the Great Divergence helped cause the recession by pushing middle-income Americans into debt.[6] The growth of household debt has followed a pattern strikingly similar to the growth in income inequality.

Raghuram G. Rajan, a business school professor at the University of Chicago, observed in his 2010 book *Fault Lines: How Hidden Fractures Still Threaten the World Economy* that at the end of the nineteenth century "small and medium-sized farmers perceived that they were falling behind." Their cause was taken up by the Populist Party, and credit was loosened as a result. But when crop prices fell in the 1920s, rural areas saw widespread, wholly predictable bank failures. Then, as now, Rajan wrote, "easy credit . . . proved an extremely costly way to redistribute." Christopher Brown, an economist at Arkansas State University, wrote a paper in 2004 affirming that "a surge in borrowing" sustained consumption otherwise dampened by inequality. Reducing inequality, he argued, would also reduce consumer debt. Westwood Capital's Daniel Alpert suggests that as his fellow capitalists financialize and edge away from the manufacture of tangible goods that once defined modern industrialism, they are replacing middle-class income with middle-class debt. Why pay the workingman and -woman when you can lend them the money instead—then make them pay it back with interest? The result, Alpert suggests, is a kind of "middle class serfdom."[7]

Perhaps I shouldn't go on so much about debt-fueled consumption, because Wilkinson ultimately argues that consumption isn't the point; what matters is utility *gained from* consumption. Joe and Sam, Wilkinson writes, both own refrigerators. Joe's is a $350 model from Ikea. Sam's is an $11,000 state-of-the-art Sub-Zero. Sam gets to consume a lot more than Joe, but whatever added utility he achieves is marginal; Joe's Ikea fridge "will keep your beer just as cold." But if getting rich is only a matter of spending more money on the same stuff you'd buy if you were poor, why bother to climb the greasy pole at all? Sam's Sub-Zero may be functionally no better than Joe's Ikea fridge, but for some reason Sam can't be persuaded to swap. Does he know something Wilkinson doesn't?

Wilkinson also places great emphasis on buying power. Food is cheaper than ever before. Since lower-income people spend their money disproportionately on food, declining food prices, Wilkinson argues, constitute a sort of raise. Never mind that Ehrenreich routinely found, in her travels among unskilled workers, people who skipped lunch to save money or brought an individual-size pack of junk food and called that lunch. Reavis reported that a day laborer's typical lunch budget was three dollars. That won't buy much. The problem isn't the cost of food alone but the cost of shelter, which has shot up so high that low-income families don't have much left over to spend on other essentials. As we saw in chapter 3, housing, health care, higher education, and automobiles are all more expensive, even factoring in inflation, than they used to be. The middle-class families that have lost the most ground in the Great Divergence can usually cover their food bills, but they struggle to pay for all these larger-ticket items.[8]

Declining food prices constitute a sort of raise for high-income people too. But Wilkinson writes that the affluent spent a smaller share of their budget on food and a much larger share on psychotherapy and yoga and cleaning services. And since services like these are unaffected by foreign competition or new efficiencies in manufacturing, Wilkinson suggests, providers can charge whatever they like. Tell that to Colleen! A couple of years ago I worked out with my cleaning lady what I would pay her. Here's how the negotiation went. I told her what I would pay her. She said, "OK." According to the Bureau of Labor Statistics, the median annual income for a housekeeper is $19,300, which is 14 percent lower than the poverty line for a family of four.

A more thoughtful version of the income-doesn't-matter argument surfaces in Mickey Kaus's *The End of Equality*. Kaus chides "Money Liberals" for trying to redistribute income when instead they might be working to diminish social inequality by creating or shoring up spheres in which rich and poor are treated the same. Everybody can picnic in the park. Everybody should be able to receive decent health care. Under a compulsory national service program, everybody would be required to perform some civilian or military duty.

As a theoretical proposition, Kaus's vision is appealing. Bill Gates will always have lots more money than I do, no matter how progressive the tax system becomes. But if he gets called to jury duty he has to show up, just like me. When his driver's license expires, he'll be just as likely to have to take a driving test. Why not expand this egalitarian zone to, say, education, by making public schools so good that Gates's grandchildren will be as likely to attend them as mine or yours?

But at a practical level, Kaus's exclusive reliance on social equality is simply inadequate. For one thing, the existing zones of social equality are pretty circumscribed. Neither Gates nor I spends a lot of time hanging around the Department of Motor Vehicles. Rebuilding or creating the more meaningful spheres—say, public education, or universal health care—won't occur overnight. Nurturing the social-equality sphere isn't likely to pay off for a very long time. Another problem is Kaus's belief that you can separate social equality from income equality. In theory, you can; in practice, you probably can't. Among industrialized nations, those that have achieved the greatest social equality are the same ones that have achieved the greatest income equality. France, for example, has a level of income inequality much lower than that of most other countries in the Organisation for Economic Co-operation and Development. Income inequality in France has actually been going *down*. (Most everywhere else in the industrialized world it's gone up, though nowhere to the degree it has in the United States.) France also enjoys what the World Health Organization calls the world's finest health-care system (by which the WHO means, in large part, the most egalitarian one; this is the famous survey from 2000 in which the United States ranks thirty-seventh).[9]

Do France's high marks on both social equality and income equality really strike you as a coincidence? As incomes become more unequal, the rich won't likely urge or even allow the government to create or expand public spheres where they must forswear special privileges and mingle with the proles. More likely, growing income inequality will make the rich want to create or expand private spheres that help maintain *separation* from the proles, with whom they will have less and less in common. The late Jonathan Rowe, a journalist and activist who wrote extensively about social equality, believed this was already happening during the aughts. In an essay titled "The Vanishing Commons" that appeared in *Inequality Matters*, a 2005 anthology, Rowe noted that Congress was busy extending copyright terms and patent monopolies and turning over public lands to mining and timber companies for below-market fees. "In an 'ownership' society especially," Rowe wrote (invoking President George W. Bush's privatization catchphrase), "we should think about what we own in common, not just what we keep apart." A more visible sign of the vanishing commons is the prevalence in the United States of gated communities. These are not a new phenomenon. (Tuxedo Park, New York, and Llewellyn Park in West Orange, New Jersey, both date to the nineteenth century.) But their construction accelerated rapidly starting in the mid-1980s, just a few years into the Great Divergence. The timing hardly seems coincidental. According to *Forbes*, between 2000 and 2003 fully 17 percent of all newly built houses costing $500,000 or more were located in gated communities. These developments are advertised as fostering a greater sense of community than can be found elsewhere; but such warm neighborliness, assuming it truly exists, is created through the conspicuous exclusion of others who dwell farther down the income scale.[10]

Inequality Doesn't Create Unhappiness

"Inequality is not what makes people unhappy," Arthur C. Brooks, president of the American Enterprise Institute, wrote in his 2010 book, *The Battle: How the Fight Between Free Enterprise and Big Government Will Shape America's Future*. Nor does material success make people happy. What drives entrepreneurs, he wrote, is the desire for *earned success* (italics his). "People who believe they have earned success—measured in whatever life currency they want—are happy," Brooks wrote. "They are much happier than people who don't believe they've earned their success." As for money, that's "just one *metric* of the value that a person is creating" (italics his).

Brooks marshaled very little evidence to support his happiness argument, and what evidence he did muster was less impressive than he thought. He made much of a 1996 survey that asked people how successful they felt, and how happy. Among the 45 percent who counted themselves "completely successful" or "very successful," 39 percent said they were very happy. Among the 55 percent who counted themselves at most "somewhat successful," only 20 percent said they were happy. Brooks claimed victory with the finding that successful people were more likely to be happy (or at least to say they were) than less-successful people, by nineteen percentage points. More striking, though, was that 61 percent of the successful people—a significant majority—did not say they were "very happy."

Let's grant Brooks his generalization that people who believe they deserve their success are likelier to be happy than people who believe they don't. It makes intuitive sense. But Brooks's claim that money is only a "metric" does not. Looking at the same survey data, the Berkeley sociologist Michael Hout found that from 1973 to 2000 the "happiness gap" between the affluent and the poor who counted themselves either "very happy" or "not too happy" ranged from twenty percentage points to twenty-seven. ("Money buys happiness after all," Hout quipped.) Among the poor, the percentage who felt "very happy" fell by nearly one third from 1973 to 1994, then crept up a couple of points during the tight labor market of the late 1990s. Hout also observed that overall happiness dropped a modest 5 percent from 1973 to 2000.[11]

In general, most surveys tend to find that happiness rises along with income until you escape poverty. After that, the correlation usually dissolves. Rising income inequality in the United States does not appear to have created a parallel trend of happiness inequality. But what if growing income inequality in a society makes *everyone* more unhappy, regardless of income? The poor might be unhappy because they're poor. The middle class might be unhappy because they're worried about *becoming* poor. And the affluent might be unhappy because they feel resented. Perhaps that's the meaning of Hout's 5 percent drop in overall happiness. A larger point is that one should take all such studies with a grain of salt, since happiness is a vague and subjective concept. How do I know whether to believe someone who describes himself as happy? It isn't even clear that the *person himself* will know the answer to this question. Moreover, one's happiness tends to vary. You can be happy today, ecstatic next week, and miserably depressed the week after that. You can feel lousy before a meal or a jog or a good talk with a friend or a session of torrid lovemaking and feel pretty terrific half an hour later. Sometimes all you need is an Advil. A lot would seem to ride on what particular moment the survey taker chooses to phone you.

Quality of Life Is Improving

This argument has been made by too many conservatives to count. An unemployed steelworker living in the twenty-first century, it is said, is better off than the royals and aristocrats of the nineteenth. Living conditions improve over time. J. P. Morgan never had access to sulfa drugs or iPhones or fresh vegetables in wintertime. And the gap between Morgan's quality of life and that of the typical American during his lifetime was in many important ways larger than the gap today between Bill Gates's quality of life and that of the typical American. In Morgan's day, as the George Mason economist Tyler Cowen puts it, "the average person had little formal education, worked six days a week or more, often at hard physical labor, never took vacations, and could not access most of the world's culture."

But people do not experience life as an interesting moment in the evolution of human living standards. They experience it in the present and weigh their own experience against that of the living. In a famous 1998 study by the economists Sara Solnick (then at the University of Miami, now at the University of Vermont) and David Hemenway of the Harvard School of Public Health, subjects were asked which they'd prefer: to earn $50,000 while knowing everyone else earned $25,000, or to earn $100,000 while knowing everyone else earned $200,000. Objectively speaking, $100,000 is twice as much as $50,000. Even so, 56 percent chose $50,000 if it meant that would put them on top rather than at the bottom. Anyone who's been the parent of more than one child will be utterly unsurprised by this finding. We are social creatures, and we establish our expectations in relation to one another.[12]

The Good Times Are Over

Cowen's 2011 book *The Great Stagnation* addresses the problem of stagnating middle-class wages, which played no small role in the Great Divergence. Cowen's diagnosis is that "we have been living off low-hanging fruit for at least three hundred years," and that now "that fruit is mostly gone." Financial gimmicks enrich the top and everyone else gets left out in the cold. The low-hanging fruit was free land (which became unavailable at the end of the nineteenth century); technological breakthroughs (Cowen thinks all the comparatively easy ones have been made); and "smart, uneducated kids" (most kids get high school educations today; most didn't at the turn of the twentieth century, as discussed in chapter 5). As with most grand theories about the future, it's impossible to say whether Cowen is right. But since today's skill threshold is no longer high school but college and graduate school, Cowen is almost certainly wrong on his last point. By twenty-first-century standards, American kids are as uneducated as ever. That leaves plenty of room for improvement, provided higher education can be made affordable.

It's the Productivity, Stupid

"Wealthy people are not wealthy because they have more money," wrote the St. Louis Fed's Garrett, in 2010. "It is because they have greater productivity. Different incomes reflect different productivity levels." But productivity has been rising in excess of median family income throughout the Great Divergence. During the aughts it rose especially steeply even as median household income declined. "Since 1978," Princeton's Alan Blinder wrote at the end of 2010, "productivity in the nonfarm business sector is up 86 percent, but real compensation per hour (which includes fringe benefits) is up just 37 percent. Does that seem fair?"[13] Of course it doesn't.

In the past, productivity increases meant prosperity for everyone. Now they mean prosperity only for the wealthy. In 2005 Ian Dew-Becker, an undergraduate at Northwestern (now an economics graduate student at Harvard), and Robert J. Gordon, an economist at Northwestern, calculated that between 1966 and 2001 only those occupying the top 10 percent in income distribution saw their incomes (excluding capital gains) grow at a rate that matched or exceeded the economy's increase in productivity.[14] That seems a dangerous situation. When ordinary people have nothing to gain from the fruits of their labors even in times of economic growth, the only motivation they have to perform their jobs well is fear of destitution. In earlier times such conditions bred radicalism. Today it seems to breed a corrosive resentment of the meritocratic elite, whose most visible and recognizable representatives inhabit the upper reaches of U.S. government, and especially the White House. That resentment probably explains the populist enthusiasm for antigovernment demagoguery that took hold during the Reagan era. ("Government is the problem," Reagan said in his 1981 inauguration speech.) With the rise of the Tea Party movement, antigovernment sentiment has intensified in recent years as the economy has struggled to recover from the 2008 financial crisis. (Even more recently, a counterweight has emerged in the

Occupy Wall Street movement. But the OWSers aren't particularly inclined to promote government as a positive good, even theoretically.)

Just *where* the benefit of these productivity increases went (besides the pockets of the top 10 percent) remains a bit of a mystery. It would be logical for health insurance premiums to have gobbled them up—certainly the rising cost of health insurance is taking an ever-larger bite out of everybody's paycheck. But the Blinder statistics quoted earlier *include* health-insurance benefits.[15]

My own preferred hypothesis is that stockholders appropriated what once belonged to middle-class wage earners. As a percentage of national income, corporate profits have (on an after-tax basis) mostly been rising since the early 1990s even as the nonwealthy's income share has dwindled, and in recent years corporate income share has reached historic levels. Is this merely coincidental? In July 2011 the *Washington Post* columnist Harold Meyerson argued that it was not. Meyerson is a political liberal strongly sympathetic to the labor movement, but his source was impeccably pro-capital: Michael Cembalest, chief investment officer at JP Morgan Chase. In a July 2011 newsletter for Morgan clients, Cembalest stated, "U.S. labor compensation is now at a 50-year low relative to both company sales and U.S. GDP." During the period from 2000 to 2007, Cembalest calculated, from the peak of one business cycle to the peak of the next, pretax profits for the Standard & Poor's 500 had increased by 1.3 percent. "Reductions in wages and benefits explain the majority of the net improvement," Cembalest wrote. That "majority" was more like 75 percent. "Profits are up," Meyerson translated, "because wages are down." In this context, of course, "wages" does not include compensation for those at the top of the income scale, who during the Great Divergence did not sacrifice any income to improve the bottom line.

But wait, you might ask: In the age of the 401(k) and mutual fund, isn't the workingman a stockholder too? Yes and no. About half of all households in America (and also about half of all households in the middle 20 percent of the income distribution) are in the stock market either directly through owning stocks or indirectly through mutual funds. But among the half of all Americans who are in the market, only about one third have stock holdings worth $7,000 or more. So stock ownership has been democratized only somewhat. Eighty-one percent of all stocks are owned by the top 10 percent; 69 percent by the top 5 percent; and 38 percent by the top 1 percent. To the extent that middle-income people possess any wealth at all, it tends to be in their houses. The collapse of housing prices in the mid-aughts was therefore particularly catastrophic for the already-pinched middle class.[16]

Inequality Isn't Increasing

This is the boldest line of attack, challenging a consensus about income trends in the United States that even most conservatives accept. Alan Reynolds, a senior fellow at Cato, made the case in a January 2007 paper. It was a technical argument hinging largely on a critique of the tax data used by Saez and Piketty in the groundbreaking paper we looked at in chapter 9. But as Gary Burtless of Brookings noted in a January 2007 reply, Social Security records "tell a simple and similar story" to Piketty and Saez's. A Congressional Budget Office analysis, Burtless wrote, addressed "almost all" of Reynolds's objections to Saez and Piketty's findings and confirmed "a sizable rise in both pre-tax and after-tax inequality." Reynolds's paper didn't deny notable increases in top incomes, but he argued that these were due to changes in tax law and/or to isolated and unusual financial events. This, Burtless answered, was akin to arguing that, "adjusting for the weather and the season, no homeowner in New Orleans ended up with a wet basement" after Hurricane Katrina.[17]

Inequality Is Increasing, but Let's Not Do Anything About It

This is the most honest conservative response to the Great Divergence. "Inequalities of condition are a fact of life," the *Weekly Standard*'s Matthew Continetti wrote in November 2011. "Some people will always be poorer than others. So too, human altruism will always seek to alleviate the suffering of the destitute. There is a place for reasonable and prudent actions to improve well-being. But that does not mean the entire structure of our polity should be designed to achieve an egalitarian ideal."

Well, no, not the *entire* structure. And no, the goal isn't to achieve a particular "ideal," egalitarian or otherwise. It is merely to reverse the trend, as occurred in the United States during the Great Compression. In the next and final chapter, let's consider how that might be achieved.

11

What to Do

HOW CAN WE REDUCE—NOT *ELIMINATE*, but reduce—income inequality in America? The answer isn't simple, because this is a problem with multiple causes that was three decades in the making. One thing we clearly can't do is set back the clock. The circumstances that created the Great Compression were particular to the times and rooted in the severe twin hardships of the Great Depression and World War II. No sane person would wish to generate comparable starting points today. But there are steps we can take to begin to reverse the Great Divergence. Some might be politically salable today. Most I introduce with few illusions that they can be enacted anytime soon. But they need to enter the political conversation.

Soak the Rich

In chapter 7 we saw that tax cuts didn't create the Great Divergence, because changes in the distribution of *pre*tax income were much larger than changes in the distribution of *post*tax income. Nonetheless, the federal tax system's ability to mitigate income inequality has diminished. In 1979 the combined effect of federal taxes and federal benefits was to reduce income inequality (as measured by the Gini index) by 23 percent. By 2007, it reduced income inequality by 17 percent.[1] A more progressive tax system would increase the government's impact on income distribution, which was (and remains) substantial.

It would also spread the burden of funding government more fairly. Today top income tax rates are at historic lows; since Ronald Reagan was elected president in 1980 they've been lower than at any time since 1931, when Herbert Hoover was president. President Obama has proposed raising, for families whose annual income exceeds $250,000, the top rate from 35 to 39.6 percent. That's where it stood during the economic boom of the 1990s. Families that earn $250,000 or more a year are richer than 97.4 percent of all Americans, and they can afford to see the top marginal tax rate increase by 4.6 percentage points. Obama's proposal is a good start.

After raising the marginal rate on incomes above $250,000, we should add some new, higher brackets. The financier Warren Buffett was ranked by *Forbes* the second-richest American in 2011, with an estimated net worth of $39 billion. In a much-discussed *New York Times* op-ed, Buffett noted that his combined bill that year for income and payroll tax came to a mere 17.4 percent of his income, a lower rate than that paid by any of the other twenty people who worked in his Berkshire Hathaway office. Buffett proposed creating brackets for incomes exceeding $1 million and $10 million, including dividends and capital gains. The Tax Policy Center, a nonpartisan nonprofit, estimated that raising the top marginal rate to 50 percent on all income over $1 million, including dividends and capital gains, would alone raise about $759 billion over the next decade. That's assuming a baseline in which the Bush tax cuts were extended indefinitely. Current law calls for the Bush tax cuts to expire at all income levels—not just for families earning more than $250,000—at the end of 2012, though it's doubtful Congress will let it happen. But if the Bush cuts did expire, the savings from raising the top rate to 50 percent on all income over $1 million, including dividends and capital gains, would be smaller—more like $296 billion over the next decade. Whatever the savings, they would probably be used to lower the budget deficit, which as of November 2011 was projected by the Congressional Budget Office to total $1.3 trillion for that year.[2] Reducing the budget deficit won't reduce income inequality, but it needs to be done, and if deficit reduction is achieved too much through budget cuts, it will likely *increase* income inequality by cutting government programs that aid the poor and middle class, such as food stamps or unemployment benefits. Better to raise the money as much as possible from those best able to pay.

I would add to Buffett's proposal that we should consider adding a *third* tax bracket for annual incomes exceeding $20 million. Buffett didn't specify what the marginal rates for his two new brackets should be, but my preferred three rates would rise gradually to 70 percent, which was the top rate during the 1960s and 1970s. The precise thresholds are less important than establishing the principle that if top income shares are going to rise faster than in the past, income tax rates need to rise faster, too. Like Buffett, I'm assuming that capital gains should be taxed at the same rate as regular income (as they were under President Ronald Reagan). S-Corporations, a common tax dodge for the self-employed, should be curtailed, and many of the various other shelter schemes and deductions and tax credits that currently pollute the tax system should be phased out, including (once the housing market stabilizes) the mortgage interest deduction.

Something else that ought to be eliminated is the payroll tax that funds Social Security and Medicare. Also known as the FICA tax (for Federal Insurance Contributions Act), the payroll tax is stubbornly regressive in two ways. It is imposed, regardless of income level, on the first dollar of earnings at the same rate for everyone (currently 7.65 percent each from employers and employees; 15.3 percent for the self-employed). And the largest portion of the tax, which pays for Social Security, is not imposed on any earnings above a certain level ($110,100 in 2012). Most Americans pay more for their FICA tax than they do for their income tax. Bill Drayton, chairman of Ashoka, a "social entrepreneurship" nonprofit, has proposed eliminating payroll taxes and replacing them with a Value Added Tax, a carbon tax, and a variety of other taxes. The idea, as the journalist Hendrik Hertzberg explained in a 2009 *New Yorker* commentary, is to tax "things that, unlike jobs, we want less rather than more of—things like pollution, carbon emissions, oil imports, inefficient use of energy and natural resources, and excessive consumption." Some of the new taxes would be regressive, but so long as they weren't capped at a certain income level they wouldn't be as regressive as the current payroll tax. And some (for instance, the Value-Added Tax) could be designed to eliminate or minimize any impact on lower-income people.[3]

Fatten Government Payrolls

Washington's bloated federal bureaucracy is a favorite punching bag for political candidates. The republican presidential contender Michele Bachmann said during the early skirmishes of the 2012 campaign that her onetime job as a lawyer for the Internal Revenue Service opened her eyes to the government's "huge bureaucracy," and not long after that, her GOP rival Mitt Romney said, "Federal employees, we've got too many of them." But in 2010 there were fewer federal employees (4.4 million) than there were in 1962 (5.4 million), even though the U.S. government was serving a population that was nearly 70 percent larger. (The civilian portion got slightly bigger, and the military portion got substantially smaller.)[4] There's no obvious reason to think that the permanent civilian and military workforces are short-staffed. But neither, given the historical trend, is there any rational argument against enlarging the federal payroll to make room for a jobs program that would provide time-limited work for middle- and lower-income people struggling to find employment. This program would be especially helpful during recessions, but given routine job dislocations even in flush times, it would also be helpful during economic expansions. (Ehrenreich did the reporting for *Nickel and Dimed*, it's worth remembering, during the tech boom.)

The New Deal's Works Progress Administration (later called the Work Projects Administration) is an obvious model. During the Great Depression it built roads and bridges, provided social services, and even made some lasting contributions to the arts. (Today the urgent public-works need isn't the creation of new roads and bridges but the repair of existing infrastructure.) Over the course of its seven-year life the WPA created 3 million jobs per year at a cost of $10.7 billion, or the equivalent of $171 billion today. Its forerunner, the Civil Works Administration, created in 1933 while U.S. unemployment was roughly 25 percent, had an even more impressive record. It lasted only four months but managed to create 4 million jobs at a cost of less than $1 billion (about $17 billion today).[5] By comparison, the upper estimate on the number of jobs created by President Barack Obama's 2009 stimulus bill as of July 2011 was 3.6 million at a cost of $221 billion in contracts, grants, and loans.[6] The stimulus passed money through the states to the private sector. Putting workers directly onto the federal payroll would be much more cost-effective.

Import More Skilled Labor

Alan Greenspan, the conservative former Federal Reserve chairman, and Dean Baker, codirector of the liberal Center for Economic and Pol-

icy Research, seldom agree about anything. But they have both proposed reducing income inequality in the United States by removing
immigration barriers for people in highly skilled professions. In his
2007 book, *The Age of Turbulence*, Greenspan proposed that we "allow
open migration of skilled workers." The United States, Greenspan complained, has created "a privileged, native-born elite of skilled workers
whose incomes are being supported at noncompetitively high levels by
immigration quotas." Eliminating these "would, at the stroke of a pen,
reduce much income inequality." Similarly, Baker argued in a 2008
speech that it is hypocritical for the U.S. government to maintain trade
barriers for professional services while it energetically seeks to remove
them for less-skilled workers. If we were consistent in our support for
free trade, Baker said,

> our trade negotiators would sit down with hospitals, law firms, uni-
> versities, and other employers of highly paid professionals and deter-
> mine the obstacles that prevent them from hiring large numbers of
> professionals from the developing world. At the top of this list would
> be immigration restrictions that sharply limit the quantity of highly
> paid professionals who can enter the country and that also require
> that foreign professionals be paid comparable wages to U.S. profes-
> sionals. If Wal-Mart can pay less than the domestic price for Chinese
> made shoes and toys, thereby depressing the wages of manufacturing
> workers in the United States, then hospitals and universities should be
> able to do the same in hiring physicians and professors.

If a foreigner in a highly skilled profession wants to work in the
United States, he typically has to get his prospective employer to apply for
an H-1B guest-worker visa on his behalf. The employer must persuade
the U.S. labor department that the highly skilled worker demonstrates
"distinguished merit and ability" that cannot be found within U.S. borders.[7] The employer must also agree to pay the prevailing wage or the
same wage the employer would pay a nonimmigrant worker, whichever
is higher. And if the employer mistimes the application, the worker
won't get the visa because there's an annual ceiling of eighty-six thousand (of which twenty thousand are reserved for holders of advanced degrees from American universities). If all those hurdles are cleared, the
worker may stay for up to six years. If he hasn't secured more permanent

status after six years, he must leave the United States. As noted in chapter 6, there are similar legal and professional barriers to the offshoring of highly skilled work such as radiology. The effect of these, Baker noted, is virtually identical to that of the immigration barriers. To the extent we reduce or eliminate this protectionism for the haute bourgeoisie, we can reduce the college wage premium and the grad-school wage premium.

Universalize Preschool

The early twentieth century gave us the high school movement, which greatly expanded the number of government-funded high schools and eventually made at least some high school education universal. Starting in the 1970s, however, the high school graduation rate dipped and then leveled off at about 75 percent. As noted in chapter 5, the U.S. high school graduation rate now trails graduation rates for Germany, Greece, the United Kingdom, Ireland, and Italy. Raising that rate will require improving the quality of public education in the United States. State and federal governments have been struggling to do that at least as far back as 1983, when a national commission report memorably stated, "If an unfriendly foreign power had attempted to impose on America the mediocre educational performance that exists today, we might well have viewed it as an act of war." I have nothing to add to the standard reform agenda—stiffen academic standards, make it easier to dismiss incompetent teachers, increase consideration of individual merit in setting teacher salaries—except to note that the reform movement's unquestioning embrace of charter schools and its relentless demonization of teachers' unions suggest, as the education writer and practicing teacher Sara Mosle noted in 2011, "that the insurgents are in danger of becoming the very thing they once (rightly) rose up against: subject to groupthink, reluctant to hear opposing views or to work with anyone perceived to be on the other side."

A more promising approach might be to do for preschool education in the early twenty-first century what was done for high school education in the early twentieth. As it happens, there is an international movement under way to universalize prekindergarten schooling—in France they've been doing it for centuries. Candidate Barack Obama came out in favor of expanding early education during the 2008 presidential campaign, and the 2009 economic stimulus bill included some funding for preschool education. Currently forty states provide funding to expand preschool education, though most limit enrollment to low-income families. Nationally, 27 percent of all four-year-olds are enrolled in pre-K programs. That's roughly equivalent to the number of four-teen- to seventeen-year-olds that were enrolled in high school during the late teens of the previous century. This might be the pool of "smart, uneducated kids" that Tyler Cowen is looking for—"low-hanging fruit" from whom we can derive future productivity gains merely by putting them in school. Research on early education suggests the benefits could be considerable. A 2011 study by the Harvard economist Raj Chetty and five others (including Berkeley's Emmanuel Saez) found that a one-percentile increase in scores on tests administered to Tennessee kinder-garteners at the end of the school year was associated with a $94 increase in annual wages at age twenty-seven—and that's *after* the numbers were adjusted to take into account variations in family background. When family background wasn't taken into consideration, the increase at age twenty-seven was $132. The trick, obviously, would be to raise scores by a lot more than a microscopic one-percentile rank. It's hard to imagine a more dramatic illustration of how early schooling can affect income distribution.[8]

Let's now consider what awaits students at the opposite end of the K–12 gantlet.

Impose Price Controls on Colleges and Universities

Price controls are a clumsy policy instrument with a checkered history. But when the price of a vitally important commodity breaks loose of fa-miliar market variables the government may have no alternatives. This happened with oil in 1973, and the government's attempts to control oil prices over the next eight years failed.[9] It is happening with health-care costs, and the government has begun taking a few baby steps toward limiting hospital and doctor fees. It is also happening with college tu-ition. Between 1981 and 2006 average tuition and fees at public and private universities, *even factoring in inflation*, more than doubled. This almost certainly helps explain why the U.S. college-completion rate for twenty-five- to thirty-four-year-olds has failed to keep up with other leading industrialized nations, among whom the United States now ranks twelfth.[10] Students enter college because they know it's the ticket to a decent income, but they often lack the financial resources to stay four years. American colleges are starting to price themselves out of the market for middle- and low-income families.

As we have seen, the long-term financial benefit of going to college and graduate school is so great that any family that can conceivably afford to pay for college will do so, no matter what the financial sacrifice and/or loan burden. There are enough such families that colleges and universities (at least in the aggregate) are experiencing no serious market pressure to control the rising price of tuition. If they did, costs wouldn't continue to rise as fast as they do. It therefore falls to the government to find creative ways to impose the downward price pressure that buyers have been unable to provide. I don't pretend to know the best way to do this, and there are more ways than I can count to do it badly. But the federal government has plenty of levers, including student loans and research grants. It needs to explore how best to use them, or threaten to use them, to force colleges to adopt long-overdue austerity measures. Otherwise the nation's pool of educated workers will remain sufficiently small in relation to demand for their skills that inequality between educated and uneducated workers will persist at an unacceptably high level.

Reregulate Wall Street

The 2008 financial crisis and bank bailout revealed one important reason that investment bankers were getting so rich: Wall Street consolidation had left the country with enormous banks that could not, for the most part, be permitted to fail. The financial world was reaping the benefit of high-risk, largely unregulated trading while offloading its losses onto the government. The 2010 Dodd-Frank financial reform bill was an important first step toward placing some limits on banks' and other corporations' most reckless (and therefore most remunerative) behavior. It imposed new capital requirements to limit bank leveraging; gave corporate shareholders the chance to approve or disapprove (in a nonbinding vote) executive compensation; removed from existing regulations explicit reliance on the major rating agencies, which had become co-opted by the

banks, as arbiters of financial soundness; restricted banks' proprietary
trading; required hedge funds, which previously operated free of government supervision, to register with the Securities and Exchange Commission; lowered the interchange fees that banks charged retailers whenever
purchases were made with debit cards; and created the Consumer Financial Protection Bureau, a new agency charged with preventing banks
from deceiving customers by imposing hidden fees and the like.

As I write, the finance industry is working furiously to persuade the
courts, the regulatory agencies, and Congress either to overturn these
new rules or to blunt their impact. Many Republican politicians are
pushing to repeal the law altogether. If the lobbyists and their proxies in
Congress and on the campaign trail succeed, households with incomes
in the top 0.1 percent will continue to increase their share of national
income even as the bankers hurtle themselves toward an inevitable next
cycle of crisis and bailout. If the lobbyists and their Republican supporters fail, the top 0.1 percent may increase its income share anyway—but
a first step will have been taken, allowing further steps to be taken in
the future that might make some difference. That's precisely why Wall
Street is fighting so feverishly the imposition of Dodd-Frank's (relatively
mild) restrictions.

The matter of proprietary trading, which is nominally banned
under Dodd-Frank (but in fact will continue in certain forms), is itself
an inequality issue, the University of Chicago's Raghuram G. Rajan
pointed out in his 2010 book *Fault Lines*. The inequality here concerns
information. "Banks that are involved in many businesses obtain an
enormous amount of private information from them," Rajan wrote.
"This information should be used to help clients, not to trade against
them." In theory, banking firewalls prevent traders from becoming
privy to information available to bankers; in practice traders have access to it. Rajan conceded that some activities that might be defined as
proprietary trading will remain necessary—for instance, to manage
risk. But "an initial crude limit," he wrote, could be "refined over time
with experience." The perfect is the enemy of the good, and the good
can be improved in the long term.

The next step in banking reform ought to be more radical. The too-big-
to-fail banks must be broken up. This is yet another left-wing-sounding
idea that has been promoted (though more tentatively) by former Fed
chairman Alan Greenspan. "If they're too big to fail, they're too big,"

Greenspan said in a 2009 speech. "In 1911, we broke up Standard Oil. So what happened? The individual parts became more valuable than the whole. Maybe that's what we need."[11] If the too-big-to-fail banks are allowed to remain as large as they are now, they will continue to pose what bankers call a "moral hazard," a market distortion in which decisions are made with no consideration of risk because the decision-makers themselves are protected from any possible downside. "Despite the widespread assumption in both New York and Washington that big banks provide societal benefits," Simon Johnson and James Kwak wrote in 13 Bankers, "there is no proof that these benefits exist and no quantification of their size—certainly no quantification sufficient to show that they outweigh the very obvious costs of having banks that are too big to fail." Breaking up the big banks ought to reduce compensation levels by introducing greater competition in the banking sector. That wouldn't be the purpose—the purpose would be to prevent catastrophic banking failures that require government bailouts—but it would be a beneficial side effect.

Elect Democratic Presidents

This sounds glibly partisan, but as I noted in chapter 7, the Vanderbilt political scientist Larry Bartels has pretty convincingly demonstrated that for the bottom 95 percent of the income distribution, Democratic administrations have since 1948 presided over income gains that diminish as you move *up* the income scale, while Republican administrations have presided over income gains that diminish as you move *down* the income scale. The hoary cliché that Republicans are the party of the rich and Democrats the party of the working class and the poor is thereby quantified and proven true. If you really want to see the Great Divergence reversed, don't vote Republican.

An important caveat. Electing Democratic presidents will help reverse the inequality that exists within the bottom 95 percent of the income distribution, but it has yet to be demonstrated that it will help reverse the inequality that exists between the top 5 percent and everybody else. The "upper-tail" inequality trend, Bartels found, was more or less unaffected by whether a Democrat or a Republican inhabited the White House.

Revive the Labor Movement

It has become fashionable, even among many liberals, to believe that unions have no place in the twenty-first-century economy. It's certainly true that private-sector unionism is in severe decline and that public-sector unionism, which fared much better during the Great Divergence, has lately come under attack in Wisconsin and elsewhere. But there's no possibility that people who lack economic clout as individuals will ever be able to count on their bosses' altruism (or even enlightened self-interest) to provide a decent wage. The age of corporate paternalism is long gone, and it would never have come into being without the existence or threat of strong unions. Businesses treat their least powerful employees as poorly as they can get away with, end of story. Blue-collar workers weren't given pensions, previously offered only in executive suites, because the nation's industrialists suffered a pang of conscience. They got them because Walter Reuther and other union leaders pushed management hard when negotiating labor contracts, with the very real threat of strikes always lurking in the background. Moreover, large forward strides toward social justice—the civil rights movement of the 1960s, the health-care reform bill in 2010—rely on support from unions because they are the only permanent institutions wielding any political power at all that are consistently dedicated to helping ordinary people.

The difficult challenge is figuring out how to nurse unions back to health. For answers I sought out Andy Stern, president from 1996 to 2010 of the Service Employees International Union, the most successful large-scale private-sector union of recent years. Much of what he said was discouraging.[12] "What we learned is you actually can grow," he told me, "but the amount of input to get an output is so uneconomical. It probably costs us, in the nonpublic sector . . . $2,000 to $3,000 a member to organize. Sometimes as high as $5,000 a member. So we had to redistribute half of the resources of the international union, 20 percent of the resources of the local unions, to grow. And the only reason the model worked was because we brought in a lot of these child-care, home-care, sort of quasi-private-sector workers, publicly funded but privately employed workers, in *huge* numbers—like seventy-four thousand in Los Angeles . . . They were on the cheap side." One logical solution would be for the labor movement to solicit outside funds. But that's largely prohibited by law (principally the 1959 Landrum-Griffin Act).

"The only way unions can get paid is by winning collective-bargaining agreements," Stern explained. Globalization is another factor that has made union leaders' jobs more difficult. "It's really hard," he said, "to create artificially high wages in tradable goods as opposed to nontradable goods." A janitor doesn't compete with offshore workers. An auto worker does.

Repealing Taft-Hartley, the 1947 law that imposed severe restrictions on labor's ability to organize, is a necessary step. As we saw in chapter 8, Taft-Hartley played a major role in labor's gradual postwar decline. But even before Republicans regained the House of Representatives in the 2010 election, labor unions were unable to persuade Congress to repeal just one part of Taft-Hartley by restoring "card check," an informal method of union certification wherein union organizers quietly collect authorization cards from employees as an alternative to secret-ballot elections (which are easily manipulated by management). "The Democrats wouldn't support it," Stern explained. "In the end, many of the Democrats don't believe in unions. It's not their funding base. In terms of their hard-dollar contributions, particularly for senators, they all come from a class of people who are not particularly pro-union. And there's always this sense that we'll always be there, and we'll never go away, even though we're sort of fading away in front of their eyes."

An alternative political path recommended in 2001 by Richard Kahlenberg, a senior fellow at the Century Foundation, is to extend civil rights protection to the right to organize. "Defining labor organizing as a civil right," Kahlenberg wrote, "breaks the deadlock by taking the focus off 'unions,' which some Americans disfavor, and putting it onto the egregious behavior of employers who fire people for reasons having nothing to do with job performance." It's an ingenious tactic in an age when liberalism has become less interested in economic justice than in identity politics. Union members and aspiring union members could be redefined as a sort of oppressed ethnic group.

Stern thinks it might be possible for labor to adopt a more collaborative approach with management through works councils and employee stock ownership plans that operate very much in the Walter Reuther spirit. As things stand now, unions prefer a more adversarial relationship with management. Employee ownership is viewed with particular suspicion because it has often taken the form of "lemon socialism"—the sharing of an unprofitable venture before it lands in bankruptcy court (for example, at the Tribune Company, which owns the *Chicago Tribune* and the *Los Angeles Times*). But Stern noted that there are some profitable employee stock ownership plans, among them the Publix supermarket chain, one of the ten largest-volume supermarket chains in the country.

Wage levels, Stern told me, should be negotiated industry-wide (as they were under the Treaty of Detroit), thereby removing wages from price competition. In exchange, Stern said, perhaps business and government could be persuaded to support easing existing restrictions on union organizing. The obvious difficulty here is that, as we saw in chapter 8, management had little inclination to let unions participate in non-labor decisions even back in the 1940s and 1950s, when unions were much more powerful. But Stern argued that heightened global competition of a sort undreamed of in the mid-twentieth century has increased pressure on government and business to work together as a team—as occurs in many countries that the United States competes with—and that labor is a logical member of that team. In his 2006 book, *A Country That Works: Getting America Back on Track*, Stern noted that the SEIU had some success working with nursing home owners in California to create statewide labor and patient-care standards, and that the union was beginning to try something similar with home health-care workers. Stern also thinks unions need to create alliances abroad and ultimately operate as global entities, much as multinational corporations do. "Imagine simultaneous protests on service contractors' global clients," Stern wrote, "or outsourcing strikes to countries where strikes are legal and will not provoke government retaliation." Workers of the world, unite!

IN HIS 1971 book *A Theory of Justice*, the Harvard philosopher John Rawls explains why equality of opportunity is not sufficient to create a just world. "Even if it works to perfection in eliminating the influence of social contingencies," Rawls writes, "it still permits the distribution of wealth and income to be determined by the natural distribution of abilities and talents." Well, that's as it should be, you might say. In a capitalist society it makes economic sense for incomes to reward the useful application of those abilities and talents. But only up to a point. Ability and talent, after all, in some ways resemble physical beauty—they are advantageous attributes that you are born with, or not born with, to one degree or another. They "are decided by the outcome of the natural lot-tery," Rawls points out, "and this outcome is arbitrary from a moral perspective." Even if you're born with ability and talent, it's far from guaranteed that you'll capitalize on them. "The extent to which natural capacities develop and reach fruition," Rawls writes, "is affected by all kinds of social conditions and class attitudes. Even the willingness to make an effort, to try, and so to be deserving in the ordinary sense is it-self dependent upon happy family and social circumstances." In Rawls's ideal society, perfect economic equality is the starting point. Any depar-ture from it has to justify itself: "All social primary goods—liberty and opportunity, income and wealth, and the bases of self-respect—are to be distributed equally," Rawls decrees, "unless an unequal distribution of any or all of these goods is to the advantage of the least favored."

Today it can feel as though we live in a society that's the precise op-posite of Rawls's ideal. The first principle isn't economic equality; it's economic inequality. Any effort to minimize income differences is held politically suspect, an intrusion on individual liberty. Whenever the government proposes any action that might redistribute income down-ward, it must demonstrate that the most economically favored will somehow benefit. If the favored few don't believe they'll benefit, they can usually persuade their allies in Congress to block it. Under Senate filibuster rules, all it takes is forty-one nays. To repeat the admirably candid words of the Procter & Gamble lobbyist (and sometime presiden-tial aide) Bryce Harlow, "When business really tries . . . it never loses a big battle in Washington."

But there's another strain in American politics, one that impressed the British essayist Henry Fairlie when he first arrived in the United States. It's the America in which a small child is as likely as a powerful president to address a complete stranger with an informal "Hi." Ameri-cans believe fervently in the value of social equality, and social equality is at risk when incomes become too dramatically unequal. It's the America that believes hard work should be rewarded, because if it isn't workers will have no reason to give their best. And it's an America that believes in equal opportunity for all to an extent that America has lately been unable to fulfill. There is even an America that recoils, on principle, from vast disparities in income. In years past, it was common to hear Americans describe with sharp disapproval societies starkly divided into the privileged and the destitute. They were oligarchies, or banana

republics. Even if their leaders were democratically elected, these countries didn't seem very democratic. Is it my imagination, or do we hear
less criticism of such societies today in the United States? Might it be
harder for Americans, as gated communities spread across the land
while middle-class enclaves disappear, to sustain in such discussions
the necessary sense of moral superiority?

   That income inequality weighs heavily on the noneconomic life of a
nation is the thesis of the 2009 book *The Spirit Level* by Richard Wilkinson and Kate Pickett, two medical researchers based in Yorkshire, England. The book has been criticized for overreaching. Wilkinson and
Pickett relate income inequality trends not only to mental and physical
health, violence, and teenage pregnancy, but also to global warming. But
their larger point—that income inequality is bad not only for people on
the losing end but also for society at large—is indisputable. "Modern societies," they write,

> will depend increasingly on being creative, adaptable, inventive, well-
> informed and flexible communities, able to respond generously to
> each other and to needs wherever they arise. Those are characteristics
> not of societies in hock to the rich, in which people are driven by sta-
> tus insecurities, but of populations used to working together and re-
> specting each other as equals.

Heightened partisanship in Washington and declining trust in government have many causes (and the latter predates the Great Divergence).
But surely growing income inequality makes it especially difficult to
maintain any spirit of *e pluribus unum*. In his 2008 book, *The Big Sort*,
Bill Bishop chronicles a geographic shift that has occurred during the
past three decades—one in which communities are increasingly segre-
gated not only by race but by politics, culture, and income. Your likelihood of even *seeing*, much less exchanging views with, anyone who
doesn't share your precise demographic identity is becoming more and
more remote. Party allegiance tracks income level more closely than in
earlier eras, according to a 2003 paper by Nolan McCarty, Keith Poole,
and Howard Rosenthal, political scientists at Princeton, the University of
Houston, and Princeton, respectively. "While American politics is certainly far from purely class-based," they write, "the divergence in party
identifications and voting between high and low income individuals has

been striking." Income inequality played a much smaller role in creating this divergence, they found, than the South's political realignment.
But income inequality can't help but reinforce class-based partisan
divisions.[13]

Meanwhile, cable TV and the Internet make it easier than ever before
to subsist on a diet of opinions and cultural reference points that con-
firm rather than challenge your worldview. Republicans and Democrats
compete to show which party more fervently opposes the elite, with
each side battling to define what "elite" means. To Republicans, the enemy is a cultural elite; to Democrats, it's the economic elite. In a less
income-divergent society, elites would still be resented. But I doubt that
opposing them would be an organizing principle of politics to the same
extent that it is today. The level of vituperation in mainstream political
discourse is frightening. Perhaps the rhetoric was more divisive in the
late 1960s and early 1970s, and if you listen to the tapes that President
Richard Nixon secretly recorded in the Oval Office you can observe that
some of the ugliest sentiments were uttered within the confines of the
White House itself. But they were uttered *in private*. In public, our politicians struggled to maintain civil discourse, and to a remarkable degree
they succeeded. Bishop found that political bipartisanship reached its
pinnacle around 1975. That was the year the Weather Underground
bombed the State Department. Nothing remotely so frightening is happening in the United States today, but you wouldn't know it from the
invective publicly spouted by Fox News commentators and some of their
Republican allies in Congress. America was an angrier place during the
1960s and 1970s, but it's a meaner place today. I think that meanness is
fueled by resentments whose origins lie in the Great Divergence.

There are some who maintain that you can't complain about income
inequality unless you're willing to state precisely what the proper distribution of income ought to be. The former U.S. treasury secretary Nicholas
Brady, after I phoned him to ask for an interview for this book, com-
manded with some indignation that I do just that.[14] I couldn't answer
him. I doubt Rawls, now deceased, could answer Brady either—not in any
nontheoretical way. And historically, much mischief has been accomplished by answering this question with any precision. But asking what
the ideal distribution in America would be is a distraction from the real
question, which is how we can align it a bit more successfully with our

democratic ideals. You'd have to be blind not to see that we are headed in the wrong direction, and we've been heading that way for too long.

We can do better. We have done better before, and other leading industrialized democracies are doing better now. Let's get started while the vast disparities in how people live and what they have still have the power to offend our sense of fair play. The worst thing we could do to the Great Divergence is get used to it.

Acknowledgments

This book began as a series of articles for *Slate* under the editorial guidance of David Plotz, Michael Newman, Rachael Larimore, and Julia Turner. Their efforts greatly improved the magazine pieces, and consequently this book. Thanks also to my two previous editors during thirteen years at *Slate*, Jacob Weisberg and especially Michael Kinsley, whose professional guidance and warm friendship I've treasured throughout my adult life. At my new home, the *New Republic*, Richard Just, Leon Wieseltier, Larry Grafstein, Rachel Morris, Chloe Schama, Cameron Abadi, Isaac Chotiner, Franklin Foer, John Judis, Jon Cohn, Walter Shapiro, Noam Scheiber, and Alec MacGillis offered various kinds of encouragement and support. Thanks also to Marty Peretz, who initiated my first tour at the *New Republic* thirty-two years ago; Roger Rosenblatt, who as my college writing teacher helped guide me there; and Charlie Peters, lifelong mentor, guru, cheerleader, and friend.

Gregg Easterbrook, James Fallows, Paul Glastris, Jacob Hacker, Mickey Kaus, and James Lardner all offered valuable opinions at the start about which topics might warrant exploration. Barbara Ehrenreich lent me a tall stack of books to read and peppered me with helpful advice along the way.

The day the first installment ran in *Slate* my friend Tom Ricks e-mailed me, "There is a book in this, I think." Tom shared this opinion with his agent, Scott Moyers of the Wylie Agency, who became my agent and guided me skillfully through the New York publishing labyrinth. When Scott decided he'd rather be publisher of Penguin Press than remain an agent, he handed me off to Andrew Wylie, with whom I already had a happy working relationship through the publication of two posthumous anthologies of writings by his client and my late wife, Marjorie Williams. As my agent, Andrew handled matters related to the book's completion with his usual aplomb.

At Bloomsbury, I benefited from the sure editorial hand of Peter Ginna, an old friend and new taskmaster. Peter spotted conceptual wrinkles, pushed me gently but firmly to make many necessary additions, and in general kept my eye on the ball. Victoria Haire copyedited the manuscript with exquisite care. Thanks also to Pete Beatty, Michelle Blankenship, Cristina Gilbert, George Gibson, Laura Keefe, Peter Miller, Mike O'Connor, Laura Phillips, Patti Ratchford, Evan Schnittman, and Ben Wiseman. Catherine Mulbrandon, whose color illustrations enlivened the dry statistics in the *Slate* series, managed a parallel feat for this book, this time with the added challenge of working in black and white. I don't know anyone better at translating complex economic data into pictures. If you've gotten this far in this book and haven't yet visited Mulbrandon's Web site (visualizingeconomics.com), a treat awaits you.

Two researchers did me the rare favor of caring as much about this project as I did. Nathan Pippenger, a gifted reporter-researcher at the *New Republic*, demonstrated characteristic intelligence and rigor in fact-checking the manuscript, on occasion startling me with an insight into the source material that had eluded me. Tanya Parlett, a graduate student in history, expertly mined the Willford I. King Papers (which reside in the special collections and university archives of the University of Oregon libraries in Eugene, Oregon), locating hard-to-find biographical details about an important American economist whom history had nearly forgotten. Bruce Tabb, special collections librarian for the University of Oregon libraries, provided various kinds of assistance.

Mark Feeney, whose formidable erudition and silken writing style are well known to readers of the *Boston Globe*, is also a generous friend. Mark volunteered to read through the entire manuscript, as he had for the two anthologies of Marjorie's writings. This therefore is the third time that my family has benefited from Mark's pitiless pencil. James Fallows, Tom Geoghegan, Claudia Goldin, Harry Holzer, Bethany McLean, Nell Minow, Charles Peters, and Peter Skerry all found time to critique individual chapters.

I am a journalist, not an economist, and I couldn't have produced this book without posing a lot of questions (in person, by phone, and by e-mail) to many of the scholars whose work is cited in this book. Thanks especially to David Autor, Marianne Bertrand, Ron Blackwell, Francine Blau, George Borjas, Gary Burtless, Larry Bartels, Joseph Ferrie, Richard Freeman, Claudia Goldin, Harry Holzer, Christopher Jencks, Lawrence Katz, Paul Krugman, Frank Levy, Emmanuel Saez, Isabel Sawhill, Jeffrey Williamson, and Scott Winship. Thanks also to the non-academics who talked to me about their own lives and work: Karen Akers, Maria Andrade, Jim Blentlinger, Chuck Gilligan, Larry Harlow, Yves-André Istel, George Koch, Joel Jankowsky, Nell Minow, and Andy Stern.

Others who in diverse ways helped support this project include Marilyn Adamo, John Alderman, Daniel Alpert, Jon Alter, Rose Marie Arce, David Atkins, Jesse Baker, Bill Barol, Jeffrey Birnbaum, Rosa Brooks, Bob Burke, Chris Caldwell, James Carville, Kevin Connelly, Reid Cramer, John Dickerson, Kevin Drum, Nina Easton, Tom Edsall, John Ehrenreich, Dan Engber, Patricia Foxen, Beth Frerking, Alan Gold, Bonnie Goldstein, Jim Grady, Don Graham, Jerome Groopman, Mark Hankin, Nathan Heller, Hendrik Hertzberg, Susan Hewitt, Ann Hulbert, Veronika Jiranova, Hilary Kantor, Elizabeth Kastor, Phil Keisling, Leslie Klein, Jim Ledbetter, Jon Leibowitz, Paul Leonard, Alexandra Lescaze, Susie Linfield, Dahlia Lithwick, Ruth Marcus, Melonyce McAfee, Susan Meiselas, Stephen Metcalf, Harold Meyerson, John Mintz, Morton Mintz, Marie Monrad, Rand Morrison, Sara Mosle, Sang Ngo, Joseph Nocera, Jocelyn Nubel, Simon Patterson, Steven Pearlstein, Beth Peters, Eric Redman, Mary Kay Ricks, the late Jonathan Rowe, Robin Rue, Will Saletan, Vivian Selbo, Jack Shafer, Steve Shere, Dana Stevens, Laura Stone, June Thomas, Jill Timmons, Kathleen Townsend, Katrina vanden Heuvel, David Von Drehle, David Weigel, Robert Weinstock, Barry Werth, Chris Wilson, Scott Winship, Dave Wood, Robert Wright, Rich Yeselson, and Emily Yoffe.

My teenage children, Will and Alice, are quite relieved to see this project reach completion. Many thanks for their forbearance when Dad became even more absentminded than usual, and for offering respite and companionship through Ping-Pong games and *Mad Men* viewings. Among the thousand reasons I will never stop missing their mother is the delight she would have taken in celebrating this, my first book. But I don't lack for a spirited cheering section. In addition to Will and Alice, they are: my parents Robert and Marian, to whom this book is dedicated; my brother, Peter; my sister, Patsy; my sisters-in-law Annie, Wistar,

Rosina, and Paula; my brothers-in-law Phil, Antonio, and Tom; my mother-in-law, Robin; my father-in-common-law, David; six wonderful nephews and nieces now beginning to start families of their own; and too many generous friends and colleagues to count. Their support sustained me through my labors, and their strong belief in the urgency of this topic were a constant source of inspiration.

Notes

Introduction

General Sources

Jenn Abelson, "Suds with Splash," *Boston Globe*, June 12, 2001, http://articles
.boston.com/2011-06-12/bostonworks/29650542_1_hispanic-population
-p-g-hispanic-consumers.

Ellen Byron, "As Middle Class Shrinks, P&G Aims High and Low," *Wall Street
Journal*, Sept. 12, 2001, http://online.wsj.com/article/SB10001424053111
90483610457655886194398924.html.

Sam Grobart, "Bells and Whistles Descend upon the Throne," *New York Times*,
Oct. 12, 2011.

Don Peck, *Pinched: How the Great Recession Has Narrowed Our Futures & What
We Can Do About It* (New York: Crown, 2011), 100.

"We Are the 99 Percent," Web testimonials, Oct. 13, 2011, accessed Oct. 14,
2011, at http://wearethe99percent.tumblr.com/page/2.

1. Alan Blinder, "The Level and Distribution of Economic Well-Being," Working Paper 488 (Cambridge, MA: National Bureau of Economic Research, 1980), 2. Hereafter the National Bureau of Economic Research will be referred to as NBER.

2. *Growing Unequal? Income Distribution and Poverty in OECD Countries* (Paris: Organisation for Economic Co-operation and Development, 2008), 27.

3. I would be remiss if I failed to note here the awkward debt that the science of income and wealth distribution owes to Italian fascism. Gini was president of Italy's Central Institute of Statistics under Benito Mussolini. Another pioneer in the field was the French-Italian Vilfredo Pareto (1848–1923), inventor of an alternative measure called the Pareto distribution.

Pareto was a dedicated Fascist who harbored truly repellant beliefs, but Gini appears to have been much less interested in politics than in statistics. Il Duce was an enthusiastic student of statistical science, presumably in the service of measuring whether the trains were in fact running on time (and other less praiseworthy efficiencies). The fascism connection is a ripe opportunity for right-wing demagogues to condemn all discussion of income distribution—one that, unaccountably, was never seized in the journalist Jonah Goldberg's 2007 tome, *Liberal Fascism: The Secret History of the American Left, from Mussolini to the Politics of Meaning*. But math is math, and Pareto's and, especially, Gini's statistical work have withstood the test of time.

4. The Gini coefficient is derived from the Lorenz curve, a graphic representation of income distribution named for an American economist named Max Otto Lorenz (1876–1959). The Lorenz curve plots cumulative percentage population share (x-axis) against cumulative percentage income share (y-axis). Perfect equality is when every population share matches every income share. This hypothetical distribution is represented by a straight line extending at a forty-five-degree angle. Actual real-world distribution, which is always unequal to some degree, is represented by a line that curves underneath the forty-five-degree line. Imagine the two lines as representing a bow that you would use to shoot an arrow (only forget the arrow and forget pulling the string, which must remain a straight line). The lower the real-world distribution dips—the more curved the bow is—the more unequal the distribution. The Gini coefficient is derived by calculating the area inside the bow and then dividing that by the sum of the area inside the bow plus the area below the bow.

5. *Growing Unequal?*, 25, 32, 51–52.

6. Facundo Alvaredo, Tony Atkinson, Thomas Piketty, and Emmanuel Saez, "The World Top Incomes Database," http://g-mond.parisschoolofeco nomics.eu/topincomes/. Hereafter referred to as WTID. All WTID data cited in this book include capital gains.

7. *Income, Poverty, and Health Insurance Coverage in the United States: 2010* (Washington: U.S. Census Bureau, 2011), 10, 14.

8. *Growing Unequal?*, 27, 51. Finland's very low Gini rating (0.27) ranks it the seventh most income-equal nation in the OECD, while New Zealand's very high Gini coefficient (0.34) ranks it a mere four places above the United States' dismal twenty-seventh out of thirty. Portugal's disturbingly high level of income inequality and high rate of increase in income inequality, which exceed those in the United States, appear to

result largely from the fact that nearly 78 percent of its households are headed by people who lack a high school degree. By European standards, that's an extraordinarily low high school graduation rate. But even in poorly educated Portugal, the top 1 percent's income share is just a little more than half what it is in the United States. To achieve American-style income inequality, you need lots of poor people, which Portugal has, and lots of rich people, which it lacks.

1: **Paradise Lost**

General Sources

Frederick Lewis Allen, *The Big Change: America Transforms Itself: 1900–1950* (New York: Transaction, reprint edition, 1993; originally published by Harper & Brothers, 1952).

Frederick Lewis Allen, *Only Yesterday: An Informal History of the 1920's* (New York: John Wiley & Sons, reprint edition, 1997; originally published by Harper & Row, 1931).

Walter E. Clark, "Everybody Is Getting Richer," *Survey* 35, no. 5 (Oct. 30, 1915), 116–17.

"Dr. Willford King Is Dead at 82; Economist, Ex-N.Y.U. Professor," *New York Times*, Oct. 19, 1962.

"Friend of the New Deal's Controlled Inflation," profile of Willford I. King, *Literary Digest*, Sept. 16, 1933, 21.

John Kenneth Galbraith, ed., *The Affluent Society & Other Writings, 1952–1967* (New York: Library of America, 2010).

C. L. Merwin Jr., "American Studies in the Distribution of Wealth and Income by Size," in *Studies in Income and Wealth*, vol. 3 (New York: National Bureau of Economic Research, 1939), 2–94.

Michael J. Thompson, *The Politics of Inequality: A Political History of the Idea of Economic Inequality in America* (New York: Columbia University Press, 2007).

Jeffrey G. Williamson, *Inequality, Poverty, and History* (Cambridge, MA: Basil Blackwell, 1991).

Jeffrey G. Williamson and Peter H. Lindert, *American Inequality: A Macroeconomic History* (New York: Academic Press, 1980).

Tom Wolfe, *The Bonfire of the Vanities* (New York: Farrar Straus, 1987).

1. Three years before Willford I. King's book appeared, Frank Hatch Streightoff, an instructor in economics at DePauw, published a book called *The Distribution of Incomes in the United States* (New York: Columbia University, 1912). But on page 155, Streightoff threw in the towel. "Knowledge of

the distribution of incomes is vital to sane legislative direction of progress," he wrote. "In a form definite enough for practical use, this knowledge does not exist. No time should be wasted in obtaining [it]." King's
groundbreaking role in the related area of national accounts—calculating
average earnings in various occupations and industries—is noted in the
memoirs of the Nobel Prize–winning economists Milton Friedman and
George Stigler.

2. Willford I. King, *The Wealth and Income of the People of the United States*
    (New York: Macmillan, 1915), 2, 232; and WTID. King was looking at the
    year 1910, whereas the WTID figure is from 1913, its earliest available
    data point (because its U.S. numbers derive from federal income-tax rec-
    ords). The point is that King made an estimate that proved remarkably
    accurate given the limited tools available.

3. WTID.

4. Willford I. King, "Desirable Additions to Statistical Data on Wealth and
    Income," *American Economic Review* 7, no. 1 (Mar. 1917), 157.

5. In fairness to Roosevelt and his predecessors, accumulated capital re-
    mained the only significant generator of sky-high incomes well into the
    twentieth century.

6. King, *Wealth and Income*, 217.

7. "Autobiographical Sketch," typescript dated Apr. 5, 1937, Willford I. King
    Papers, Coll. 089, Special Collections and University Archives, Univer-
    sity of Oregon Libraries, Eugene, Oregon.

8. King, *Wealth and Income*, 249, 251, 254, 255.

9. Another Wisconsin Progressive who figures in the story of income distri-
    bution was Max Otto Lorenz. Lorenz, who invented the Lorenz curve
    (from which the Gini coefficient, the most common measure of income
    inequality, is derived), received his Ph.D. in economics at the University
    of Wisconsin in 1906 and coauthored an economics textbook with Ely in
    1908. He worked for four years as Wisconsin's deputy commissioner of
    labor and industrial statistics before decamping in 1910 for Washington,
    D.C. After working briefly at the Census Bureau and the Bureau of Rail-
    way Economics, Lorenz settled in for thirty-eight years at the Interstate
    Commerce Commission.

10. King, *Wealth and Income*, 218.

11. Solomon Fabricant, "Toward a Firmer Basis of Economic Policy: The
     Founding of the National Bureau of Economic Research," (Cambridge, MA:
     NBER, 1984). Other significant institutions the Progressive movement be-
     queathed include Hull House, the *New Republic*, Consumers Union, the
     Federal Trade Commission, and the Food and Drug Administration.

12. Wesley C. Mitchell, Willford I. King, Frederick R. Macaulay, and Oswald W. Knauth, *Income in the United States: Its Amount and Distribution, 1909–1919*, vol. 1 (New York: NBER, 1921), 147; and Willford I. King ("assisted by Lillian Epstein"), *The National Income and Its Purchasing Power* (New York: NBER, 1930), 173, 178. The contemporary recalculations are all from WTID. Strikingly, the income share for the top 1 percent in 1928, the year before the crash, and in 2007, the year before the subprime crash, was the same proportion: 24 percent.

13. WTID.

14. King Papers: letter to President Franklin Roosevelt, June 19, 1933; letter to O. E. Baker, Bureau of Agricultural Economics, Oct. 28, 1938; letter to John C. Gebhart, the National Economy League, March 24, 1939; and letter to George E. Roberts, Apr. 18, 1940. See also "Biographical Note" in the NWDA online guide to the King Papers (http://nwdadb.wsulibs.wsu.edu/findaid/ark:/80444/xv64995#bioghistID). King called the minimum wage "dangerous" in the *Literary Digest* profile listed in General Sources.

15. In *The Haves and the Have-Nots: A Brief and Idiosyncratic History of Global Inequality* (New York: Basic Books, 2011), Branko Milanovic points out (pp. 7–8) that Alexis de Tocqueville made a strikingly similar observation in his 1835 *Memoir on Pauperism*. Equality, Tocqueville wrote, "is prevalent only at the historical poles of civilization. Savages are equal because they are equally weak and ignorant. Very civilized men can all become equal because they all have at their disposal similar means of attaining comfort and happiness. Between these two extremes is found inequality of condition, wealth, knowledge—the power of the few, the poverty, ignorance and weakness of all the rest."

16. In fairness to Kuznets, he himself characterized his income-inequality theory as "5 percent empirical information and 95 percent speculation, some of it possibly tainted by wishful thinking."

17. Simon Kuznets, "Economic Growth and Income Inequality," *American Economic Review* 45, no. 1 (Mar. 1955), 1–28.

18. Steven R. Weisman, *The Great Tax Wars* (New York: Simon & Schuster, 2002), 353.

19. Claudia Goldin and Robert Margo, "The Great Compression: The Wage Structure in the United States at Mid-Century," *Quarterly Journal of Economics* 107, issue 1 (Feb. 1992), 1–34.

20. The factory workers were all in New York State.

21. WTID.

22. King Papers, letter to O. E. Baker, Oct. 28, 1938.

23. WTID.

24. When you read this passage today, your heart breaks a little at the realization that these class distinctions reasserted themselves with a vengeance during the Great Divergence. Automobiles and (to a lesser extent) clothing are once again conspicuous class markers.

25. Claudia Goldin and Lawrence F. Katz, *The Race Between Education and Technology* (Cambridge: Harvard University Press, 2008) 290. Hereafter referred to as *Education and Technology*.

26. Robert Reich, *The Work of Nations: Preparing Ourselves for 21st Century Capitalism* (New York: Vintage, 1992), 105; David Vogel, *Fluctuating Fortunes: The Political Power of Business in America* (Frederick, MD: Beard Books, 2003; originally published by Basic Books, 1989), 113.

27. WTID; Vogel, *Fluctuating Fortunes*, 113; and U.S. Energy Information Administration, *Annual Energy Review, 2010* (Washington: U.S. Government Printing Office, 2010), 73. This last can be found at http://www.eia .gov/totalenergy/data/annual/pdf/aer.pdf.

28. Commission on Presidential Debates, Oct. 28, 1980, debate transcript, http://www.debates.org/index.php?page=october-28-1980-debate-tran script.

29. Goldin and Katz, *Education and Technology*, 52; WTID.

30. Interview with Paul Krugman, Aug. 28, 2010.

31. Frank Levy and Peter Temin, "Inequality and Institutions in 20th Century America," Industrial Performance Center MIT Working Paper Series (Cambridge, MA, 2007), 5. Levy and Temin derived their 80 percent figure from Thomas Piketty and Emmanuel Saez's income data. Capital gains were not included. The Georgetown economist Stephen J. Rose, in his contrarian 2010 book *Rebound: Why America Will Emerge Stronger from the Financial Crisis* (New York: St. Martin's, 2010), 254, used a different method for calculating inflation; adjusted the numbers for family size; and found the top 1 percent *still* captured 39 percent of all income gains. The 36 percent figure is from Jacob Hacker and Paul Pierson, *Winner-Take-All Politics: How Washington Made the Rich Richer—And Turned Its Back on the Middle Class* (New York: Simon & Schuster, 2010), 3, 311–12. Hacker and Pierson worked from data supplied by the Congressional Budget Office, which used census and IRS data. Capital gains were included.

32. Census Bureau, "Median Household Income by State," http://www.census .gov/hhes/www/income/data/historical/household/index.html; Jared Bernstein and Lawrence Mishel, "Economy's Gains Fail to Reach Most Workers' Paychecks," Economic Policy Institute Briefing Paper (Washington, 2007), http://www.epi.org/publication/bp195/; and Anthony B. Atkinson, Thomas

Piketty, and Emmanuel Saez, "Top Incomes in the Long Run of History," *Journal of Economic Literature* 49, no. 1 (Mar. 2011), 3–71.

33. Thomas Byrne Edsall, *The New Politics of Inequality* (New York: W. W. Norton, 1984), 13.

34. Milanovic, *Haves and the Have-Nots*, 84–85.

35. CIA World Factbook, "Distributions of Family Income—Gini Index," https://www.cia.gov/library/publications/the-world-factbook/fields/2172 .html.

36. Luis Felipe López-Calva and Nora Claudia Lustig, eds., *Declining Inequality in Latin America: A Decade of Progress?* (Washington: Brookings Institution Press, 2010), 1. In the first chapter, the editors write: "After rising in the 1990s, inequality in Latin America declined between 2000 and 2007. Of the seventeen countries for which comparable data are available, twelve experienced a decline in their Gini coefficient. The average decline for the twelve countries was 1.1 percent a year."

2: Going Up

General Sources

James Truslow Adams, *The Epic of America* (Garden City, NY: Garden City Books, 1933; first published by Little Brown, 1931).

Horatio Alger Jr., *Luke Walton; or, the Chicago Newsboy* (Chicago: M. A. Donohue, 1905), Project Gutenberg e-text at http://www.gutenberg.org/files/ 26083/26083-h/26083-h.htm.

Horatio Alger Jr., *Ragged Dick; or, Street Life in New York with the Bootblacks* (Boston: Loring, 1868), University of Virginia e-text at http://etext.vir ginia.edu/etcbin/toccer-new2?id=AlgRagg.sgm&images=images/ modeng&data=/texts/english/modeng/parsed&tag=public&part=all.

Barbara Ehrenreich, *Bright-Sided: How Positive Thinking Is Undermining America* (New York: Metropolitan Books, 2009).

James Fallows, *More Like Us: Making America Great Again* (Boston: Houghton Mifflin, 1989).

Henry Fairlie, *Bite the Hand That Feeds You: Essays and Provocations*, Jeremy McCarter, ed. (New Haven: Yale University Press, 2009).

Anne Trubek, "What Muncie Read," *New York Times Book Review*, Nov. 27, 2011, 43.

1. 1999 Social Inequality III survey, International Social Survey Program. Quoted in Julia B. Isaacs, Isabel V. Sawhill, and Ron Haskins, *Getting Ahead or Losing Ground: Economic Mobility in America* (Washington: Brookings Institution, 2008), 37. Scott Winship, an economic studies

fellow at Brookings's Center on Children and Families, informs me that the question about whether coming from a wealthy family was "essential" or "very important" to getting ahead was asked once again in the 2009 Social Inequality IV survey. This time the international median was an even higher 32 percent. But the countries polled in 2009 were different from those polled in 1999, and in 2009 the United States wasn't polled on this question at all.

2.   Greenberg Quinlan Rosner poll for Pew Charitable Trusts Economic Mobility Project, Mar. 12, 2009, at http://www.pewtrusts.org/uploaded Files/wwwpewtrustsorg/Reports/Economic_Mobility/EMP%202009% 20Survey%20on%20Economic%20Mobility%20FOR%20PRINT%203 .12.09.pdf; Gallup poll, "Half of Young People Expect to Strike It Rich," Mar. 11, 2003, at http://www.gallup.com/poll/7981/half-young-people -expect-strike-rich.aspx; and Thomas A. DiPrete, "Is This a Great Country? Upward Mobility and the Chance for Riches in Contemporary America," Nov. 28, 2005, at http://www.ssc.wisc.edu/soc/faculty/docs/diprete/ riches112805.pdf.

3.   Isaacs et al., *Getting Ahead*, 19.

4.   Bhashkar Mazumder, "Sibling Similarities, Differences and Economic Inequality," Working Paper 2004-13 (Chicago: Federal Reserve Bank, 2004), 23.

5.   *Getting Ahead*, 17, 21. The calculations are based on real family income from 1995 to 2002 for Americans who were children in 1968 as compared with their parents' real family income from 1967 to 1971.

6.   Panel Study of Income Dynamics brochure at http://psidonline.isr.umich .edu/Guide/Brochures/PSID.pdf; and PSID video at http://psidonline.isr .umich.edu/videos.aspx. The PSID was created as an outgrowth of some research undertaken by the Office of Economic Opportunity, the short-lived federal agency tasked with conducting President Lyndon Johnson's War on Poverty. But where the OEO research had focused on low-income families, the PSID expanded the sampling group to include households at all income levels.

7.   Interview with Isabel Sawhill, Feb. 4, 2011.

8.   Chul-In Lee and Gary Solon, "Trends in Intergenerational Income Mobility" (Cambridge, MA: NBER, 2006), 16.

9.   Katharine Bradbury and Jane Katz, "Trends in U.S. Family Income Mobility, 1967–2004," Working Paper 09-7 (Boston: Federal Reserve Bank, 2009).

10. Gary Solon, "Intergenerational Income Mobility in the United States," *American Economic Review* 82, no. 3 (June 1992), 393–408.

11. Thomas Piketty, "Theories of Persistent Inequality and Intergenerational Mobility," in *Handbook of Income Distribution*, vol. 1, A. B. Atkinson and F. Bourguignon, eds. (Oxford: Elsevier North Holland, 2000), 457.

12. Bhashkar Mazumder, "Earnings Mobility in the U.S.: A New Look at Intergenerational Inequality," Working Paper 2001-18 (Chicago: Federal Reserve Bank, 2001), 34; Mazumder, "Revised Estimates of Intergenerational Income Mobility in the United States," Working Paper 2003-16 (Chicago: Federal Reserve Bank, 2003), 18–19; and Mazumder, "Sibling Similarities, Differences, and Economic Inequality," Working Paper 2004-13 (Chicago: Federal Reserve Bank, 2004), 4, 27, 32–33.

13. Wojciech Kopczuk, Emmanuel Saez, and Jae Song, "Earnings Inequality and Mobility in the United States: Evidence from Social Security Data Since 1937," *Quarterly Journal of Economics* 125, no. 1 (Feb. 2010), 123; *Getting Ahead*, 66–67, 74–77.

14. Anna Cristina d'Addio, "Intergenerational Transmission of Disadvantage: Mobility or Immobility Across Generations? A Review of the Evidence for OECD Countries," OECD Social, Employment and Migration Working Papers 52 (Paris: OECD, 2007), 33; and Miles Corak, "Do Poor Children Become Poor Adults? Lessons from a Cross Country Comparison of Generational Earnings Mobility," Discussion Paper No. 1993 (Bonn: Institute for the Study of Labor [IZA], 2006), 53, 63.

15. Miles Corak, "Chasing the Same Dream, Climbing Different Ladders: Economic Mobility in the United States and Canada" (Washington,: Pew Economic Mobility Project, 2010), 2, 20. The calculations of the dollar thresholds for the bottom and top household income tenths are from Andrew Sum and Ishwar Khatiwada, "The Nation's Underemployed in the 'Great Recession' of 2007–09," *Monthly Labor Review*, Nov. 2010, 11–12.

16. Corak, "Chasing the Same Dream," 4.

17. The same term would subsequently be borrowed by the American political journalist Richard Rovere to describe a similar phenomenon in the United States. But Rovere's appropriation was tongue-in-cheek and a bit self-conscious. That was partly because Rovere, as chief political correspondent for the *New Yorker*, arguably qualified as a member of the Establishment himself, but mainly because the American Establishment exercised much less power than its British counterpart.

18. Gary Scharnhorst with Jack Bales, *The Lost Life of Horatio Alger, Jr.* (Bloomington: Indiana University Press,1985), 5.

19. Allan Nevins, *James Truslow Adams: Historian of the American Dream* (Urbana: University of Illinois Press, 1968), 3.

20. Scharnhorst with Bales, *Lost Life*, 66, 67, 70.
21. Nevins, *James Truslow Adams*, 20.
22. Scharnhorst with Bales, *Lost Life*, 127, 129.
23. Adams, *Epic of America*, 317–23.
24. Scharnhorst with Bales, *Lost Life*, 127–30; Nevins, *James Truslow Adams*, 58, 243, 246, 249; and Adams, *Epic of America*, 317.
25. Scharnhorst with Bales, *Lost Life*, 7, 144.
26. Joseph P. Ferrie, "The End of American Exceptionalism? Mobility in the U.S. Since 1850," *Journal of Economic Perspectives* 19, no. 3 (Summer 2005), 199–215.
27. *Getting Ahead*, 30.
28. Jason Long and Joseph Ferrie, "A Tale of Two Labor Markets: Intergenerational Occupational Mobility in Britain and the U.S. Since 1850," Working Paper 11253 (Cambridge, MA: NBER, 2005).

3: Usual Suspects

General Sources

"The *Forbes* 400: The Richest People in America," *Forbes*, Sept. 2011, at http://www.forbes.com/forbes-400/.

Betty Friedan, *The Feminine Mystique* (New York: W. W. Norton, 1963).

Mary Patillo-McCoy, *Black Picket Fences: Privilege and Peril Among the Black Middle Class* (Chicago: University of Chicago Press, 1999).

"Races: America's Rising Black Middle Class," *Time*, June 17, 1974, at http://www.time.com/time/magazine/article/0,9171,879319-1,00.html.

1. Carmen DeNavas-Walt, Bernadette D. Proctor, and Jessica C. Smith, *Income, Poverty, and Health Insurance Coverage in the United States: 2010* (Washington: Census Bureau, 2011), 6, 12.

2. My source for historical median income data here and in most instances throughout this book is the Census Bureau's Web page for historical income tables at http://www.census.gov/hhes/www/income/data/historical/household/index.html. It is possible to argue that the black/white wage gap grew worse during the past three decades, for instance, by factoring in blacks' higher incarceration rate and lower participation in the job market. And as we saw in chapter 2, blacks are less upwardly mobile than whites. But the Great Divergence is a phenomenon that's typically measured according to median household or family income, and by those measures the black/white wage gap is virtually unchanged.

3. Some people prefer to compare median weekly incomes because women

are more likely to take time off over the course of the year. But weekly incomes followed a near-identical trend. Among part-time workers, women now enjoy a higher median weekly income than men. This is mainly because female part-time workers are typically older than male part-time workers. Source: "The Gender Wage Gap: 2010," fact sheet (Washington: Institute for Women's Policy Research, Mar. 2011; updated Apr. 2011), at http://www.iwpr.org/publications/pubs/the-gender-wage-gap-2010-up dated-march-2011.

4. Male college graduates still make about 16 percent more in their first post-college jobs than female college graduates. That's perplexing. Women don't usually bear children immediately after graduating from college, so you can't blame this disparity on child-rearing (the duties of which typically fall most heavily on women). This 16 percent gap would appear to be a legacy of the prefeminist era. It's hard to imagine it will persist very far into the future. Source: Jessica Godofsky, Cliff Zukin, and Carl Van Horn, "Unfulfilled Expectations: Recent College Graduates Struggle in a Troubled Economy" (New Brunswick, NJ: Rutgers John J. Heldrich Center for Workforce Development, 2011), at http://www.heldrich.rutgers.edu/sites/default/files/content/Work_Trends_May_2011.pdf.

5. Claudia Goldin, Lawrence Katz, and Ilyana Kuziemko, "The Homecoming of American College Women: The Reversal of the College Gender Gap," *Journal of Economic Perspectives* 20, no. 4 (Fall 2006), 133–56; *Gender Equity in Higher Education* (Washington: American Council on Education, 2010), 7; Daniel de Vise, "More Women Than Men in U.S. Earned Doctorates Last Year for the First Time," *Washington Post*, Sept. 14, 2010, at http://www.washingtonpost.com/wp-dyn/content/article/2010/09/14/AR2010091400004.html; and Nathan E. Bell, *Graduate Enrollment and Degrees: 1999 to 2009* (Washington: Council of Graduate Schools, 2010), 8.

6. Claude Fischer, "Women Graduating," *The Berkeley Blog*, May 26, 2011, at http://blogs.berkeley.edu/2011/05/26/women-graduating/.

7. National Center for Education Statistics, *NAEP 2008: Trends in Academic Progress* (Washington: U.S. Department of Education), 18–19; Sara Mead, "The Truth About Boys and Girls" (Washington: Education Sector, 2006), 6; "NAEP: Measuring Student Progress Since 1964," National Center for Education Statistics, at http://nces.ed.gov/nationsreportcard/about/naephistory.asp.

8. Goldin, Katz, and Kuziemko, "Homecoming of College Women," 133, 140; Goldin and Katz, *Education and Technology* (see chapter 1, note 25), 231.

9. *Women in the Labor Force: A Databook*, Report 1018 (Washington: U.S. Bureau of Labor Statistics, 2009), 8.

10. Claudia Goldin, "The Quiet Revolution That Transformed Women's Employment, Education, and Family" (Richard T. Ely Lecture, American Economic Association Papers and Proceedings, May 2006). The most recent NAEP report (*NAEP 2009: Year in Review*, at http://nces.ed .gov/nationsreportcard/pdf/about/2011471.pdf) found that in 2009 the percentages of the nation's schoolchildren at or above "proficient" in science were, in fourth grade, 35 percent for boys and 32 percent for girls. The gaps are bigger in higher grades, but still not very big. In eighth grade, 34 percent of boys and 27 percent of girls are "proficient" in science; in twelfth grade, it's 24 percent of the boys and 18 percent of the girls. The more worrisome trend at this point isn't the male/female gap, but the decline in science proficiency for *both* boys and girls as they get older.

11. Men hadn't always outnumbered women at colleges. Between 1900 and 1930, according to Goldin, Katz, and Kuziemko, "Homecoming of College Women," their representation was roughly equal. (However, a disproportionate number of the women attended two-year teachers colleges. It's also worth remembering that during this period college attendance by a man *or* a woman was still a comparatively rare occurrence in American life.) Male undergrads started to displace females during the Great Depression, and did so even more after World War II thanks to the GI bill. The trend slowly began to reverse itself in the 1950s.

12. David Autor, "The Polarization of Job Opportunities in the U.S. Labor Market" (Washington: Center for American Progress, 2010), 10–11.

13. Hanna Rosin, "The End of Men," *Atlantic*, July–Aug 2010, at http://www .theatlantic.com/magazine/archive/2010/07/the-end-of-men/8135/.

14. Goldin "Quiet Revolution," 14.

15. Census historical tables at http://www.census.gov/hhes/www/income/ data/historical/families/index.html ; "Income of Families and Persons in the United States: 1949," in *Current Population Reports: Consumer Income* (Washington: U.S. Census Bureau, 1951), 1, at http://www2.census.gov/ prod2/popscan/p60-007.pdf; and *Money Income of Families and Persons in the United States: 1979* (Washington: U.S. Census Bureau, 1981), 1, 2, at http://www2.census.gov/prod2/popscan/p60-129.pdf.

16. Bob Davis and David Wessel, *Prosperity: The Coming 20-Year Boom and What It Means to You* (New York: Times Business, 1999; hardcover published by Times Books in 1998). As the title suggests, the book did a lousy job predicting the future, especially with regard to the fortunes of the middle class. But Wessel and Davis combined library research with on-the-ground reporting to document in minute and revealing detail how

economic changes affected the lives of ordinary people throughout the twentieth century, particularly during its latter half.

17. Ibid., 75.

18. Elizabeth Warren and Amelia Warren Tyagi, *The Two-Income Trap: Why Middle-Class Parents Are Going Broke* (New York: Basic Books, 2004; hardcover published in 2003), 8, 16–20. Warren's calculation is based on a comparison of two-income couples with two young children.

19. Interview with Jim Blentlinger, June 25, 2011; Census Table 697, "Money Income of Families—Distribution by Family Characteristics and Income Level: 2008," at http://www.census.gov/compendia/statab/2011/tables/11s0696.pdf; federal civilian employment chart, U.S. Office of Personnel Management, Sept. 2010, at http://www.opm.gov/feddata/html/gcoagy10.asp; "The Employment Situation—September 2011," U.S. Bureau of Labor Statistics, Oct. 7, 2011, at http://www.bls.gov/news.release/empsit.nro.htm.

20. Jacob S. Hacker, *The Great Risk Shift: The Assault on American Jobs, Families, Health Care, and Retirement and How You Can Fight Back* (New York: Oxford University Press, 2006), 31–33, 203–04.

21. Warren and Tyagi, *Two-Income Trap*, 130, 233; Charles J. Tabb, "Consumer Bankruptcy Filings: Trends and Indicators," Working Paper 67 (Champaign, IL: University of Illinois College of Law, 2006), 24.

22. Hacker, *Great Risk Shift*, 67, 112.

23. Christine R. Schwartz and Robert D. Mare, "Trends in Educational Assortative Marriage from 1940 to 2003," Working Paper 017-05 (Los Angeles: UCLA, California Center for Population Research, 2005), fig. 2.

24. Christine R. Schwartz, "Earnings Inequality and the Changing Association Between Spouses' Earnings" (Washington: National Institutes of Health, 2010), 1, 15; Christine R. Schwartz and Nikki L. Graf, "Assortative Matching Among Same-Sex and Different-Sex Couples in the United States, 1990–2000," *Demographic Research* 21 (Dec. 8, 2009), 843–78, at http://www.demographic-research.org/volumes/vol21/28/21-28.pdf.

25. David T. Ellwood and Christopher Jencks, "The Spread of Single-Parent Families in the United States since 1960," Working Paper RWP04-008 (Cambridge, MA: Harvard University, Kennedy School of Government, 2004), 2, at http://ssrn.com/abstract=517662.

26. Maria Cancian and Deborah Reed, "Family Structure, Childbearing, and Parental Employment: Implications for the Level and Trend in Poverty," *Focus* 26, no. 2 (Fall 2009), 24; "Poverty Rates for Single Mothers Are Higher in the U.S. Than in Other Higher Income Countries," Women's Legal Defense Fund memo, June 2011, at http://www.legalmomentum

.org/our-work/women-and-poverty/resources--publications/single-moth
ers-poverty-higher-us.pdf; and Warren and Tyagi, *Two-Income Trap*, 9,
104.

27. "Growing Income Inequality in OECD Countries: What Drives It and
How Can Policy Tackle It?" (Paris: OECD, 2011), 11.

28. By 1980 the proportion of children living with one parent (about 26 percent today) was already 20 percent. The especially worrisome trend of
teenage births peaked in the early 1990s.

29. Interview with Christopher Jencks, July 12, 2010; Bruce Western, Dier-
dre Bloome, and Christine Percheski, "Inequality Among American
Families with Children, 1975 to 2005," *American Sociological Review* 73
(Dec. 2008), 903–20.

30. Stephen J. Rose, *Rebound: Why America Will Emerge Stronger from the
Financial Crisis* (New York: St. Martin's, 2010), 91, 98, 125; *Income, Poverty, and Health Insurance Coverage in the United States: 2010*, 10–11;
Timothy Noah, "Inequality Petard," *Slate*, Sept. 28, 2010, at http://www
.slate.com/articles/news_and_politics/politics/2010/09/inequality_
petard.html.

4: Teeming Shores

General Sources

Damien Cave, "Better Lives for Mexicans Cut Allure of Going North," *New York
Times*, July 6, 2011, at http://www.nytimes.com/interactive/2011/07/06/
world/americas/immigration.html.

Roger Daniels, *Guarding the Golden Door: American Immigration Policy and Immigrants Since 1882* (New York: Hill & Wang, 2005; originally published
in 2004).

Daniel Tichenor, *Dividing Lines: The Politics of Immigration Control in America*
(Princeton, NJ: Princeton University Press, 2002).

Aristide R. Zolberg, *A Nation by Design: Immigration Policy in the Fashioning of
America* (Cambridge, MA: Harvard University Press, 2008).

1. Interview with Maria Andrade, Oct. 21, 2011.

2. By the century's end, about one third of these immigrants settled in
California. Most of the rest ended up in New York, Texas, Florida, New
Jersey, and Illinois. See George Borjas, *Heaven's Door: Immigration Policy
and the American Economy* (Princeton, NJ: Princeton University Press,
1999), 64.

3. Randall Monger and James Yankay, "U.S. Legal Permanent Residents:
2010," *Annual Flow Report* (Washington: Homeland Security Office of

Immigration Statistics, 2011), at http://www.dhs.gov/xlibrary/assets/statistics/publications/lpr_fr_2010.pdf; and Michael Hoefer, Nancy Rytina, and Bryan C. Baker, "Estimates of the Unauthorized Immigrant Population Residing in the United States: January 2001," *Population Estimates* (Washington: Homeland Security Office of Immigration Statistics, 2011), at http://www.dhs.gov/xlibrary/assets/statistics/publications/ois_ill_pe_2010.pdf. The estimated undocumented population peaked in Jan. 2007 at about 12 million and has since dropped to just below 11 million.

4. Elizabeth M. Grieco and Edward N. Trevelyan, "Place of Birth of the Foreign-Born Population: 2009," American Community Survey Briefs (Washington: U.S. Census Bureau, 2010), and Campbell J. Gibson and Emily Lennon, "Historical Census Statistics on the Foreign-Born Population of the United States, 1850 to 1990," Population Division Working Paper 29 (Washington: U.S. Census Bureau, 1999). The percentage figure given for 1966 was recorded in the 1970 census, before the immigration law's impact was felt.

5. Benjamin Franklin, "Observations Concerning the Increase of Mankind," 1755, from The Papers of Benjamin Franklin, an online archive sponsored by the American Philosophical Society and Yale University, at http://franklinpapers.org/franklin/framedVolumes.jsp?vol=4& page=225a; Edmund S. Morgan, *Benjamin Franklin* (New Haven: Yale University Press, 2002), 77; Thomas Jefferson, *Notes on the State of Virginia* (New York: Penguin Books, 1999; originally published in France in 1785), 91–92.

6. Andrew Gyory, "Closing the Gate: Race, Politics, and the Chinese Exclusion Act," in *Race and Racialization: Essential Readings*, ed. Tania Das Gupta (Toronto: Canadian Scholars Press, 2007), 220.

7   Woodrow Wilson, *A History of the American People*, vol 5: *Reunion and Nationalization* (New York: Harper & Brothers, 1906; originally published in 1902), 212–13.

8. Senator William Dillingham et al., *Reports of the Immigration Commission: Dictionary of Races or Peoples* (Washington: U.S. Government Printing Office, 1911), 84.

9. Gibson and Lennon, "Historical Statistics," at http://www.census.gov/population/www/documentation/twps0029/tab01.html.

10. In the State Department the chief obstacle was an anti-Semitic assistant secretary of state named Breckenridge Long. Thanks in large part to Long's bureaucratic delaying tactics, between 1942 and 1945 fully 90 percent of the existing immigrant quotas for countries under German and Italian control went unfilled.

11. Grieco and Trevelyan, "Place of Birth"; "Unauthorized Immigrant Popu-
     lation: National and State Trends, 2010" (Washington: Pew Hispanic
     Center, 2011), 9; "U.S. Immigration and Economic Growth: Putting Pol-
     icy on Hold" (Dallas: Federal Reserve Bank, 2003), at http://dallasfed
     .org/research/swe/2003/swe0306a.html; Census Table 2-14, "Poverty
     Status Among Foreign-Born Families by Family Type and Year of Entry
     of the Householder: 2008."

12. Claudia Goldin, "The Political Economy of Immigration Restriction in
     the United States, 1890 to 1921," Working Paper 4345 (Cambridge, MA:
     NBER, 1993), 21–22.

13. Timothy J. Hatton and Jeffrey G. Williamson, *Global Migration and the
     World Economy: Two Centuries of Policy and Performance* (Cambridge,
     MA: MIT Press, 2006), 125, 305.

14. Cited in George Borjas, "Increasing the Supply of Labor Through Immi-
     gration: Measuring the Impact on Native-Born Workers," Center for Im-
     migration Studies Backgrounder, May 2004, at http://www.cis.org/
     articles/2004/back504.pdf.

15. James P. Smith and Barry Edmonston, eds., *The New Americans: Eco-
     nomic, Demographic and Fiscal Effects of Immigration* (Washington: Na-
     tional Academy Press, 1997), 6, 337.

16. Federal Reserve Bank, Dallas "U.S. Immigration."

17. *Miami Herald* timeline on the Mariel boatlift at http://www.miamiherald
     .com/2010/04/16/1583475/el-mariel-timeline.html.

18. David Card, "The Impact of the Mariel Boatlift on the Miami Labor Mar-
     ket," *Industrial and Labor Relations Review* 43, No. 2. (Jan. 1990), 245–57.

19. Borjas, "Increasing the Supply of Labor Through Immigration."

20. In a subsequent study with the Harvard economist Lawrence Katz, this
     one focusing solely on immigration from Mexico, Borjas calculated that
     from 1980 to 2000, Mexican immigrants reduced income for native-
     born high school dropouts by 8.2 percent on average, or a little more
     than 0.4 percent per year. Wage competition from Mexican immigrants
     posed a greater burden than wage competition from all immigrants be-
     cause Mexican immigrants were more likely to lack a high school educa-
     tion. See Borjas and Katz, "The Evolution of the Mexican-Born Workforce
     in the United States," Working Paper 11281 (Cambridge, MA: NBER,
     2005), 37.

21. Goldin and Katz, *Education and Technology* (see chapter 1, note 25), 195.

22. "More Working Women Than Men Have College Degrees, Census Bu-
     reau Reports," Census Bureau press release, April 26, 2011, at http://
     www.census.gov/newsroom/releases/archives/education/cb11-72.html;

and "The Role of Immigrants in the U.S. Labor Market" (Washington: Congressional Budget Office, 2005), 1.

23. Borjas, *Heaven's Door*, 83–84.

24. Census-derived charts posted online by the University of Maryland sociologist Reeve Vanneman in 2002, at http://www.bsos.umd.edu/socy/vanneman/socy441/trends/ratio13.html, accessed on Oct. 22, 2011. See also Arloc Sherman and Chad Stone, "Income Gaps Between Very Rich and Everyone Else More Than Tripled in Last Three Decades, New Data Show" (Washington: Center on Budget and Policy Priorities, 2010), which is based on data from the Congressional Budget Office, at http://www.cbpp.org/files/6-25-10inc.pdf. The economic downturn of the early aughts and especially the economic crisis of 2008 hit low-income people very heavily. Since 2008 the bottom 20 percent, census figures show, has seen its mean household income lowered not just in constant (inflation-corrected) dollars but also in current (uncorrected) dollars between 2007 and 2010.

25. "Occupations with the Largest Job Growth," Bureau of Labor Statistics, at http://www.bls.gov/emp/ep_table_104.htm.

26. Sherman and Stone, "Income Gaps."

27. Gary Burtless, "Impact of Immigration on the Distribution of American Well-Being," Working Paper 2009-34 (Boston: Boston College Center for Retirement Research, 2009), 8, 24.

28. Sabrina Kay Golden, "Immigration and Construction: An Analysis of the Impact of Immigration on Construction Project Costs" (College Park, MD: University of Maryland doctoral thesis, 2008), 78.

29. Sir Charles, "In Which I Call Bullsh*t on Yglesias," *Cogitamus* (blog), Feb. 24, 2010, at http://www.cogitamusblog.com/2010/02/in-which-i-call-bullsht-on-yglesias.html#tp%22%20target=%22_blank, accessed on Oct. 22, 2011.

30. Grieco and Trevelyan, "Place of Birth," 1, 2.

31. "Unauthorized Immigrant Population: National and State Trends, 2010" (Washington: Pew Hispanic Center, 2001), 10.

32. Interview with George Borjas, Aug. 16, 2010.

5: Kudoka and the College Premium

General Sources

Frederick Lewis Allen, *The Big Change: America Transforms Itself: 1900–1950* (New Brunswick, NJ: Transaction, 2007; originally published by Harper & Brothers in 1952).

Bill Bishop, *The Big Sort: Why the Clustering of Like-Minded America Is Tearing Us Apart* (Boston: Houghton Mifflin, 2008).

Barrington Moore Jr., *Social Origins of Dictatorship and Democracy: Lord and Peasant in the Making of the Modern World* (Boston: Beacon Press, 1993; originally published in 1966).

Robert B. Reich, *The Work of Nations: Preparing Ourselves for 21st-Century Capitalism* (New York: Vintage Books, 1992; originally published in 1991 by Knopf).

Jeannette Walls, *The Glass Castle* (New York: Scribner, 2005).

1. Bishop, *Big Sort*, 137; 2010 and 2000 U.S. census data on Welch, West Virginia, at http://factfinder2.census.gov/faces/nav/jsf/pages/index.xhtml.

2. Bishop, *Big Sort*, 137; Ronald Garay, *U.S. Steel and Gary, West Virginia: Corporate Paternalism in Appalachia* (Knoxville: University of Tennessee Press, 2011), 117; 2010 U.S. census data on Welch, West Virginia.

3. Jason C. Booza, Jackie Cutsinger, and George Galster, "Where Did They Go? The Decline of Middle-Income Neighborhoods in Metropolitan America," Living Cities Census Series (Washington: Brookings Institution, 2006).

4. *Statistical Abstract of the United States* (Washington: U.S. Census Bureau, 2011), Table 689, at http://www.census.gov/compendia/statab/2011/tables/11s0689.pdf; and Rick Newman, "How the Middle Class Is Shrinking," *U.S. News & World Report*, Oct. 15, 2010, at http://money.usnews.com/money/blogs/flowchart/2010/10/15/how-the-middle-class-is-shrinking. Measuring middle-class shrinkage is not an exact science. Using a different methodology, Georgetown's Stephen J. Rose calculated that the middle class shrank by about 8 percent between 1979 and 2004. See Rose, *Social Stratification in the United States* (New York: New Press, 2007), 28. Newman of *U.S. News*, working in consultation with the economist Heidi Shierholz of the Washington-based Economic Policy Institute, a liberal-leaning think tank, calculated that the middle class shrank by about 6 percent between 1980 and 2009.

5. Rose, *Social Stratification*, 27–28; and Rose, *Rebound*, 103.

6. Economists call this the "lump of labor fallacy." The term was coined by the British economist David F. Schloss, who wrote in 1891: "The theory of the Lump of Labour will be seen to rest upon the utterly untenable supposition that a fixed amount of work exists, which has to be done, and will be done, irrespective of the conditions under which the work is done, and, in particular, irrespective of the efficiency of the labour employed; and that, the more work is done by any one workman, the less work re-

mains to be done by all other workmen . . . The character of this fallacy will best be understood [through] . . . the precisely similar objection to a man's using the best available tools; in other words, with the popular objection to the use of motor power and machinery. No clear thinker believes that, in order to provide labour for the unemployed, it is advisable that we should give up steam-ploughs for ordinary iron ploughs, these again for wooden ploughs, and, in the ultimate resort, should abandon these instruments and scratch the ground with the fingers." See David F. Schloss, "Why Working-Men Dislike Piece-Work," *Economic Review* 1, no. 3 (July 1891), 311–26.

7. A decade after the Nobelists sent their letter, the Harvard sociologist (and onetime *Fortune* magazine journalist) Daniel Bell observed that it was "one more instance of the penchant for overdramatizing a momentary innovation and blowing it up far out of proportion to its actuality." See Daniel Bell, *The Coming of Post-Industrial Society: A Venture in Social Forecasting* (New York: Basic Books, 1999; originally published in 1973), 463.

8. Frank Levy and Richard J. Murnane, *The New Division of Labor: How Computers Are Creating the Next Job Market* (Princeton, NJ.: Princeton University Press, 2004), 13–25; and Farhad Manjoo, "Will Robots Steal Your Job?," *Slate*, Sept. 26–30, 2011, at http://www.slate.com/articles/ technology/robot_invasion/2011/09/will_robots_steal_your_job.html. Levy and Murnane's book grew out of a 2003 paper that they wrote with MIT's David Autor.

9. Erik Brynjolfsson and Andrew McAfee, *Race Against the Machine: How the Digital Revolution Is Accelerating Innovation, Driving Productivity, and Irreversibly Transforming Employment and the Economy* (Lexington, MA: Digital Frontier Press, e-book, 2011), chap. 2; and Sebastian Thrun, "What We're Driving At," *The Official Google Blog*, Oct. 9, 2010, at http://google blog.blogspot.com/2010/10/what-were-driving-at.html.

10. Carol Boyd Leon, "Occupational Winners and Losers: Who They Were During 1972–1980" (Washington,· U.S. Bureau of Labor Statistics, 1982), 23, at http://www.bls.gov/opub/mlr/1982/06/art4full.pdf; Paula England, "Women and Occupational Prestige: A Case of Vacuous Sex Equality," *Signs* 5, no. 2 (Winter 1979), 265; Kim Zetter, "Sept. 2, 1969: First U.S. ATM Starts Doling Out Dollars," *Wired* (Web-only), Sept 2, 2010, at http://www.wired.com/thisdayintech/2010/09/0902first-us -atm/.

11. Karen Akers, interview with author, Aug. 13, 2011.

12. "Tellers," in *Occupational Outlook Handbook, 2010–2011 Edition*

(Washington: U.S. Bureau of Labor Statistics, 2010), at http://www.bls.gov/oco/ocos126.htm: Bureau of Labor Statistics, Occupational Employment Statistics Survey, National Employment and Wage data, May 2010. At http://www.bls.gov/news.release/ocwage.t01.htm.

13. David Autor and David Dorn, "The Growth of Low-Skill Service Jobs and the Polarization of the U.S. Labor Market," June 2011, at http://www.cemfi.es/~dorn/Autor-Dorn-LowSkillServices-Polarization.pdf; and David Autor, interview with author, June 7, 2010.

14. Harry Holzer, Julia I. Lane, David Rosenblum, and Fredrik Andersson, *Where Are All the Good Jobs Going?: What National and Local Job Quality and Dynamics Mean for U.S. Workers* (New York: Russell Sage Foundation, 2011); Harry Holzer, "Is the Middle of the U.S. Job Market Really Disappearing? A Comment on the 'Polarization' Hypothesis," Center for American Progress, May 13, 2010, at http://www.americanprogress.org/issues/2010/05/pdf/Holzer_memo.pdf; and Harry Holzer, interview with author, April 19, 2011.

15. David Autor, "The Polarization of Job Opportunities in the U.S. Labor Market," Center for American Progress, Apr. 2010, 16–18, at http://www.americanprogress.org/issues/2010/04/pdf/job_polarization.pdf; Robert G. Valletta, "Computer Use and the U.S. Wage Distribution, 1984–2003," Working Paper 2006-34 (San Francisco: Federal Reserve Bank, 2006), 14–15.

16. "As he grew accustomed to the great gallery of machines, he began to feel the forty-foot dynamos as a moral force, much as the early Christians felt the Cross. The planet itself seemed less impressive, in its old-fashioned, deliberate, annual or daily revolution, than this huge wheel, revolving within arm's length at some vertiginous speed, and barely murmuring—scarcely humming an audible warning to stand a hair's-breadth further for respect of power—while it would not wake the baby lying close against its frame. Before the end, one began to pray to it; inherited instinct taught the natural expression of man before silent and infinite force." See Henry Adams, *The Education of Henry Adams* (New York: Oxford University Press, 1999; originally published in 1918 by Riverside Press), 318.

17. Goldin and Katz, *Education and Technology* (see chapter 1, note 25), 102; Ruth Schwartz Cowan, "The 'Industrial Revolution' in the Home: Household Technology and Social Change in the 20th Century," *Technology and Culture* 17, no. 1 (Jan. 1976), 4; Valletta, "Computer Use and the U.S. Wage Distribution," 1.

18. This in itself was remarkable and new. Goldin and Katz write that prior

to the twentieth century technological advances were not associated with increased demand for more skilled employees. If anything, it went the other way, as artisans—for instance, gun makers, butchers, bakers, glassblowers, and shoemakers—were replaced by unskilled workers on assembly lines. But as production processes streamlined further, machines replaced the unskilled workers and higher-skilled workers were sought to manipulate the machines (Goldin and Katz, *Education and Technology*, 122).

19. Goldin and Katz, *Education and Technology*, 140, 161, 185.

20. Ibid., 198.

21. Ibid., 113, 177.

22. Ibid., 114, 118; Richard Feynman, quoted in *Surely You're Joking, Mr. Feynman! Adventures of a Curious Character,* ed. Edward Hutchings (New York: W. W. Norton, 1997; originally published in 1985), 18–21.

23. Goldin and Katz, *Education and Technology*, 178–80, 248–49, 264.

24. Albert Parker Fitch, *The College Course and the Preparation for Life: Eight Talks on Familiar Undergraduate Problems* (Boston: Houghton Mifflin, 1914), 177–78.

25. Goldin and Katz, *Education and Technology*, 95, 248–49, 261–62, 278.

26. This calculation omits a fleeting and fairly predictable falloff during World War II.

27. Goldin and Katz, *Education and Technology*, 326–27, 330–31.

28. "Education at a Glance 2008: OECD Indicators" (Paris: OECD, 2008), 65, at http://www.oecd.org/dataoecd/23/46/41284038.pdf; U.S. Census Bureau, "Educational Attainment: 2000" (Washington, 2003), 3–4; 2010 OECD data cited in Anthony P. Carnevale and Stephen J. Rose, "The Undereducated American," report (Washington: Georgetown University Center on Education and the Workforce, 2011), 14; Lawrence Katz and Claudia Goldin, interview with author, June 8, 2010.

29. Goldin and Katz, *Education and Technology*, 290; Frank Levy and Tom Kochan, "Addressing the Problem of Stagnant Wages" (Champaign, IL: Employment Policy Research Network, March 17, 2011), 2, at http://www employmentpolicy.org/topic/12/research/addressing-problem-stagnant -wages.

30. Carnevale and Rose, "Undereducated American," 18–20.

31. Goldin and Katz, *Education and Technology*, 278; Laura Pappano, "The Master's as the New Bachelor's," *New York Times*, July 22, 2011, at http://www.nytimes.com/2011/07/24/education/edlife/edl-24masters-t.html?_ r=3&ref=education; Cecelia Capuzzi Simon, "R.O.I.," *New York Times*, July 22, 2011, at http://www.nytimes.com/2011/07/24/education/edlife/

edl-24roi-t.html?pagewanted=all; Levy and Kochan, "Addressing the Problem," 2–3.

32.   David Card and Thomas Lemieux, "Going to College to Avoid the Draft: The Unintended Legacy of the Vietnam War," *American Economic Review* 91, no. 2 (May 2001), 101.

33.   Richard B. Freeman, *The Overeducated American* (New York: Academic Press, 1976), 4, 31.

34.   Claudia Goldin and Lawrence F. Katz, "Education and Technology: Supply, Demand, and Income Inequality" (London: Center for Economic Policy Research, 2009), 3, at http://www.voxeu.org/index.php?q=node/3640. See also Thomas, Lemieux, "Postsecondary Education and Increased Wage Inequality," *American Economic Review* 96 (May 2006), 195–99.

35.   Goldin and Katz, *Education and Technology*, 278; Freeman, *Overeducated American*, 22–23; Andrew Ferguson, *Crazy U: One Dad's Crash Course in Getting His Kid into College* (New York: Simon & Schuster, 2011), 171; Erik Larson, "Why Colleges Cost Too Much," *Time*, June 24, 2001, at http://www.time.com/time/magazine/article/0,9171,137412,00.html; Barry Werth, "Why Is College So Expensive?," *New England Monthly*, Jan. 1988, 35–43, 99. The dean who explained the Chivas Regal strategy was Joseph Ellis Jr., who later achieved national fame as the author of *Founding Brothers* and other popular works of American history.

6: Offshore

General sources

Rone Tempest, "Barbie and the World Economy," *Los Angeles Times*, Sept. 22, 1996, at http://articles.latimes.com/1996-09-22/news/mn-46610_1_hong-kong.

"Top Companies: Most Profitable," *Fortune*, July 25, 2011, at http://money.cnn.com/magazines/fortune/global500/2011/performers/companies/profits/.

"Top Companies: Biggest Employers," Fortune, July 25, 2001, at http://money.cnn.com/magazines/fortune/global500/2011/performers/companies/biggest/.

1.   Wayne M. Morrison, "China's Economic Conditions" (Washington: Congressional Research Service, 2011), 1–5, 11; Ronald E. Kutscher, "Historical Trends, 1950–92, and Current Uncertainties," *Monthly Labor Review*, Nov. 1993, 5; "Country Comparison: Exports," *CIA World Factbook*, at

https://www.cia.gov/library/publications/the-world-factbook/rankorder/2078rank.html; and "Country Comparison: GDP (Purchasing Power Parity)," at https://www.cia.gov/library/publications/the-world-factbook/rankorder/2001rank.html?countryName=China&countryCode=ch&regionCode=eas&rank=3#ch.

2. "World Development Indicators" July 2011, at http://data.worldbank.org/data-catalog/world-development-indicators.

3. Morrison, "China's Economic Conditions," 16–18. China's growing inequality problem is severe, but not in ways that shed any light on U.S. inequality. China's more egalitarian government policies of the past included mass starvation and some of the most brutal political repression achieved during the twentieth century—a reminder that there are problems that are worse than income inequality. Whatever China's path forward, it won't be informed by hopeful lessons from its past eighty years.

4. Wolfgang F. Stolper and Paul A. Samuelson, "Protection and Real Wages," *Review of Economic Studies* 9, no. 1 (Nov. 1941), 58–73; Paul A. Samuelson, "Tribute to Wolfgang Stolper on the Fiftieth Anniversary of the Stolper-Samuelson Theorem," in *The Stolper-Samuelson Theorem: A Golden Jubilee*, ed. Alan V. Deardorff and Robert M. Stern (Ann Arbor: University of Michigan Press, 1994), 343; and Jagdish Bhagwati, "The Stolper-Samuelson Theorem: Then And Now," in *Stolper-Samuelson Golden Jubilee*, 219.

5. Taussig, who for many years had chaired Harvard's Economics Department (he was succeeded by Joseph Schumpeter), was a highly influential figure in modern trade theory. He died the year before Stolper and Samuelson published their paper. In the passage they quoted, Taussig went on at cringe-inducing length: "It is a belief held especially in countries of high wages like the United States, and it goes with—indeed, is a part of—the most persuasive argument in favor of a policy of tariff protection. It seems plain as a pikestaff to the average person—to the average employer not less than to the average workman—that the country in which money wages are low can undersell the country paying high money wages; and that if the two compete without restriction, wages must become the same in both. The reasoning of the preceding chapters shows that *there is no such tendency* [italics mine] to equalization. Countries with high money wages trade with those of low money wages, to the advantage of both, and with permanent maintenance of the divergences in wages . . . Yet to most persons it seems perplexing and anomalous, and remains so even tho the main lines are followed and accepted on the first summary presentation. In the field of economics, as in every intellectual

field, fundamental principles, however simple, are not really understood until they are applied, repeated, turned over, gradually worked into the full intellectual equipment of the recipient." See Frank William Taussig, *International Trade* (New York: Macmillan, 1936; originally published in 1927), 37–39, at http://www.sotsium.ru/books/122/186/taussig1927 .html. Let Taussig's condescension in making a since-discredited argument stand as a lesson to all overconfident social scientists and experts of every kind.

6. Adrian Wood, "How Trade Hurt Unskilled Workers," *Journal of Economic Perspectives* 9, no. 3 (Summer 1995), 57–80.

7. Paul R. Krugman and Robert Z. Lawrence, "Trade, Jobs, and Wages," *Scientific American*, Apr. 1994, 44–49. That same year Krugman argued elsewhere that if trade were creating greater income inequality in the United States, one would expect to see it creating greater income equality in, say, Mexico, which "ships low-skill goods to the United States and imports high-skill goods in return." But income inequality, Krugman wrote, was increasing in Mexico. That was true at the time, but the trend has since reversed itself. For the past decade and a half income inequality has been decreasing in Mexico. See Paul Krugman, *Peddling Prosperity: Economic Sense and Nonsense in the Age of Diminished Expectations* (New York: W. W. Norton, 1994), 148.

8. This calculation was weighted according to how much trade any given country had with the United States.

9. Paul Krugman, "Trade and Wages, Reconsidered," Brookings Papers on Economic Activity, (Washington: Brookings, Spring 2008), 103.

10. Ibid., 104.

11. Paul Krugman, interview with author, Aug. 24, 2010; Krugman, "Trouble with Trade," *New York Times*, Dec. 28, 2007, at http://www.nytimes .com/2007/12/28/opinion/28krugman.html; Krugman, "Trade and Wages," 107–10.

12. Lee Hudson Teslik, "NAFTA's Economic Impact," Council on Foreign Relations Backgrounder, July 7, 2009, at http://www.cfr.org/economics/ naftas-economic-impact/p15790#p6. NAFTA may be lowering middle-skilled wages in the United States, but as we saw in chapter 4 there are also some tentative signs that the treaty's favorable impact on Mexico's economy helped reduce the flow of undocumented workers into the United States. That would raise unskilled wages here.

13. Krugman, "Trade and Wages," 135; Josh Bivens, "Globalization, American Wages, and Inequality," Working Paper 279 (Washington: Economic Policy Institute, 2007), 1.

14. Robert Z. Lawrence, "Slow Real Wage Growth and U.S. Income Inequality: Is Trade to Blame?," paper for Brandeis University conference "Is Free Trade Still Optimal in the 21st Century?," June 15, 2007, 12–13, 40, at http://www.hks.harvard.edu/fs/rlawrence/Lawrence%20for%20Brandeis.pdf. The Brandeis paper was a preliminary draft of Robert Z. Lawrence, *Blue-Collar Blues: Is Trade to Blame for Rising U.S. Income Inequality?* (Washington: Peterson Institute for International Economics, 2008). In the final version Lawrence conceded, "It does appear that imports from China in 2006 are still in relatively low-wage industries, but this is not the case for manufactured goods from developing countries as a whole" (p. 43). Even with that caveat, Lawrence's conclusion was not in the end notably different from Krugman's: "While increased trade has made some contributions, both to wage and [to] super rich inequality, it should be acknowledged that trade is just one of many sources of structural change in the U.S. economy, and isolating its particular contribution to both inequality and displacement is difficult" (p. 73).

15. The Princeton economists Gene Grossman and Esteban Rossi-Hansberg, in a well-received 2006 paper ("The Rise of Offshoring: It's Not Wine for Cloth Anymore," at http://www.kc.frb.org/PUBLICAT/SYMPOS/2006/PDF/Grossman-Rossi-Hansberg.paper.0728.pdf), argued that the increase in world trade can *raise* wages for low-skilled manufacturing workers, not lower them—that Ricardo, in effect, got this right after all, though for reasons neither Ricardo nor Stolper nor Samuelson could have anticipated. Grossman and Rossi-Hansberg wrote that productivity gains from the internationalized manufacture of individual items— they called it "trade in tasks"—outweighed the Stolper-Samuelson effects, to low-wage manufacturing workers' benefit. But the economists concluded, "Our calculations admittedly are crude and so must be taken with a grain of salt." A 2008 follow-up paper ended by stating that they "would dearly like" to find empirical data to test their theory. Grossman and Rossi-Hansberg, "Trading Tasks: A Simple Theory of Offshoring," *American Economic Review* 98, no. 5 (Dec. 2008), 1996. Pending the discovery of real-world evidence that lower-wage production workers really are benefiting from trade with low-wage nations, I will follow their advice.

16. Greg Linden, Jason Dedrick, and Kenneth Kraemer, "Innovation and Job Creation in a Global Economy: The Case of Apple iPad," *Journal of International Commerce and Economics* 3, no. 1 (May 2011), 223–32; and Kramer, Linden, and Dedrick, "Capturing Value in Global Networks: Apple's iPad and iPhone," July 2011, 11, at http://pcic.merage.uci.edu/papers/2011/Value_iPad_iPhone.pdf.

17. Philip Elmer-DeWitt, "Apple's Headcount, Up 30 %, Still Industry's Most Productive," *Fortune*, Oct. 30, 2011, at http://tech.fortune.cnn.com/2011/10/30/apples-headcount-up-30-still-industrys-most-productive/; "History of the Rouge," Henry Ford Museum Web site, at http://www.thehenry ford.org/rouge/historyofrouge.aspx.

18. Marianne Bertrand, "From the Invisible Handshake to the Invisible Hand? How Import Competition Changes the Employment Relationship," *Journal of Labor Economics* 22, no. 4 (2004), 723–65; Mine Zeynep Senses, "The Effects of Outsourcing on the Elasticity of Labor Demand" (Washington: Center for Economic Studies, 2006).

19. Alan Blinder, "Offshoring: The Next Industrial Revolution?" *Foreign Affairs* 85, no. 2 (Mar.–Apr. 2006), 113–28; and Blinder, "How Many U.S. Jobs Might Be Offshorable?," *World Economics* 10, no. 2 (Apr.–June 2009), 41–78.

20. Janet Norwood, Carol Carson, et al., *Off-Shoring: An Elusive Phenomenon* (Washington: National Academy of Public Administration, 2006), 58; Blinder, "Offshoring," 114.

21. Blinder, "Offshoring: Big Deal, or Business as Usual?," Working Paper 149 (Princeton, NJ.: Center for Economic Policy Studies, 2007), 5.

22. "Offshoring in Six Human Service Programs" (Washington: U.S. Government Accounting Office, 2006), 12–13; and Timothy Noah, "Hello Bangalore? Where's My Unemployment Check," *Slate*, Apr. 6, 2006, at http://www.slate.com/articles/news_and_politics/hot_document/features/2006/hello_bangalore_wheres_my_unemployment_check/_2.html.

23. Tell it, brother. In my own profession of journalism, I note with some regret, Reuters already has a Bangalore office that employs dozens of Indian reporters to cover the New York Stock Exchange at a fraction of what it would cost to hire reporters in the United States. Some of their sources may be only a stone's throw away; all the big investment banks have hired offshore research analysts in India and/or Asia. See Steve Schifferes, "Here Is the U.S. News from Bangalore," BBC News, Feb. 2, 2007, at http://news.bbc.co.uk/2/hi/business/6289521.stm; Heather Timmons, "Cost-Cutting in New York, but a Boom in India," *New York Times*, Aug. 12, 2008, at http://www.nytimes.com/2008/08/12/business/worldbusiness/12indiawall.html?pagewanted=print; and Shaheen Pasha, "The Outsourcing Wave Hits Investment Bankers," CNNMoney.com, Feb. 22, 2006, at http://money.cnn.com/2006/02/22/news/companies/banks_outsourcing/index.htm.

24. Jan Vang and Cristina Chaminade, "East Asian Growth: Policy Lessons

from Bangalore, India" (Luxembourg: Joint Research Centre/Institute
for Prospective Technological Studies, 2011), 7.

25. Blinder, "How Many U.S. Jobs."

26. Frank Levy and Kyoung-Hee Yu, "Offshoring Radiology Serivces to
India," Working Paper 06-005 (Cambridge, MA: MIT Industrial Performance Center, 2006), 17–19.

27. Dean Baker, "Trade and Inequality: The Role of Economists," paper delivered to the "Inequality, Democracy, and the Economy" plenary session
of the Association for Social Economics in New Orleans, Jan. 3, 2008, at
http://www.cepr.net/documents/publications/trade_2008_01.pdf.

28. Paul McDougall, "In a Reversal, Feds Say Outsourced Programmers Are
Eligible for Assistance," *Information Week*, Apr. 24, 2006, at http://www
.informationweek.com/news/186700365.

7: Unequal Government

General Sources

"Bryce Harlow Dies; Aide to Presidents," Associated Press, in *New York Times*,
Feb. 18, 1987, at http://www.nytimes.com/1987/02/18/obituaries/bryce
-harlow-dies-aide-to-presidents.html.

Bob Burke and Ralph G. Thompson, *Bryce Harlow: Mr. Integrity* (Oklahoma
City: Oklahoma Heritage Association, 2000).

Thomas Byrne Edsall, *The New Politics of Inequality* (New York: W. W. Norton,
1984).

William Greider, "The Education of David Stockman," *Atlantic*, Dec. 1981, at
http://www.theatlantic.com/magazine/archive/1981/12/the-education-of
-david-stockman/5760/.

Michael Harrington, *The Next Left: The History of a Future* (New York: Henry
Holt, 1987).

Mickey Kaus, *The End of Equality* (New York: Basic Books, 1992).

Henry Kissinger, *Years of Renewal* (New York: Simon & Schuster, 1999).

Henry Kissinger, *Years of Upheaval* (Boston: Little Brown, 1982).

Paul Krugman, *The Conscience of a Liberal* (New York: W. W. Norton, 2007).

William E. Simon, *A Time for Truth* (New York: McGraw-Hill, 1978).

David Vogel, *Fluctuating Fortunes: The Political Power of Business In America*
(Washington: Beard Books, 2003; originally published by Basic Books
in 1989).

1. For instance, a May 2002 Congressional Budget Office report responded
to "claims that the cut in top rates in the 1980s caused tax receipts and
the size of the economy to double in that decade. They did double in

nominal terms (including the effect of inflation and the size of the economy), but by that standard, they rose even more in the 1970s [when the 70 percent top marginal income-tax rate was never lowered]. Real GDP, a more relevant measure, grew by almost exactly the same amount—37 percent—in the 1980s as it did in the 1970s. Moreover, some of the rise in overall revenues reflected an increase in payroll tax rates in 1983. Individual income tax receipts, the component of taxes that should have been affected by the decline in the top tax rate, actually grew more slowly than GDP grew over that period." See "Supplement to CBO's May 9, 2002, Testimony on Federal Budget Estimating" (Washington: Congressional Budget Office, May 2002), 6. Reagan's support for supply-side economics attracted skepticism even at the time; during the 1980 GOP primaries George H. W. Bush, subsequently Reagan's vice president, called it "voodoo economic policy."

2. After this and other impolitic comments in the magazine piece generated a wave of bad publicity, Stockman was only mildly reprimanded. At the time Stockman told the media that a meeting he had had with the president "was more in the nature of a visit to the woodshed after supper," but in a subsequent memoir Stockman admitted this had been a fabrication. Reagan had merely asked why he'd made comments that hurt him and, after Stockman apologized, told Stockman he was "a victim of sabotage by the press." See David Stockman, *The Triumph of Politics: Why the Reagan Revolution Failed* (New York: Harper & Row, 1986).

3. Lou Cannon, *President Reagan: The Role of a Lifetime* (New York: Public Affairs, 2000; originally published by Simon & Schuster in 1991), 456–57; and "Chicago Relief Queen Guilty," Associated Press, Mar. 18, 1977, in *New York Times*, Mar. 19, 1977.

4. The Congressional Budget Office says it was 24 percent; the White House Office of Management and Budget says it was 25 percent. See *2011 Long-Term Budget Outlook* (Washington: Congressional Budget Office, 2011), 3, at http://www.cbo.gov/ftpdocs/122xx/doc12212/06-21-Long-Term _Budget_Outlook.pdf; and "Historical Tables," White House Office of Management and Budget Web page, Table 1.3, at http://www.whitehouse .gov/omb/budget/Historicals. In its June 2011 report CBO said government spending dropped to 22 percent of GDP in 2010 and was expected to remain at that level through 2011 before dropping to 20 percent for the remainder of the decade.

5. Brad DeLong, "The Primacy of Politics for Income Distribution?," *Grasping Reality with Both Hands* (blog), Aug. 20, 2006, at http://delong.type pad.com/sdj/2006/08/the_primacy_of_.html. Accessed on Nov. 1, 2011.

6. "Historical Effective Tax Rates, 1979 to 2005: Supplement with Additional Data on Sources of Income and High-Income Households," memo from Congressional Budget Office to Senator Max Baucus, Dec. 2008, Table 1, at http://www.cbo.gov/ftpdocs/98xx/doc9884/12-23 -EffectiveTaxRates_Letter.pdf.

7. Thomas Piketty and Emmanuel Saez, "How Progressive Is the U.S. Federal Tax System? A Historical and International Perspective," *Journal of Economic Perspectives* 21, no. 1 (Winter 2007), 3–24. Their calculations for effective tax rates appear in Table 2.

8. Jacob Hacker and Paul Pierson, *Winner-Take-All Politics: How Washington Made the Rich Richer—and Turned It's Back on the Middle Class* (New York: Simon & Schuster, 2010), 49.

9. "Historical Effective Tax Rates, 1979 to 2005," Table 1; and Atkinson, WTID (World Top Incomes Database; see Introduction, note 6). The change in the effective tax rate on the bottom 20 percent (i.e., poor and lower-middle-class people) was more dramatic than the change at the top 0.01 percent, but not in a direction that would increase income inequality. During the same period it fell by nearly half, from 7.7 to 4.3 percent. This was largely due to President Clinton's expansion of the Earned Income Tax Credit.

10. *Trends in the Distribution of Household Income Between 1979 and 2007* (Washington: Congressional Budget Office, 2011), 19. The Gini index, it should be said, is better at capturing inequality trends between large subgroups (like college versus high school graduates) than between the top 1 percent, or 0.1 percent, or 0.01 percent, and everybody else.

11. WTID.

12. Levy and Temin, "Inequality and Institutions in 20th Century America" (see chapter 1, note 31), 5.

13. Paul Krugman, "Introducing This Blog," *The Conscience of a Liberal* (blog), Sept. 18, 2007, at http://krugman.blogs.nytimes.com/2007/09/ 18/introducing-this-blog/.

14. Larry Bartels, *Unequal Democracy: The Political Economy of the New Gilded Age* (Princeton, NJ: Princeton University Press, 2008), ix, 30–43. See especially Table 2.1 on p. 32 and Table 2.2 on p. 37.

15. Bryce Harlow, "Business and the Federal Government," remarks to the 1962 annual management conference of the Merchants and Manufacturers Association in Palm Springs, Oct. 1962, in Bryce N. Harlow Collection at the Carl Albert Center, University of Oklahoma, Norman, OK. This speech and all others cited hereafter are (unless otherwise indicated) online at http://www.ou.edu/special/albertctr/archives/HarlowInventory/ harlowbox.htm. Accessed on Nov. 2, 2011.

16. "About the Foundation," Web page for the Bryce Harlow Foundation, at http://www.bryceharlow.org/aboutf/index.cfm. Accessed on Nov. 2, 2011. Harlow's son Larry assured me (interview, Aug. 12, 2011) that although his father "was proud of what he accomplished at Procter & Gamble, and he was proud of the company, too," Bryce Harlow derived "his greatest satisfaction in life . . . serving the president." The foundation was created (with Harlow's consent) by others in Washington's lobbying community after a postretirement one-hundred-dollar-a-plate tribute dinner in Harlow's honor left behind an unexpected surplus. Still, it's an odd way to remember a man who, among other accomplishments, played a key role in the selection of Gerald Ford as Nixon's vice president, a decision that ultimately amounted to choosing the next president.

17. "Advocacy" is a Washington euphemism for "corporate lobbying." In his memoirs, Kissinger described Harlow as "a man not of soaring imagination but of encompassing prudence" (*Years of Upheaval*, 1982) and, more generously, as "one of the most respected figures in the permanent Washington establishment," someone who "often advised me on how to navigate the shoals of high-level politics" (*Years of Renewal*, 1999). Harlow learned a lesson or two from Kissinger as well. Taking a vacation while serving as Nixon's congressional liaison, Harlow returned to find that Kissinger and Chief of Staff Bob Haldeman had appropriated the much-coveted private bathroom off his West Wing office by walling up the entrance and creating a new one off a hallway leading to Kissinger's office. (See Burke and Thompson, *Mr. Integrity*, 184.)

18. Joel Jankowsky, interview with author, Aug. 10, 2011; Harlow, "Corporate Representation," Bryce Harlow Foundation Web site, 1984, at http://www.bryceharlow.org/resources/Corporate_Representation.pdf. Also in *Mr. Integrity*, appendix, 293.

19. George Koch interview, Bryce Harlow Foundation oral history, at http://www.bryceharlow.org/aboutbh/oral_history/Koch_George_Interview.pdf.

20. George Koch, interview with author, Aug. 11, 2011.

21. Harlow, "Business and the Federal Government"; Vogel, *Fluctuating Fortunes*, 38–53; and Harlow, "Remarks," meeting of the Better Business Bureau's Research and Education Foundation in Chicago, Aug. 30, 1966, Harlow Collection at Carl Albert Center.

22. Vogel, *Fluctuating Fortunes*, 135, 145.

23. Lewis Powell, "Confidential Memorandum: Attack on American Free-Enterprise System," memo to Eugene B. Snydor Jr. of the U.S. Chamber of Commerce, Aug. 23, 1971, Lewis F. Powell Jr. Archives, Washington & Lee

School of Law, online at http://law.wlu.edu/deptimages/Powell%20
Archives/PowellMemorandumTypescript.pdf.

24. William H. Jones, "Powell Advises Business on Politics," *Washington
Post*, Nov. 12, 1973, Powell Archives, at http://law.wlu.edu/deptimages/
Powell%20Archives/PowellSCSFChamberofCommerce.pdf.

25. Harlow, "Remarks," Business Roundtable, June 17, 1974, Harlow Collection at Carl Albert Center.

26. Harlow, untitled speech to the Grocery Manufacturers Association, Jan.
18, 1972, Harlow Collection at Carl Albert Center.

27. Harlow, "Remarks," meeting of the Better Business Bureau's Research
and Education Foundation in Chicago, Aug. 30, 1966. Harlow Collection
at Carl Albert Center.

28. William Raspberry, "Give Poor a Tax Break," *Washington Post*, June 28,
1971; and Jack Newfield, "A Populist Manifesto: The Making of a New
Majority, *New York*, July 19, 1971, 39–46; both at Powell Archives, http://
law.wlu.edu/deptimages/Powell%20Archives/PowellSpeechResearch
AOFESMemo.pdf.

29. Joel Jankowsky, interview with author, Aug 10, 2011.

8: The Fall of Detroit

General Sources

"Fordism vs. Unionism," *Time*, July 26, 1937, 13–14.

Frederick Lewis Allen, *The Big Change: America Transforms Itself: 1900–1950*
(New Brunswick, NJ: Transaction, 2007; originally published by Harper &
Brothers in 1952).

Daniel Bell, "The Treaty of Detroit," *Fortune*, July 1950, 53–55.

Thomas Geoghegan, *Which Side Are You On?: Trying to Be for Labor When It's
Flat on Its Back* (New York: Farrar, Straus, 1991).

David Halberstam, *The Reckoning* (New York: William Morrow, 1986).

Laurie Collier Hillstrom, "Labor Organizations and Reform Movements," in
The Industrial Revolution in America, vol. 9, ed. Kevin and Laurie Hillstrom (Santa Barbara, CA: ABC-CLIO, 2006), 120–21.

Irving Howe and B. J. Widick, *The UAW and Walter Reuther* (New York: Da
Capo, 1973; originally published by Random House in 1949).

Thomas Kochan, *Restoring the American Dream: A Working Families' Agenda for
America* (Cambridge, MA: MIT Press, 2005).

Martin Jay Levitt with Terry Conrow, *Confessions of a Union Buster* (New York:
Crown, 1993).

Nelson Lichtenstein, *Walter Reuther: The Most Dangerous Man in Detroit* (Urbana:

University of Illinois Press, 1997; originally published by Basic Books in 1995 under the title *The Most Dangerous Man in Detroit: Walter Reuther and the Fate of American Labor*).

Richard Reeves, *President Kennedy: Profile of Power* (New York: Simon & Schuster, 1993).

Judith Stein, *Pivotal Decade: How the United States Traded Factories for Finance in the Seventies* (New Haven: Yale University Press, 2010).

1. The 2011 Walmart corporate financial fact sheet is at walmartstores.com/ download/2230.pdf; Kari Lydersen, "Wal-Martyrs," *In These Times*, May 15, 2000, at http://www.inthesetimes.com/issue/24/12/lydersen2412. html; "Wal-Mart to Eliminate Some Meat-Cutters," *Washington Post*, Mar. 4, 2000, reprinted in *Los Angeles Times* at http://articles.latimes.com/ 2000/mar/04/business/fi-5280; Carol Pier, Carly Tubbs, et al., *Discounting Rights: Wal-Mart's Violation of U.S. Workers' Right to Freedom of Association* (New York: Human Rights Watch, 2007), 139–40; *United Food and Commercial Workers v. National Labor Relations Board*, decision by U.S. Court of Appeals for the District of Columbia No. 06-1358, Mar. 14, 2008, at http://www.cadc.uscourts.gov/internet/opinions.nsf/359DC350 B643DA708525744000470BBD/$file/06-1358a.pdf.

2. Arindrajit Dube and Steve Wertheim, "Wal-Mart and Job Equality— What Do We Know, and Should We Care?" Center for American Progress report, October 2005, 3–4; Steven Greenhouse, "At a Small Shop in Colorado, Wal-Mart Beats a Union Once More," *New York Times*, Feb. 26, 2005, at http://www.nytimes.com/2005/02/26/politics/26walmart .html?fta=y&pagewanted=print&position=; Christopher Hayes, "Symbol of the System," *In These Times*, Nov. 6, 2005, at http://www.inthese-times.com/article/2377/; Pier, Tubbs, et al., *Discounting Rights*, 191–202; and Robert Greenwald, *Wal-Mart: The High Cost of Low Price*, Brave New Films, 2005.

3. Gerald Mayer, "Union Membership Trends in the United States" (Washington: Congressional Research Service, 2004), 22, Table A1; "Union Members: 2010," U.S. Bureau of Labor Statistics press release, Jan. 21, 2011, at http://www.bls.gov/news.release/union2.nro.htm; David Madland, Karla Walter, and Nick Bunker, "Unions Make the Middle Class" (Washington: Center for American Progress, 2011), 2.

4. Mayer, "Union Membership Trends," 6; David Card, Thomas Lemieux, and W. Craig Riddell, "Unions and Wage Inequality," *Journal of Labor Research* 25, no. 4 (Fall 2004), 519; and Richard Freeman, "Unionism and the Dispersion of Wages," *Industrial and Labor Relations Review* 34, no. 1 (Oct. 1980), 3–23.

5. Richard Freeman, "What Can We Learn from NRLA to Create Labor Law for the 21st Century?," paper presented at George Washington University conference on the National Labor Relations Act at fifty, Oct. 28, 2010, 3; David Card, "The Effect of Unions on Wage Inequality in the U.S. Labor Market," *Industrial and Labor Relations Review* 54, no. 2 (Jan. 2001), 311; Richard Freeman, *America Works: Critical Thoughts on the Exceptional U.S. Labor Market* (New York: Russell Sage Foundation, 2007), 50; Bruce Western and Jake Rosenfeld, "Unions, Norms, and the Rise in U.S. Wage Inequality," *American Sociological Review* 76, no. 4 (Aug. 2011), 532–33. As we saw in chapter 5, Goldin and Katz would call one third a lowball estimate of the education premium's impact on income inequality. They put it at 60 percent. I won't attempt to referee. Education and the decline of labor are both significant factors.

6. Levy and Temin, "Inequality and Institutions" (see chapter 1, note 31), 20–21; and "The Presidency: Momentous Meeting," *Time*, Nov. 12, 1945, at http://www.time.com/time/magazine/article/0,9171,792482-1, 00.html. The U.S. Chamber of Commerce's current position on unions is quite different from what it was in 1945. A recent white paper reads: "Unions are not the answer to increasing prosperity for Americans workers or the economy." See "Is Unionization the Ticket to the Middle Class?" (Washington: U.S. Chamber of Commerce, 2008), 8, at http://www.uschamber.com/sites/default/files/issues/labor/files/Chap%202%20-%20Unionization%20Not%20Ticket%20to%20Middle%20Class.pdf. Accessed on Nov. 3, 2011.

7. Charlie Wilson is best remembered as the Eisenhower-era defense secretary who said, at his confirmation hearing, "What's good for General Motors is good for the country." But Wilson never said that. What he said was: "I cannot conceive of [a decision I'd make as defense secretary that would harm General Motors] because for years I thought what was good for the country was good for General Motors and vice versa." The correct version was less pithy and arrogant-sounding, but it was also more damning because Wilson was in effect pledging never, as defense secretary, to make any decision that might hurt GM.

8. Everybody remembers the 1973 oil embargo and the clout enjoyed by the newly potent OPEC cartel, but few people remember the accompanying food shock of that same year, which saw a 20 percent increase in U.S. food prices. The latter was caused partly by rising food consumption in more prosperous economies abroad and partly by a deliberate policy by the Nixon administration to reduce domestic agricultural production (and thereby increase food prices) to court the farm vote in 1972.

9. Frank Levy, interview with author, Apr. 22, 2011.

10. The disruptive oil shocks of the 1970s—in 1973 and 1974 alone oil prices quadrupled—likely played a significant role.

11. William J. Baumol and Alan S. Blinder, *Macroeconomics: Principles and Policy* (Mason, OH: South-Western College Publishing, 2010), 145; Paul Krugman and Robin Wells, *Macroeconomics* (New York: Worth, 2009), 233; Susan Fleck, John Glaser, and Shawn Sprague, "The Compensation-Productivity Gap: A Visual Essay," *Monthly Labor Review*, Jan. 2011, 57–69.

12. Barry T. Hirsch, "Sluggish Institutions in a Dynamic World: Can Unions and Industrial Competition Coexist?" Discussion Paper 2930 (Bonn: Institute for the Study of Labor, 2007), at http://www2.gsu.edu/~ecobth/IZA _Unions&Competition_dp2930.pdf.

13. OECD chart on trade union density, 1960–2010, at http://www.oecd.org/ LongAbstract/0,3425,en_2649_33927_39891562_1_1_1_1,00.html; Freeman, *America Works*, 37.

14. Joseph Shister, "The Impact of the Taft-Hartley Act on Union Strength and Collective Bargaining," *Industrial and Labor Relations Review* 11, no. 3 (Apr. 1958), 339–51; Mayer, "Union Membership Trends," 22, Table A1.

15. This is a sentence I've had to resist writing multiple times throughout this book. It's particularly applicable to changes in financial regulation discussed in chapter 9.

16. Steven E. Abraham, "How the Taft-Hartley Act Hindered Unions," *Hofstra Labor Law Journal* 12, no. 1 (Fall 1991), 1–37. I rely heavily on Abraham's article in my analysis here. This is not a topic that interested social scientists much after, say, 1980, and Abraham's analysis, which incorporates previous analyses, is admirably clear and comprehensive.

17. Ibid., 9.

18. There were 112 decertification elections in 1950, 237 in 1960, and 301 in 1970. When unions entered the crisis years of the late 1970s and early 1980s, decertification elections spiked. Between 1970 and 1980 they tripled to 902, and during the first half of the 1980s decertification elections averaged 882 per year. (NLRB annual reports at http://www.nlrb. gov/annual-reports.)

19. Abraham, "Taft-Hartley," 16.

20. NLRB annual reports.

21. Freeman, "What Can We Learn from the NRLA?," 3.

22. Ironic, given that Reagan was himself a onetime union president (of the Screen Actors Guild). In those days he was an Americans for Democratic Action–style liberal.

23. Ron Blackwell, interview with author, Apr. 20, 2011.

24. Melvyn Dubofsky, *The State and Labor in Modern America* (Charlotte: University of North Carolina Press, 1994), xiii; Henry S. Farber and Bruce Western, "Round Up the Usual Suspects: The Decline of Unions in the Private Sector, 1973–1998," Working Paper 437 (Princeton, NJ: Princeton University, Industrial Relations Section, 2000), 16–18.

25. Jared Bernstein and Isaac Shapiro, "Buying Power of Minimum Wage at 51-Year Low" (Washington: Economic Policy Institute, 2006), at http://epi.3cdn.net/68c6d93de23ecfe692_esm6bhzzw.pdf.

26. See David Autor, Alan Manning, and Christopher L. Smith, "The Contribution of the Minimum Wage to U.S. Wage Inequality over Three Decades: A Reassessment," Finance and Economics Discussion Series (Washington: Federal Reserve Board, 2010); and David S. Lee, "Wage Inequality in the United States During the 1980s: Rising Dispersion or Falling Minimum Wage?" *Quarterly Journal of Economics* 114, no. 3 (Aug. 1999), 977–1023.

9: Rise of the Stinking Rich

General Sources

Ken Auletta, *Greed and Glory on Wall Street: The Fall of the House of Lehman* (New York: Random House, 1985).

Robert Frank, *Richistan: A Journey Through the American Wealth Boom and the Lives of the New Rich* (New York: Crown, 2007).

Robert H. Frank and Philip J. Cook, *The Winner-Take-All Society. Why the Few at the Top Get So Much More Than the Rest of Us* (New York: Penguin, 1996; originally published by the Free Press, 1995).

Charles R. Geisst, *Wall Street: A History* (New York: Oxford University Press, 1997).

Daniel Henninger, "The Obama Rosetta Stone," *Wall Street Journal*, Mar. 12, 2009, at http://online.wsj.com/article/SB123681860305802821.html.

Karen Ho, *Liquidated: An Ethnography of Wall Street* (Durham, NC.: Duke University Press, 2009).

"How Bill Clinton Helped Boost CEO Pay," *Businessweek*, Nov. 27, 2006, at http://www.businessweek.com/magazine/content/06_48/b4011079.htm.

Rakesh Khurana, *Searching for a Corporate Savior: The Irrational Quest for Charismatic CEOs* (Princeton, NJ: Princeton University Press, 2002).

Paul Krugman, *The Conscience of a Liberal* (New York: W. W. Norton, 2007).

Jeff Madrick, *The Age of Greed: The Triumph of Finance and the Decline of America, 1970 to the Present* (New York: Knopf, 2011).

James Sterngold, "Too Far, Too Fast: Salomon Brothers' John Gutfreund," *New York Times Magazine,* Jan. 10, 1988, at http://www.nytimes.com/1988/01/10/magazine/too-far-too-fast-salomon-brothers-john-gutfreund.html?pagewanted=all&src=pm.

1. Thomas Piketty and Emmanuel Saez, "Income Inequality in the United States, 1913–1998," *Quarterly Journal of Economics* 118, no. 1 (Feb. 2003), 1–39; Saez, "Striking It Richer: The Evolution of Top Incomes in the United States," *Pathways* (Palo Alto, CA: Stanford Center for the Study of Poverty and Inequality, 2008), 6–7, updated at http://elsa.berkeley.edu/~saez/saez-UStopincomes-2008.pdf; Paul Krugman, "On Tracking Inequality," *The Conscience of a Liberal* (blog), Sept. 19, 2006, at http://krugman.blogs.nytimes.com/2006/09/19/on-tracking-inequality/.

2. Between 1913, when the income tax was introduced, and 1916 even many in the top decile were excused from having to file. Piketty and Saez therefore confined their analysis for this brief period to filers within the top 1 percent.

3. Irving Kristol, "Some Personal Reflections on Economic Well-Being and Income Distribution," in *The American Economy in Transition,* ed. Martin Feldstein (Chicago: University of Chicago Press, 1980), 484. Note the publication date. Kristol's claim was even less persuasive in 1980, when $100,000 was the equivalent of $274,000 in current dollars. Were he still alive, Kristol might answer that my A-student analogy overlooks the contemporary epidemic of grade inflation. Point taken.

4. All calculations of fractile thresholds are from WTID (World Top Incomes Database; see Introduction, note 6), which when this book went to press was current through 2008, and include capital gains. The 2007–09 recession drove the thresholds down between 2007 and 2008, and almost certainly they came down a bit further in 2009, but those numbers are not yet available. Probably they rebounded with the economic recovery (such as it was) in 2010 and 2011. It should by now be clear, from the many citations here, that much of this book couldn't have been written without this fantastically useful Web tool.

5. SOI Tax Stats, Historical Table 3, IRS Web page at http://www.irs.gov/taxstats/article/0,,id=175800,00.html. The figure is for 2009.

6. Another difference—there's no polite way to say this—is that the economics profession takes Piketty and Saez much more seriously than it ever took Laffer. As the journalist Jonathan Chait put it, "Laffer believed it was possible to simultaneously expand the economy and tamp down inflation by cutting taxes, especially the high tax rates faced by upper-

income earners. Respectable economists—not least among them conservative ones—considered this laughable." See Jonathan Chait, *The Big Con: The True Story of How Washington Got Hoodwinked and Hijacked by Crackpot Economics* (Boston: Houghton Mifflin, 2007), 14.

7. All these calculations, and the ones that follow, are from the WTID, include capital gains, and are current through 2008.

8. Emmanuel Saez, interview with author, Aug. 18, 2010.

9. Anthony B. Atkinson, Thomas Piketty, and Emmanuel Saez, "Top Incomes in the Long Run of History," *Journal of Economic Literature* 49, no. 1 (Mar. 2011), 45–47, Tables 6–8. The paper's authors note that their data for the Netherlands, Germany, and Switzerland went only through the late 1990s and that there's a "reasonable presumption" that when twenty-first-century data become available an upward trend will be observed there, too.

10. For consistency, numbers in this international comparison excluded capital gains. Income share for the U.S. top 1 percent is 21 percent if you include capital gains and 18 percent if you exclude them. But that's as of 2008, the most recent year for which U.S. data are available. The study, remember, goes up only through 2005, when income share for the U.S. top 1 percent was 17 percent, excluding capital gains.

11. The study goes through 2005, but the actual end point dates for these nine countries varied, depending on data availability at the time of the study. Three were ten years distant or more: India (1999), Canada (2000), and Australia (2002). Of these three, only Canada seemed (when last heard from) within striking range of the United States' 18 percent income share.

12. These figures don't include capital gains. Despite my usual preference to include capital gains, I use these, because later I will compare 2005 percentages to 1979 percentages. The study, alas, did not provide multiyear data that included capital gains. If you include capital gains for 2004—the paper doesn't show these figures for 2005—the percentages are only slightly different: 41 percent for nonfinancial executives, 18 percent for financiers, 6 percent for lawyers, and 4 percent for doctors. Jon Bakija, Adam Cole, and Bradley T. Heim, "Jobs and Income Growth of Top Earners and the Causes of Changing Income Inequality: Evidence from U.S. Tax Return Data," Williams College Economics Department Working Paper No. 2010-24 (Nov. 2010), 49–51, Tables 1–3. Membership in the somewhat less-exclusive top 1 percent had fewer nonfinancial executives (31 percent), more doctors (16 percent), fewer financiers (14 percent), and slightly more lawyers (8 percent).

13. Pradnya Joshi, "We Knew They Got Raises. But This?," *New York Times*, July 2, 2011, at http://www.nytimes.com/2011/07/03/business/03pay .html?_r=2; "Usual Weekly Earnings of Wage and Salary Workers Fourth Quarter 2010," U.S. Bureau of Labor Statistics press release, Jan. 20, 2011, at http://www.bls.gov/news.release/archives/wkyeng_01202011.pdf; "North Haven Voters Have Until 8 P.M. to Cast Ballot on Budget," *New Haven Register*, May 17, 2011, at http://www.newhavenregister.com/articles/2011/ 05/17/news/metro/doc4dd2e6e1349b6751514042.txt.

14. By 2009 the recession had driven CEO pay down to 185 times that of the average worker. See Hay Group report, "How Chief Executives Are Paid: Rewards in the Largest Companies in Europe and the US," Jan. 2008, 4, at http://www.haygroup.com/downloads/uk/How_chief_ executives_are_paid_30.11.07.pdf; Carola Frydman and Raven E. Saks, "Historical Trends in Executive Compensation, 1963–2003," Working Paper, Nov. 15, 2005, at http://faculty.chicagobooth.edu/workshops/ AppliedEcon/archive/pdf/FrydmanSecondPaper.pdf; and Lawrence Mishel, "CEO-to-Worker Pay Imbalance Grows" (Washington: Economic Policy Institute, 2006) at http://www.epi.org/publication/web-features_snapshots_20060621/.

15. A study by James Ang and Gregory Nagel, professor and associate professor of business at Florida State and Mississippi State, respectively, examined CEO hires between 1986 and 2005 and found that corporations that promoted the top boss from within experienced 24 percent greater financial performance than corporations that hired the top boss from outside. See James S. Ang and Gregory L. Nagel, "Outside and Inside Hired CEOs: A Performance Surprise," working paper, at http://69.175.2.130/~ finman/Reno/Papers/Outside_and_Inside_Hired_CEOs-A_Financial_ Surprise_FMA-Turin-blind.pdf.pdf.

16. Nell Minow, interview with author, April 14, 2011.

17. Suman Banerjee, Vladimir Gatchev, and Thomas Noe, "Doom or Gloom? CEO Stock Options After Enron," working paper, Jan. 2008, 37, Table 1; Nell Minow interview; Franklin R. Edwards, "U.S. Corporate Governance: What Went Wrong and Can It Be Fixed?," paper for B.I.S. and Federal Reserve Bank of Chicago conference, Oct. 30–Nov. 1 2003, 5; Brian J. Hall and Kevin Murphy, "Stock Options for Undiversified Executives," Working Paper 8052 (Cambridge, MA: NBER, 2000), 43, Figure 3; Donald P. Delves, *Stock Options and the New Rules of Corporate Accountability: Measuring, Managing, and Rewarding Executive Performance* (New York: McGraw-Hill, 2004), 47–49; "Congress and the Accounting Wars," Web page for PBS *Frontline* documentary, Hedrick Smith interview with Ar-

thur Levitt, March 12, 2002, at http://www.pbs.org/wgbh/pages/front
line/shows/regulation/interviews/levitt.html.

18. Alexandra Higgins, "The Effect of Compensation Consultants: A Study
of Market Share and Compensation Policy Advice" (New York: Corporate
Library, Oct. 2007), 4–5 and 12–13; Roel C. Campos, "Remarks Before
the 2007 Summit on Executive Compensation," Jan. 23, 2007, at http://
www.sec.gov/news/speech/2007/spch012307rcc.htm; Nell Minow interview; Warren Buffett, Berkshire Hathaway Chairman's Letter, Feb. 28,
2007, 20, at http://www.berkshirehathaway.com/letters/2006ltr.pdf.

19. Bakija, Cole, and Heim, "Jobs and Income Growth of Top Earners," 51,
Table 3.

20. Simon Johnson and James Kwak, 13 Bankers: The Wall Street Takeover and
the Next Financial Meltdown (New York: Vintage, 2011; originally published by Pantheon in 2010), 85–86.

21. Justin Lahart, "Has the Financial Industry's Heyday Come and Gone?,"
Wall Street Journal, Apr. 28, 2008, at http://online.wsj.com/article/
SB120933096635747945.html; Christine Hauser, "G.E. Posts Earnings
That Exceed Forecasts and Raises Dividend," New York Times, Apr. 21,
2011, at http://www.nytimes.com/2011/04/22/business/22electric.html?_
r=2; David Welch, "G.M.'s Dwindling Options," Businessweek, Mar. 16,
2006, at http://www.businessweek.com/autos/content/mar2006/
bw20060316_306932.htm; Kathleen Madigan, "Like the Phoenix, U.S.
Finance Profits Soar," Real Time Economics (blog), Wall Street Journal, Mar.
25, 2011, at http://blogs.wsj.com/economics/2011/03/25/like-the-phoenix-u
-s-finance-profits-soar/; Sameer Khatiwada, "Did the Financial Sector
Profit at the Expense of the Rest of the Economy? Evidence from the
United States," Discussion Paper no. 206, International Institute for Labor
Studies, Jan. 1, 2010, 2, at http://digitalcommons.ilr.cornell.edu/cgi/view
content.cgi?article=1101&context=intl.

22. "Business Grads Look Beyond Wall Street," Dealbook (blog), Apr. 20, 2009,
at http://dealbook.nytimes.com/2009/04/20/business-grads-looking-be-
yond-wall-street/.

23. Yves-Andre Istel, interview with author, May 26, 2011.

24. Robert H. Frank and Philip J. Cook, The Winner-Take-All Society: Why the
Few at the Top Get So Much More Than the Rest of Us (New York: Penguin,
1996; originally published by Free Press in 1995), 48.

25. The bankers' "last hurrah," according to the financial journalists Beth-
any McLean and Joe Nocera, was the Internet bubble of the late 1990s.
See Bethany McLean and Joe Nocera, All the Devils Are Here: The Hidden
History of the Financial Crisis (New York: Penguin, 2010), p. 154.

26. Alan D. Morrison and William J. Wilhelm Jr., "The Demise of Investment-Banking Partnerships: Theory and Evidence," working paper, Dec. 2005, 1, at http://www.finance.uni-frankfurt.de/master/brown/98.pdf.

27. Daniel Alpert, e-mail to the author, Nov. 9, 2011.

28. McLean and Nocera, *All the Devils*, 151–52.

29. Calvin Trillin, "Wall Street Smarts," *New York Times*, Oct. 13, 2009, at http://www.nytimes.com/2009/10/14/opinion/14trillin.html: and Rose, *Rebound*, 2n.

30. Thomas Philippon and Ariell Reshef, "Wages and Human Capital in the U.S. Financial Industry: 1909–2006," Working Paper 14644 (Cambridge, MA: NBER, 2009), 29–31.

31. Sherwin Rosen, "The Economics of Superstars," *American Economic Review* 71, no. 5 (Dec. 1981), 845–58. Mickey Kaus, in *The End of Equality*, called it "the Hollywood effect."

32. Frank and Cook argue that corporate boards' desire to hire known-quantity chief executives from outside the company, described earlier in this chapter, has made the market for CEOs winner-take-all as well.

10: Why It Matters

General Sources

Arthur C. Brooks, *The Battle: How the Fight Between Free Enterprise and Government Will Shape America's Future* (New York: Basic Books, 2010).

Matthew Continetti, "About Inequality," *Weekly Standard*, Nov. 14, 2011, at http://www.weeklystandard.com/articles/about-inequality_607779.html?page=1.

Tyler Cowen, *The Great Stagnation: How America Ate All the Low-Hanging Fruit of Modern History, Got Sick, and Will (Eventually) Feel Better* (New York: Dutton, 2011).

———— "The Inequality That Matters," *American Interest* 6, no. 3 (Jan.–Feb. 2011), at http://www.the-american-interest.com/article.cfm?piece=907.

Barbara Ehrenreich, *Nickel and Dimed: On (Not) Getting By in America* (New York: Metropolitan Books, 2001).

Mickey Kaus, *The End of Equality* (New York: Basic Books, 1992).

Dick Reavis, *Catching Out: The Secret World of Day Laborers* (New York: Simon & Schuster, 2010).

Jonathan Rowe, "The Vanishing Commons," in *Inequality Matters: The Growing Economic Divide in America and Its Poisonous Consequences*, ed. James Lardner and David A. Smith (New York: New Press, 2005).

1. Finis Welch, "In Defense of Inequality," *American Economic Review* 89,

no. 2 (May 1999), 1–17; Paul Solman, "Does U.S. Economic Inequality Have a Good Side?," interview with Richard Epstein, PBS *NewsHour*, Oct. 26, 2011, at http://www.pbs.org/newshour/bb/business/july-dec11/mak ingsense_10-26.html; Thomas Garrett, "U.S. Income Inequality: It's Not So Bad," *Inside the Vault* 14, no. 1 (Spring 2010), 3.

2. By the candidate Rick Santorum. In an Oct. 18, 2011, debate in Las Vegas, Santorum said, "Believe it or not, studies have been done that show that in Western Europe, people at the lower parts of the income scale actually have a better mobility going up the ladder now than in America. And I believe that's because we've lost our manufacturing base." See CNN transcript at http://archives.cnn.com/TRANSCRIPTS/1110/18/se.05 .html. Santorum also mentioned the issue in an Oct. 11 debate in Hanover, NH. See *Time* transcript at http://thepage.time.com/2011/10/11/ complete-transcript-of-hanover-economic-debate/.

3. Paul Ryan, "Saving the American Idea: Rejecting Fear, Envy, and the Politics of Division," speech to the Heritage Foundation, Oct. 26, 2011, at http://blog.heritage.org/2011/10/26/video-rep-paul-ryan-on-saving-the -american-idea/. A number of commentators, including Garrett, cite a 2007 Treasury Department study to argue that U.S. upward mobility is in fact quite robust. It found that about half of those in the bottom income quintile in 1996 moved to a higher quintile by 2005. But as explained in chapter 2, this isn't a good way to measure income mobility, because people's incomes follow a predictable pattern over time: The more work experience you acquire, the better you tend to get paid. That isn't mobility. It's life. A better measure—one closer to the way most of us actually think about upward mobility—is to compare one generation's relative position in the income distribution with the next generation's. Did the barber's son become a dentist, or did he become a janitor? It's here that the United States now falls behind most of western Europe. See "Income Mobility in the U.S. from 1996 to 2005," U.S. Department of the Treasury, Nov. 13, 2007, at http://www.treasury.gov/ resource-center/tax-policy/Documents/incomemobilitystudy03-08re vise.pdf.

4. LaDonna Pavetti and Liz Schott, "TANF's Inadequate Response to Recession Highlights Weakness of Block-Grant Structure," report, Center on Budget and Policy Priorities, July 14, 2011, at http://www.cbpp.org/ cms/index.cfm?fa=view&id=3534. See also Jason DeParle, "Welfare Aid Isn't Growing as Economy Drops Off," *New York Times*, Feb. 1, 2009, at http://www.nytimes.com/2009/02/02/us/02welfare.html? pagewanted=all.

5. Will Wilkinson, "Thinking Clearly About Economic Inequality," Policy Analysis 640 (Washington: Cato Institute, 2009), at http://www.cato .org/pubs/pas/pa640.pdf; and Bruce D. Meyer and James X. Sullivan, "The Material Well-Being of the Poor and Middle Class Since 1980," Working Paper 2011-04, Oct. 25, 2011, at http://www.aei.org/files/2011/ 10/25/Material-Well-Being-Poor-Middle-Class.pdf.

6. Louise Story, "Income Inequality and Financial Crises," *New York Times*, Aug. 21, 2010, at http://www.nytimes.com/2010/08/22/weekinreview/ 22story.html; Paul Krugman, "Inequality and Crises: Coincidence or Causation?," lecture slides, 2010, at https://webspace.princeton.edu/ users/piirs/pdf/krugman_inequality_crises.pdf.

7. Raghuram G. Rajan, *Fault Lines: How Hidden Fractures Still Threaten the World Economy* (Princeton, NJ: Princeton University Press, 2010), 42–44; Christopher Brown, "Does Income Distribution Matter for Effective Demand? Evidence from the United States," *Review of Political Economy* 16, no. 3 (July 2004), 303–05; Daniel Alpert, "Macroeconomic Challenges to the U.S. Middle Class," PowerPoint presentation at New America Foundation retreat, Apr. 30, 2011. See also Daniel Alpert, Robert Hockett, and Nouriel Roubini, "The Way Forward: Moving from the Post-Bubble, Post-Bust Economy to Renewed Growth and Competitiveness," New America Foundation, Oct. 2011, at http://growth.newamerica.net/sites/newamerica.net/files/pol icydocs/NAF—The_Way_Forward—Alpert_Hockett_Roubini.pdf.

8. A much-cited 2009 study by Christian Broda and John Romalis at the University of Chicago's Booth School of Business examined differing consumption patterns for the affluent and nonaffluent and found that "poorer households consume fewer food products than richer households." This fact, oddly, was deployed to buttress an argument for worrying less about income inequality, not more. The idea was that "non-durable inflation for poorer households has been substantially lower than for richer households." Rough translation: It's cheaper to be poor than to be rich. Well, duh. The authors didn't appear to consider how being poor got to be such a bargain in the first place. Might it be because . . . poor people don't have the money to buy expensive stuff? The study didn't include automobiles (they're a durable good), health insurance, or higher education, but I'm going to guess that these items, too, are consumed much less by lower-income households than by higher-income households. By the perverse logic of this study, that means their steep price increases are a worry only for the rich. (In fairness, I think Broda and Romalis were out mainly to demonstrate that Walmart and cheap Chinese imports help poor people buy certain necessities of life more cheaply than they could before. No ar-

gument there, but two other parts of this bargain are the low wages Walmart provides its own employees (see chapter 8) and the job losses for less-skilled U.S. workers attributable to trade with China (see chapter 6). See Christian Broda and John Romalis, "The Welfare Implications of Rising Price Dispersion," working paper, July 4, 2009, at http://faculty.chicagobooth.edu/john.romalis/research/Draft_v7.pdf.

9. *Growing Unequal?* (see Introduction, note 2), 27; and *World Health Report 2000* (Geneva: World Health Organization, 2000), Annex Table 1, 152. Since the mid-1980s income inequality has declined not only in France but also in Austria, Greece, Ireland, Spain, and Turkey, as measured by the Gini coefficient.

10. Edward J. Blakely and Mary Gail Synder, *Fortress America: Gated Communities in the United States* (Washington: Brookings Institution, 1997), 3, 18–19; and Sara Clemence, "Most Expensive Gated Communities in America 2004," *Forbes* Web site (Nov. 19, 2004), at http://www.forbes.com/2004/11/19/cx_sc_1119home.html.

11. Michael Hout, "Money and Morale: What Growing Inequality Is Doing to Americans' Views of Themselves and Others," Survey Research Center Working Paper (Berkeley: University of California, 2003), at http://ucdata.berkeley.edu/rsfcensus/papers/Morale_Working_Paper.pdf.

12. Sara J. Solnick and David Hemenway, "Is More Always Better? A Survey on Positional Concerns," *Journal of Economic Behavior & Organization* 37, no. 3 (Nov. 30, 1998), 373–83.

13. Alan Blinder, "Our Dickensian Economy," *Wall Street Journal*, Dec. 17, 2010, at http://online.wsj.com/article/SB10001424052748704828104576022002280730440.html?mod=googlenews_wsj.

14. Ian Dew-Becker and Robert J. Gordon, "Where Did the Productivity Growth Go? Inflation Dynamics and the Distribution of Income," Working Paper 11842 (Cambridge, MA: NBER, 2005).

15. The economist Susan Houseman of the Upjohn Institute, a Michigan-based nonprofit, has been arguing for some time that recent productivity increases were overstated for technical reasons traceable to the federal Bureau of Economic Analysis's inability to properly account for the full cost saving associated with offshoring. In a 2007 *Businessweek* cover story based on Houseman's research, Michael Mandel estimated that when you corrected for the resultant "phantom GDP," the unusually high productivity growth of the aughts was more in line with the lower productivity growth of the 1980s. The Bureau of Economic Analysis disputed this, but three economists at the Federal Reserve Board recently collaborated on a paper with Houseman that upheld her earlier findings. Assuming

Houseman is correct, phantom GDP still doesn't account for all of the gap between productivity increases and wage increases. See Michael Mandel, "The Real Cost of Offshoring," *Businessweek,* June 18, 2007, at http://www.businessweek.com/magazine/content/07_25/b4039001.htm; "Is Offshoring Causing GDP and Productivity Growth to Be Overstated?" (Washington: U.S. Bureau of Labor Statistics, 2007) at http://www.bea.gov/faq/index.cfm?faq_id=447&searchQuery=&start=140&cat_id=0; and Susan Houseman, Christopher Kurz, Paul A. Lengermann, and Benjamin J. Mandel, "Offshoring Bias in U.S. Manfacturing," *Journal of Economic Perspectives* 25, no. 2 (2011), 111–32.

16. Harold Meyerson, "Corporate America's Chokehold on Wages," *Washington Post,* July 19, 2011, at http://www.washingtonpost.com/opinions/corporate-americas-chokehold-on-wages/2011/07/19/gIQAL2ieOI_story.html; Michael Cembalest, "Eye on the Market," JP Morgan newsletter, July 11, 2011, at http://www.investorvillage.com/uploads/44821/files/07-11-11_-_EOTM_-_Twilight_of_the_Gods__PWM_.pdf; Justin Fox, "The Real Story Behind Those 'Record' Corporate Profits," *HBR Blog Network,* Nov. 24, 2010, at http://blogs.hbr.org/fox/2010/11/the-real-story-behind-those-re.html; Edward N. Wolff, "Recent Trends in Household Wealth in the United States: Rising Debt and the Middle-Class Squeeze," Working Paper No. 589, Levy Economics Institute (Annandale-on-Hudson, NY: Bard College, 2010), at http://www.levyinstitute.org/pubs/wp_589.pdf. See also Wolff, *Top Heavy: The Increasing Inequality of Wealth in America and What Can Be Done About It* (New York: New Press, 2002; originally published in 1996). Wealth distribution in the United States is much more skewed than income distribution. I don't discuss wealth in this book because for all practical purposes nobody in America but the rich has any. The housing crash was a catastrophe for the middle class because of the debt they took on, not because of the wealth that they lost. That wealth was always a mirage. Like Willford King and the Progressives of the early twentieth century, I believe the industrial revolution made income a much better indicator than wealth of economic well-being (or lack thereof).

17. Reynolds argued that when Piketty and Saez stated income share for the top 1 percent, or 0.1 percent, or 0.001 percent, the ratio was skewed by a too-high numerator and a too-low denominator. The numerator was too high, Reynolds wrote, because it didn't take into account the fact that after passage of the 1986 income-tax reform law rich people took advantage of the lower top marginal rate by reporting as personal income money that they'd previously "concealed, deferred,

or reported on *corporate* income tax returns." For example, businesses that once reported as "C-corporations" and therefore filed corporate returns switched to reporting as "S-corporations" and therefore filed personal returns. When you drop the top marginal tax rate, Reynolds wrote, reported income increases because rich people have less incentive to shelter their money. The denominator was too low, Reynolds argued, because the Great Divergence coincided with the advent of tax-favored 401(k)s; the income socked away into these accounts no longer appeared on tax returns.

In reply, Piketty and Saez pointed out that in addition to calculating personal income they had calculated personal income plus capital gains and that both calculations showed a doubling of income between 1980 and 2004. (Virtually all of the Piketty-Saez data that I use in this book include capital gains income.) Piketty and Saez also wrote that any increase in reported income resulting from a drop in the top marginal rate would have been short-term and therefore wouldn't have had much impact on the thirty-year trend. As for the denominator being too small, Piketty and Saez pointed out that when you draw money out of your 401(k), that gets reported on your income tax returns, so 401(k)s are "implicitly included in our income measure." Before the advent of 401(k)s, they added, workers had defined-benefit plans that were similarly unreported on income tax returns until the money was withdrawn during retirement.

See Alan Reynolds, "Has U.S. Income Inequality *Really* Increased?," Policy Analysis No. 586 (Washington: Cato Institute, 2007), at http://www.cato.org/pubs/pas/pa586.pdf; Reynolds, "Taxes and the Top Percentile Myth," *Wall Street Journal*, Dec. 23, 2010, at http://online.wsj.com/article/SB10001424052748703581204576033861522959234.html; "Response to Alan Reynolds by Thomas Piketty and Emmanuel Saez" (includes text of earlier Reynolds *WSJ* article, "The Top 1 % . . . of What?"), at http://elsa.berkeley.edu/~saez/answer-WSJreynolds.pdf; and Gary Burtless, "Comments on 'Has U.S. Income Inequality Really Increased'" (Washington: Brookings Institution, 2007), at http://www.brookings.edu/~/media/Files/rc/papers/2007/0111useconomics_burtless/20070111.pdf.

11: What to Do

General Sources

Dean Baker, "Trade and Inequality: The Role of Economists," paper delivered at the conference of the Association for Social Economics, New Orleans, Jan. 3, 2008.

Bill Bishop, *The Big Sort: Why the Clustering of Like-Minded America Is Tearing Us Apart* (Boston: Houghton Mifflin, 2008).

Alan Greenspan, *The Age of Turbulence: Adventures in a New World* (New York: Penguin, 2007).

June Hopkins, *Harry Hopkins: Sudden Hero, Brash Reformer* (New York: Palgrave Macmillan, 1999).

Richard Kahlenberg, "Labor Organizing as a Civil Right," *American Prospect*, Dec. 19, 2001, at http://prospect.org/article/labor-organizing-civil-right.

Sara Mosle, "Steve Brill's Report Card on School Reform," *New York Times*, Aug. 18, 2001, at http://www.nytimes.com/2011/08/21/books/review/class-warfare-by-steven-brill-book-review.html?_r=3&pagewanted=1.

A Nation at Risk: The Imperative for Educational Reform, National Commission on Excellence in Education (Washington: Education Department, 1983).

Raghuram G. Rajan, *Fault Lines: How Hidden Fractures Still Threaten the World Economy* (Princeton, NJ: Princeton University Press, 2010).

John Rawls, *A Theory of Justice* (Cambridge, MA: Harvard University Press, 1971).

Andy Stern, *A Country That Works: Getting America Back on Track* (New York: Free Press, 2008; originally published in 2006).

Richard Wilkinson and Kate Pickett, *The Spirit Level: Why Greater Equality Makes Societies Stronger* (New York: Bloomsbury, 2009).

1. *Trends in the Distribution of Household Income*, Congressional Budget Office, 19.

2. Warren Buffett, "Stop Coddling the Super-Rich," *New York Times*, Aug. 14, 2011, at http://www.nytimes.com/2011/08/15/opinion/stop-coddling-the-super-rich.html; "Options to Tax Individuals with Incomes over $1 Million," Table T11-0302, Tax Policy Center (Washington: Brookings Institution, 2011), at http://www.taxpolicycenter.org/numbers/Content/PDF/T11-0302.pdf; "Monthly Budget Review," Congressional Budget Office, Nov, 7, 2011, at http://www.cbo.gov/ftpdocs/125xx/doc12541/2011_Nov_MBR.pdf.

3. Bill Drayton, "Engage People, Retire Things," *Innovations* 4, no. 4 (Fall 2009), 49–55; and Hendrik Herzberg, "Not Insane," *New Yorker*, Mar. 23, 2009, at http://www.newyorker.com/talk/comment/2009/03/23/090323taco_talk_hertzberg.

4. "Historical Federal Workforce Tables: Total Government Employment Since 1962" (Washington: U.S. Office of Personnel Management), at http://www.opm.gov/feddata/HistoricalTables/TotalGovernmen-

tSince1962.asp. The civilian workforce actually grew by about 8 percent during Ronald Reagan's presidency, compared to an increase in the military workforce of about 4 percent. So perhaps it's appropriate that the biggest government office building in Washington, D.C. (also the District's biggest building, period) was named after the Gipper. The comparatively modest personnel increase in uniformed military during Reagan's two terms demonstrates that the much-touted military buildup of the Reagan years consisted mainly of spending vast sums on expensive military hardware.

5. Charles Peters and Timothy Noah, "Wrong Harry," *Slate*, Jan. 26, 2009, at http://www.slate.com/articles/news_and_politics/chatterbox/2009/01/wrong_harry.html.

6. This constituted one of three categories of stimulus spending. The other two were tax cuts ($260 billion) and entitlement payments ($187 billion). See "The Economic Impact of the American Recovery and Reinvestment Act of 2009," Council of Economic Advisers (Washington: Executive Office of the President, 2011), at http://www.whitehouse.gov/sites/default/files/cea_7th_arra_report.pdf.

7. "Work Authorization for Non-U.S. Citizens: Workers in Professional and Specialty Occupations (H 1-B, H-1B1, and E-3 Visas)," U.S. Labor Department Web page, Sept. 2009, at http://www.dol.gov/compliance/guide/h1b.htm. Hilariously, mixed in with all the usual wonky occupations eligible for H-1B visas is "fashion model," which typically requires not even a high school diploma. What "distinguished merit and ability" means in this context would be a fruitful topic for extended research. Any volunteers?

8. W. Steven Barnett, Dale J. Epstein, et al., "The State of Preschool 2010," National Institute for Early Education Research (New Brunswick, NJ: Rutgers, 2010), 4–5; Raj Chetty, John N. Friedman, Nathaniel Hilger, Emmanuel Saez, Diane Whitmore Schanzenbach, and Danny Yagan, "How Does Your Kindergarten Classroom Affect Your Earnings? Evidence from Project Star," Mar. 2011, at http://obs.rc.fas.harvard.edu/chetty/STAR.pdf, 1.

9. The effort grew out of broader but much shorter-term wage and price controls that also failed.

10. "Trends in College Pricing 2011" (New York: College Board, 2011), 13, at http://trends.collegeboard.org/downloads/College_Pricing_2011.pdf; and "The College Completion Agenda 2010 Progress Report" (New York: College Board, 2010), 5–6, at http://completionagenda.collegeboard.org/sites/default/files/reports_pdf/Progress_Report_2010.pdf.

11. Simon Johnson and James Kwak, *13 Bankers: The Wall Street Takeover and the Next Financial Meltdown* (New York: Vintage, 2011; originally published by Pantheon in 2010), 210–11.

12. Andy Stern, interview with author, Sept. 22, 2011. Unless otherwise indicated, all quotations by Stern are from this interview.

13. Nolan McCarty, Keith Poole, and Howard Rosenthal, "Political Polarization and Income Inequality," Russell Sage Foundation Working Paper No. 201 at www.russellsage.org/sites/all/files/u4/McCarty%20et%20al .pdf, 148.

14. Nicholas Brady, telephone conversation with author, May 25, 2011.

Index

Note: Page numbers in *italic* refer to figures.

AARP (American Association of Retired Persons), 124
ability, 191–192
Abraham, Steven, 139
ABS (alkylbenzene sulfonate), 119
absolute mobility, 29–30, 31
Abu Ghraib, 102
accounting standards, 154
accumulated capital, 204n.5
Achieving Society, The (McClelland), 43
Adams, Henry, 83, 220n.16
Adams, James Truslow, 38–42, 43, 167
Adams, John, 62
Addams, Jane, 13
advertising controls, 122
advocacy industry, 118, 230n.17
AEA (American Economic Association), 12, 165
AES Corporation, 153
African Americans. *See also* black/white income gap
    citizenship rights of, 2
    the Great Divergence impact on, 47
    median incomes for, 44–45
    upward mobility for, 34–35
Age of Greed (Madrick), 160
Age of Turbulence, The (Greenspan), 183
Aid to Families with Dependent Children, 168
Akers, Karen, 80–81
Akin Gump Strauss Hauer & Feld, 118, 124
Albert, Carl, 118
Alger, Horatio, Jr., 28, 38–42, 43, 167
Algeria, 95

Alien and Sedition Acts, 62
alkylbenzene sulfonate (ABS), 119
Allen, Frederick Lewis, 15, 21–22, 83–84
Allen, Woody, 97
Alpert, Daniel, 159, 170
American Association of Retired Persons (AARP), 124
American dream, the
    in American fiction, 39, 40
    enduring belief in, 27
    upward mobility in, 41–43
American Economic Association (AEA), 12, 165
American Medical Association, 124
Anderson, Jack, 121
Andersson, Frederik, 82–83
Andrade, Maria, 60–61
Andrade, Rafael, 61
antigovernment movements, 176–177
Apple Inc., 100–101
appraisals, real estate, 154–155
Argentina, 27, 150, 151
Asian immigrants, 62, 65, 66
assortative mating, 54–55, 57
athletes, professional, 162–163
Atkinson, Anthony B., 150
ATMs (automatic teller machines), 80–81
Auletta, Ken, 158
Australia, 89, 150
automatic teller machines (ATMs), 80–81
auto mechanics, 78
Autor, David, 47, 82, 83
average earnings, 204n.1

baby-boom generation, 46–47
Bachmann, Michele, 181–182
Baekeland, Leo, 84
bailouts, 161–162
Baker, Dean, 105–106, 182–184
Bakija, Jon, 151, 162
Bakke, Dennis, 153
banana republics, 192–193
Bank of America, 159
bankruptcy
    and job loss, 54
    of Lehman Brothers, 159
    of single-parent households, 57
banks and banking
    bailouts of, 161–162
    commercial, 160
    deregulation of, 158, 160–162
    failures of, 168, 170
    investment, 158–160, 162
    reform of, 186–188
    tellers, 80–81
    too-big-to-fail, 187–188
    trading vs., 158–159
Barbie doll, 100
Bartels, Larry, 114–117, 129, 143, 188
Basically Rich, 146, 147
Battle, The (Brooks), 173
Battle of the Overpass, 130
Bear Stearns, 160
Becker, Gary S., 33
Belgium, 89, 98
Bell, Alexander Graham, 84
Bell, Daniel, 134
Bell & Howell, 158
Bertrand, Marianne, 102
Big Change, The (Allen), 83
Big Sort, The (Bishop), 193
bipartisanship, 194
Bishop, Bill, 75, 193, 194
Bivens, Josh, 98–99
Blackwell, Ron, 142
black/white income gap
    growth of, 210n.2
    income gains with, 167
    median incomes in, 44–45
Blentlinger, Ann-Marie, 51, 52
Blentlinger, Jim, 51–53
Blentlinger, Matthew, 52
Blentlinger family, 50–52
Blinder, Alan, 3, 103–105
blue-collar workers, 86–87, 189
Bonfire of the Vanities, The (Wolfe), 27

Booza, Jason, 75
Borjas, George, 69–72, 74, 97, 216n.20
boycotts, secondary, 140
Bradbury, Katharine, 32
Brady, Nicholas, 194
Bright-Sided (Ehrenreich), 43
Broda, Christian, 242–243n.8
Brooks, Albert, 104
Brooks, Arthur C., 173
Brown, Christopher, 170
Brynjolfsson, Erik, 79
Buffett, Warren, 155, 161, 164, 180
Bulgaria, 95
bureaucracy, federal, 181–182
Burtless, Gary, 72, 178
Bush, George H. W., 108, 111, 114,
    228n.1
Bush, George W., 1, 8, 108, 111, 114, 143,
    172
Business-Government Relations
    Council, 122
business-related government policy,
    120–124
Business Roundtable, 122
butlers, 152
Butlers and Household Managers (Ferry),
    152
buying power, 170–171
Byllesby, Langton, 11

cable TV, 194
California, 60–61
Campos, Roel C., 154–155
Canada, 35–37, 89, 98, 150
capital gains
    in income shares calculation, 206n.31,
        237n.10, 245n.17
    taxation of, 119, 181
capitalist economies
    ability and talent in, 191–192
    income inequality in, 166
    inequality in, 165
Capra, Frank, 164
Card, David, 68, 69, 128
card checks, 139–140, 190
Carlton Group, 122
Carnegie, Andrew, 84, 86
Carnevale, Anthony, 90
Carter, Jimmy, 6, 23, 69, 114, 116, 142
Castro, Fidel, 66, 68
Catching Out (Reavis), 166
Cave, Damien, 73

CBO (Congressional Budget Office),
112–113
C-corporations, 245n.17
Cembalest, Michael, 177
Center for Responsive Politics, 124
Central America, 67
CEOs (chief executive officers), 154–155
Chait, Jonathan, 236–237n.6
Chamber of Commerce, 124
Chetty, Raj, 185
chief executive officers (CEOs), 151–155
children's advertising, 122
China, 94–95, 98–101, 104, 223n.3,
225n.14
Chinese immigrants, 62, 63
Chivas Regal strategy, 93
Chrysler, 130
Citigroup, 160
citizenship, 2, 62
civil rights, 190
Civil Rights Act, 65
Civil Works Administration, 182
class status, 206n.24. See also middle
class; top-income shares
class warfare, 11
Clifford, Clark, 117
Clinton, Bill, 79, 111, 114, 143, 153
Clooney, George, 164
closed shops, 140
Coen, Harry, 133
Cole, Adam, 151, 162
collective action, 43
collective bargaining, 142
colleges and universities
compensation for graduates of, 72, 90
female-to-male ratios in, 45, 46,
211n.4, 212n.11
feminization of, 45–46
in governance, 13
graduation rates for, 185–186
incentives to attend, 167
increase in students attending, 87–89
tuition, 92–93, 185–186
and wage premium, 89–93
commercial banks, 160
Committee for Constitutional Government, 16
compensation. See also wages
for college graduates, 72, 90
for corporate executives, 151–155
computer technology
and educational attainment, 85–93

in finance industry, 161
and job polarization, 81–83
offshoring of jobs related to, 105
and rule-based jobs, 77–81
Confessions of a Union Buster (Levitt), 141
Congressional Budget Office (CBO),
112–113
Conscience of a Liberal, The (Krugman),
5, 113–114, 148
construction industry, 72–73
consultants, 155
Consumer Product Safety Commission,
120
consumer protection, 119–124
consumption
and debt, 54, 168, 169, 170
patterns of, 242–243n.8
Continetti, Matthew, 178
Cook, Philip, 163
Coolidge, Calvin, 64
Corak, Miles, 36–37
corporate executives, 151–155. See also
top-income shares
corporate lobbying
as "advocacy," 230n.17
in finance industry regulation, 188
and government policy, 117–124
growing influence of, 160
corporate profits, 120–121
cost-of-living adjustments, 134
Counsel to the President (Clifford), 117
Country That Works, A (Stern), 191
Cowen, Tyler, 175–176, 185
credit card debt, 54
Cuba, 68–69, 95
Current Population Survey, 144–145
Cutsinger, Jackie, 75
cycles, U-shaped, 16–19

data
on economic trends, 6
on income distribution, 10–11
on income inequality, 3
for income inequality calculations,
206n.31
for statistical research, 11
on top-income shares, 144–146,
236n.4
used by economists, 72–73
Dauman, Philippe, 151
Davis, Bob, 50
"death tax," 18

Debs, Eugene V., 130
debt
    consumer, 54, 168, 169, 170
    and inequality, 168, 169
deciles, income, 145
Declaration of Independence, 164
DeLong, Brad, 109, 110
democracies, industrialized, 3
Democratic party
    on economic elite, 194
    immigration policy of, 62
    income inequality with, 114–116
    presidents from, 188
    union policy of, 190
Democratic-Republican party, 62
democratization of incomes, 1
Deng Xiaoping, 94
denial of inequality, 178
Denmark, 57, 89
deregulation, 160–162
Dew-Becker, Ian, 176
Dictionary of Races or Peoples (Jenks),
    63–64
Dillon Read, 157
Distribution of Incomes in the United
    States (Streightoff), 203–204n.1
Dividing Lines (Tichenor), 62
Dodd-Frank financial reform bill,
    186–188
Dorn, David, 82
Dotson, Donald, 142
Drayton, Bill, 181
drugs, 119
durable goods, 242n.8

earned success, 173
eastern Europeans, 13, 62–64
economic cycles, 16–19
economic growth
    immigrants' contributions to, 68–70
    in 1980s and 1990s, 25
    tax cuts to stimulate, 108–109
Economic Policy Institute, 218n.4
economic risk, 54, 57
"Economics of Superstars, The" (Rosen),
    163
economists
    data used by, 72–73
    denial of Great Divergence by, 25–26
    on income inequality, 6
Edison, Thomas, 86
Edsall, Thomas Byrne, 25–26, 122

educational attainment
    computer technology and, 85–93
    in employment rates, 48
    high school, 45–46
    for immigrants, 67
    and marriage patterns, 55
    and preschool attendance, 184–185
    of women, 46
effective tax rates, 110–113
egalitarian institutions, 110
egalitarianism
    in economic cycles, 16–17, 19
    educational, 88, 89
    as embedded in language, 37–38
    increases in, 5
    as portrayed by pro-business interests,
        123–124
    in United States, 19
Ehrenreich, Barbara, 43, 164, 171, 182
Eisenhower, Dwight, 110, 114, 117, 118
elections, 139–141, 188
electricity, 83–84, 86
"elite," the, 194
Ellwood, David, 56
Ely, Richard T., 12–13, 165
employee stock ownership, 190–191
employment
    changes in occupational shares,
        by education and sex, 48
    employee-employer relationship in,
        102–103
    and technological advances, 77
End of Equality, The (Kaus), 109–110, 171
English Classical School, 85
entertainers, top, 162–163
Environmental Protection Agency, 120
Epic of America, The (Adams), 39, 40, 41
Epstein, Richard, 165–166
equality
    and civilization, 205n.15
    and corporate lobbying, 123
    federal government role in, 117
    in industrialized democracies, 3
    property ownership as measure of,
        11–12
    and service-sector offshoring, 103–104
Establishment, the, 37, 208n.17
eugenics, 13
Europe, 35–37, 42, 88, 89, 167
European immigrants, 62–64, 66
European Union, 83
"Everybody Ought to be Rich" (Raskob), 15

Fair Credit Reporting Act, 160
Fairlie, Henry, 37–38, 192
fall of Saigon, 67
Fallows, James, 42–43
families
    examples of, 50–52
    median incomes for, 49–50
    single-parent, 57
    and social inequality, 207–208n.1
    two-income, 53–54, 56, 57
family reunification, 66
fascism, 201–202n.3
Fault Lines (Rajan), 170, 187
Federal Express, 124
federal government
    bureaucracy of, 181–182
    as cause of Great Divergence, 108
    payroll of, 181–182
    role of, in equality, 117
    in Treaty of Detroit, 134–135
    workforce in, 53
Federal Insurance Contributions Act
        (FICA) tax, 181
Federal Reserve Board, 142
Felsenthal, Peter, 162
Feminine Mystique, The (Friedan), 46
Ferguson, Andrew, 93
Ferrie, Joseph P., 40, 41, 42
Ferry, Steven M., 152
Feynman, Richard, 86
FICA (Federal Insurance Contributions
        Act) tax, 181
finance industry. See also Wall Street
    computer models used in, 161
    growth of, 155–157
    reregulation of, 186–188
    in top-income shares, 155–158
Financial Accounting Standards Board, 154
financial crisis of 2008. See 2008
        financial crisis
financial reform bill (2010), 186
Finland, 4, 150, 202n.8
First National City, 160
Fischer, Claude, 45
Fisher, Irving, 15
Fitch, Albert Parker, 87
Flesh and the Devil (film), 162
Fluctuating Fortunes (Vogel), 122
food prices, 170–171, 233n.8
Ford, Gerald, 110, 114, 120, 230n.16
Ford, Henry, 84, 101–102, 130
Ford Motors, 130

foreign trade. See international trade
France, 5, 14, 57, 150, 172, 184
Franck Muller, 152
Frank, Robert, 151–152, 163
Franklin, Benjamin, 62
Freeman, Richard B., 90, 128, 137, 141
Friedan, Betty, 46
Friedman, Milton, 88, 204n.1
Frydman, Carola, 152
Full Monty, The (film), 49, 56

Galster, George, 75
Garbo, Greta, 162
Garrett, Thomas, 166, 176
gated communities, 172–173
gender, 44
General Electric (GE), 124, 156
General Motors (GM), 122, 130, 132–134,
        156, 233n.7
Geoghegan, Thomas, 140, 141
geographic shifts, 60, 193
German-speaking immigrants, 62
Germany, 14, 17, 57, 65, 89, 94, 150, 184
G.I. Bill, 88, 212n.11
Gilligan, Chuck, 72–73
Gini, Corrado, 4, 201, 202n.3
Gini coefficient
    for income inequality, 3–5
    in Latin American nations, 207n.36
    and Lorenz curve, 202n.4, 204n.9
Gini index, 229n.10
Glass Castle, The (Walls), 75
Glass-Steagall Act, 160
globalization, 94–107
    exports and supply chains in, 99–103
    and labor organizing, 190, 191
    and service sector, 103–106
    in wage competition, 95–99
    Wall Street and, 157
Glucksman, Lew, 158, 159
GMAC, 156
Goldberg, Arthur, 135
Goldberg, Jonah, 202n.3
Golden, Sabrina Kay, 72
Golden Age, the, 19, 23
Goldin, Claudia, 19–22, 25, 46–47, 67,
        69, 83–86, 88, 92–93, 167,
        220–221n.18
Goldman Sachs, 159, 160
Gompers, Samuel, 63, 67
Google, 79
Gordon, Robert J., 176

Gore, Albert, Sr., 119
government policy, 108–124
    business-related, 120–124
    for consumer protection, 120–124
    and corporate lobbying, 117–124
    on immigration, 61, 62, 64–67
    and income tax structure, 110–113
    institutions and norms theory on,
        113–117
    and labor movement, 138–143
    long-term effects of, 26
    of Reagan administration, 108–110
    on wealth, 18
graduate school
    benefits of, 186
    degree rates for, 90
    female-to-male ratio for, 45
graduation rates, 184–186
Great Britain, 42
Great Compression, The
    causes of, 179
    college tuition during, 92
    emergence of, 19
    and immigration, 67–68
    income equality with, 148, 150
    income tax brackets in, 110
    middle class prosperity during, 76, 82
    reversal of, 24, 25–27
Great Depression, The, 142
    in emergence of Great Compression,
        179
    income distribution during, 19–23
    and income patterns, 19–20
    income tax brackets in, 110
    jobs programs from, 182
    labor movement in, 131
    women's educational attainment
        and, 46
Great Divergence, The
    beginning of, 49, 83
    denial of, 26, 58
    evidence for existence of, 58–59
    and the Great Compression, 24, 25, 50
    income inequality in, 5–9, 113
    major factors in, 57, 108–109, 117
    middle class in, 76, 78
    Part 2, 144, 151, 155
    and quality of life, 71–72
    resentments about, 194
    Stolper-Samuelson theorem in, 96–97
    supply-side economics in, 109–110
    in 2008 financial crisis, 168, 170

Great Risk Shift, The (Hacker) 54
Great Society program, 61
Great Stagnation, The (Cowen), 175
Great Train Robbery, The (film), 84
Greece, 5, 89, 184
Greed and Glory on Wall Street (Auletta),
    158
Greeley, Horace, 62
Greenspan, Alan, 182–183, 187–188
Greider, William, 109
Grocery Manufacturers of America,
    121–122
gross domestic product (GDP)
    of China, 94–95
    and government spending, 109
    and productivity rates, 243–244n.15
    ratio of U.S. debt to, 169
Grossman, Gene, 225n.15
gross national income, 95
growth, economic. See economic
        growth
guest-worker visas, 183–184
Gutfreund, John, 159
Guyana, 27

Haberler, Gottfried von, 96
Hacker, Jacob, 54, 57, 112, 116–117,
    206n.31
Haight, Henry, 62
Haldeman, Bob, 120, 230n.17
happiness, 173–174
Harding, Warren G., 64
Harlow, Bryce, 108, 117–123, 192,
    229n.15, 230n.16, 230n.17
Harrington, Michael, 108
Hatton, Timothy, 67
Haves and the Have-Nots, The (Mila-
    novic), 26, 205n.15
health insurance, 177
Heaven's Door (Borjas), 71
Heim, Bradley, 151, 162
Heller, Walter, 135
Hemenway, David, 175
Henley, William Ernest, 33
Henninger, Daniel, 147
heritability, income, 32–33
Hertzberg, Hendrik, 181
higher education. See colleges and
        universities
high school(s)
    development of, 85–87
    dropouts of, 70–71

educational achievement in, by gender,
  45–46
graduation rates, 203n.8
movement to increase number of, 184
and wage premium, 89–90
Hirsch, Barry, 137
historical background, 2–3
History of the American People (Wilson),
  63
Hitler, Adolf, 65
Ho, Karen, 161–162
Holzer, Harry, 82–83
Hong Kong, 98, 100
Hooper, Herb, 51
Hoover, Herbert, 180
households, 58. *See also* families
Houseman, Susan, 243–244n.15
housing prices, 171, 178
Hout, Michael, 174

immigrants
  Asian, 62, 65, 66
  backlash against, 61–64
  education level of, 67
  European, 62–64, 66
  Mexican, 66, 67, 73, 216
  undocumented, 72–73
  upward mobility for, 30
immigration, 60–74
  barriers to, 183–184
  and decline in wages, 67–74
  government policies on, 64–67
  quotas, 13, 215n.10
Immigration and Nationality Act, 61
income(s)
  democratization of, 1
  in determining class status, 76, 77
  and economic growth, 17–18
  and inequality, 168–173
  in intergenerational mobility, 31–33
  pre- and post-tax, 112–113, 179–181
  of union members, 128
  of women vs. men, 49
income distribution, 10–27
  data on, 10–11
  equality of, 148, 150
  and fascism, 202n.3
  Great Compression of, 25–27, 148, 150
  from Great Depression to post-World
    War II, 19–23
  Great Divergence of, 5–9, 113
  ideal, 194–195

in Lorenz curve, 202n.4
and marriage patterns, 55–56
measurement of, 3–5
Progressive era policies for, 11–16
and stagnation of median incomes,
  23–25
U-shaped cycle of, 16–19
and wealth distribution, 244n.16
income growth rates, 115
income heritability, 32–37
income inequality, 1–9
  as beneficial, 165–166
  in China, 223n.3
  data for calculations of, 206n.31
  with Democratic administrations,
    114–116
  Gini coefficient for, 3–5
  in Great Divergence, 5–9
  with Republican administrations,
    eholds in, 57
    ly, 171–172

  14
  also top-income shares
  calculation of, 237n.10,
  , 202n.4
  of middle class, 1–2
  for top decile, 24, 149
  and 2008 financial crisis, 4
income tax rates
  effective tax rates, 229n.9
  recommended policies for, 179–181
  reform of, 244–245n.17
  structure of, 110–113
  in supply-side theory, 227–228n.1
India, 164, 150
Indonesia, 100
industrialization, 16–18
industrialized democracies
  equality in, 3
  income inequality in, 5
  policies on income disparities in, 18
industrial unions, 131–132
inequality, 164–178
  of access to information, 187
  causes of, 44
  complacency about, 178
  and debt, 168, 169

inequality (*continued*)
  denial of, 178
  as good, 165–168
  and income, 168–173
  marriage patterns in, 55–56
  and productivity, 176–178
  and quality of life, 174–176
  social, 171–173
  think tank's avoidance of term, 26
  and unhappiness, 173–174
  in U.S. history, 2–3
"Inequality and Institutions in 20th
    Century America" (Levy & Temin),
    206n.31
Inequality Matters (anthology), 172
inflation
  guideposts for, 135, 136
  partisan views of, 116
  and tax cuts, 135, 236–237n.6
  and wage demands, 135
inheritance tax, 18
institutions and norms theory, 113–117
intergenerational mobility
  absolute vs. relative, 30–37
  measuring of, 241n.3
  post-World War II, 41, 167
Internal Revenue Service (IRS), 145
international finance, 157
international trade
  with China, 225n.14
  employee-employer relationship with,
    102–103
  and manufacturing sector, 99–103
  in modern trade theory, 223–224n.5
  in wage competition, 95–99, 225n.15
  Wall Street and, 157
Internet, the, 194
investment banks, 158–159, 160, 162
"Invictus" (Henley), 33, 43
iPad, 101
iPhone, 101
iPods, 100–101
Ireland, 5, 89, 99, 184
IRS (Internal Revenue Service), 145
Isaacs, Julia B., 31
Istel, Yves-André, 156–161
Italy, 89, 98, 184, 201–202n.3
It's a Wonderful Life (film), 164

Jamaica, 95
James, William, 39
Jane Austen Paradigm, 55

Jankowsky, Joel, 118, 124
Japan, 89, 97, 99, 100, 101, 150
Japanese immigrants, 62
Jefferson, Thomas, 11
Jefferson National Bank, 80–81
Jencks, Christopher, 56, 57
Jenks, Jeremiah, 63–64
Jennings, Ken, 77
job loss
  and bankrupty, 54
  computer-driven, 7, 77–78
  increasing risk of, 53–54
job polarization, 83
jobs
  for immigrants, 68–70
  low wage, 71
  opportunities for men, 47, 49
  in private sector, 52
  programs for, 182
  rule-based, 78–81, 104
  in service sector, 103–106
  in top-income share, 146, 151, 153
Jobs, Steve, 101
Johnson, Lyndon, 61, 65, 66, 114, 136,
    208n.6
Johnson, Simon, 155–156, 160, 188
Johnston, Eric, 129
Joseph, Jeffrey, 121
journalists, 225n.23

Kahlenberg, Richard, 190
Katz, Jane, 32
Katz, Lawrence F., 25, 46, 83–86,
    88, 92–93, 97, 167, 216n.20,
    220–221n.18
Kaus, Mickey, 109–110, 171, 172
Kennedy, John F., 65, 114, 135
Kennedy, Robert, 135
Kerley, Ann, 51
Kerley, Dennis, 51
Kerley family, 50–52
Khurana, Rakesh, 153
King, Martin Luther, Jr., 35, 129
King, Willford I., 10–16, 19, 165,
    203–204nn.1–2
Kissinger, Henry, 118, 230n.17
Koch, George, 119, 121
Korea, 89, 101
Kristol, Irving, 145, 236n.3
Krugman, Paul, 5, 25, 96–99, 113–114,
    117, 129, 148, 150, 170, 224n.7
kudoka (job polarization), 81, 83

Obama, Barack, 6, 18, 42, 50, 110, 139, 147, 180, 182, 184
Observations on the Sources and Effects of Unequal Wealth (Byllesby), 11–12
Occupational Safety and Health Administration, 120
Occupy Wall Street movement, 2, 147, 167, 168, 177
OECD. *See* Organisation for Economic Co-operation and Development
offshoring. *See* globalization
oil embargo, 23, 233n.8
Only Yesterday (Allen), 15
opinion, 193–194
OPM (other people's money), 159
Organisation for Economic Co-operation and Development (OECD), 3–5, 89, 172
Organization of Arab Petroleum Exporting Countries (OPEC), 23
Other America, The (Harrington), 108
other people's money (OPM), 159

Palmer, A. Mitchell, 11
Panel Study of Income Dynamics (PSID), 31–32, 34, 208n.6
Pareto, Vilfredo, 17, 201–202n.3
Pareto distribution, 201–202n.3
Paris Exposition, 83
partisanship, 193–194
Pauling, Linus, 77
payroll tax, 181
pensions, 54
performers, 162–163
Peterson, Pete, 158, 159
PG&E, 124
Phibro Corporation, 159
Philippines, 101
Philippon, 161
picketing, mass, 140, 141
Pickett, Kate, 193
Pierson, Paul, 112, 116–117, 206n.31
Piketty, Thomas, 111, 112, 144–148, 150, 178, 206n.31, 245n.17
policy recommendations, 179–195
    college and university price controls, 185–186
    distribution of wealth, 191–195
    government payrolls, 181–182
    importation of skilled labor, 182–184
    income tax rates, 179–181
    labor movement, 189–191

preschool universalization, 184–185
presidential elections, 188
Wall Street regulation, 186–188
political factors, 105
political refugees, 66–67
Poole, Keith, 193–194
"A Populist Manifesto" (Powell), 123
Porter, Cole, 162
Porter, Edwin S., 84
Portugal, 4–5, 202–203n.8
positive thinking, 43
post-tax income, 112–113, 179–181
poverty
    elimination of, 15
    and Great Divergence, 71
    of immigrants, 67
    rates of, 4
Powell, Lewis, 121, 123
Prague Spring, 67
preschool education, 184–185
presidents, 188
pre-tax income
    policy recommendations for, 179–181
    and political party in power, 116–117
    for top decile, 112–113
price controls, 135–136, 185–186
price shifts, 50
private sector, 52, 171–172
Procter & Gamble, 108, 118–119, 121, 122, 230n.16
productivity
    decline in, 137–138
    and inequality, 176–178
    and inflation, 136
    meaning of, 134
    overstatement of increases in, 243–244n.15
professional athletes, 162–163
profits, 120–121, 177
Progressive era, 11–16, 63
property ownership, 11–12
proprietary trading, 187
prosperity, 19, 176–177
protection, consumer, 119–124
PSID. *See* Panel Study of Income Dynamics
public corporations, 158, 159–160
public-employee unions, 127
public schools, 85–87
public sector, 53, 171–173
Publix supermarket chain, 191

quality of life, 71–72, 174–176
quiet revolution, 47
quota laws, 64, 65–66

*Race Between Education and Technology,
    The* (Goldin & Katz), 25, 84
"race suicide," 13
racism, 44
radiologists, 105
Ragged Dick (Alger), 28, 38
Rajan, Raghuram, 170, 187
Raskob, John J., 15
Raspberry, William, 123
Rawls, John, 191–192, 194
RBA (Russ Brown Associates), 142
Reagan, Ronald, 6, 22, 23–24, 108,
    110–111, 114, 122, 148, 176, 179–181,
    228n.2
Reagan administration
    antigovernment rhetoric of, 176
    anti-union stance of, 142–143
    policies of, 108–110
    workforce growth during, 246–247n.4
real estate appraisals, 154–155
Really Rich, 146–148, 150, 151, 155, 162,
    163
Reavis, Dick J., 166, 171
*Rebound: Why America Will Emerge
    Stronger from the Financial Crisis*
    (Rose), 58
refugees, 65, 66–67
regressive taxes, 111
regulation, 119–121, 158. *See also*
    deregulation
Reich, Robert, 79–80, 104
relative mobility, 30, 31
rentiers, 146
Republican party
    and corporate lobbying, 124, 187
    on cultural elite, 194
    income inequality with, 114–116
    presidents from, 188
    Reagan administration, 108–110
    union policy of, 138
Reshef, Ariell, 161
retirement funds, 54
Reuther, Valentine, 129–130
Reuther, Victor, 130
Reuther, Walter, 129–138, 190
Reynolds, Alan, 178, 244–245n.17
Ricardo, David, 95, 225n.15
rich, the, 146. *See also* top-income shares

Richistan (Frank), 151–152
risk, economic, 54
River Rouge (Ford plant), 102
robocars, 79
Romalis, John, 242–243n.8
Romney, George, 132
Romney, Mitt, 132, 182
Roosevelt, Franklin D., 16, 18, 40, 53, 65,
    131, 138, 204n.5
Roosevelt, Theodore, 12
Rorty, Malcolm, 14
Rose, Stephen J., 58, 76, 90, 218n.4
Rosen, Sherwin, 163
Rosenblum, David, 82–83
Rosenfeld, Jake, 128
Rosenthal, Howard, 193–194
Rosin, Hanna, 47, 49, 56
Ross, Edward A., 13
Rossi-Hansberg, Esteban, 225n.15
Rothschild's Global Financial Advisory,
    156
Rovere, Richard, 208n.17
Rowe, Jonathan, 172
rule-based jobs, 78–81, 104
Russ Brown Associates (RBA), 142
Ryan, Paul, 167

Saez, Emmanuel, 111, 112, 144–148, 150,
    178, 185, 206n.31, 245n.17
safety standards, 119–120
Saks, Raven, 152
salaries, CEO, 154–155
salaries, tax-deductible, 153
Salomon Brothers, 159
Salomon Smith Barney, 162
sampling data, 144–145
Samuelson, Paul, 68, 95, 96, 106
Santorum, Rick, 241n.2
Sarnoff, David, 84
Sawhill, Isabel, 32
Schloss, David F., 218–219n.6
schools, public, 85–87
Schwartz, Christine R., 55–56
sciences, 47, 212n.10
S-corporations, 181, 245n.17
Scudere, Carol, 152
Searching for a Corporate Savior
    (Khurana), 152
Sears Roebuck and Company,
    119
secondary boycotts, 140
secondary strikes, 140

Securities and Exchange Commission, 154, 160
self-employed people, 181
Senses, Mine Zeynep, 103
Service Employees International Union, 189
service sector, 82, 103–106
sexism, 44
Sheen, Charlie, 162
shielding agreement, 102–103
Shierholz, Heidi, 218n.4
Shister, Joseph, 138
Simon, William, 120, 123–124
Singapore, 98, 101, 150
single-parent families, 56–59
sit-down strikes, 140
skilled labor
    importation of, 182–184
    offshoring of, 105
    supply and demand for, 91
    and technological advances, 220–221n.18
    wage gap with unskilled labor, 101
    on Wall Street, 161
    women in, 48
Slate (Manjoo), 78
Sleeper (film), 97
social inequality
    egalitarian institutions for, 110
    and family background, 207–208n.1
    and income inequality, 171–173
Social Security, 181
Social Stratification in the United States (Rose), 58
Solnick, Sara, 175
Solon, Gary, 32–33, 34, 37
Soros, George, 157
Sort of Rich, 146
South America, 67
Southeast Asia, 98
southern Europeans, 13, 62–63, 64
South Korea, 98
Spain, 5
Spirit Level, The (Wilkinson & Pickett), 193
"stagflation," 23
stagnation of median incomes, 23–25, 54
Standard Oil, 188
Stein, Judith, 135
Stern, Andy, 189–190, 191
Stewart, William Morris, 62
Stigler, George, 204n.1

Stinking Rich, 146–148, 150, 151, 155, 162, 163. See also top-income shares
Stockman, David, 109, 228n.2
stock options, 153–154
stock ownership, 90–191, 177–178
Stolper, Wolfgang, 95, 96, 106
Stolper-Samuelson theorem, 95–97, 225n.15
Stone, Nahum, 14
Streightoff, Frank Hatch, 203–204nn.1–2
strikes, 140, 141
strikes, sit-down, 140
Suadi Arabia, 100
success, 173
Sullivan, James, 168
supply-side theory, 108–109, 227–228n.1
Survey, The ($journal), 10
Sweden, 95, 150
Switzerland, 150
Sylvia, Alicia, 125, 126–127, 141

Taft-Hartley Act, 138–141, 190
Taiwan, 98, 100, 101
talent, 191–192
TANF (Temporary Assistance for Needy Families), 167–168
tariffs, 96
Taussig, F. W., 96, 223–224n.5
tax brackets, 180–181
tax cuts
    and corporate lobbying, 122–123
    with highest impact, 111–112
    and inflation, 135, 236–237n.6
    in supply-side theory, 108–109
    for top income brackets, 179–180, 227–228n.1
tax-deductible salaries, 153
Tax Policy Center, 180
Taylor, Linda, 109
Teamster union, 140
Tea Party movement, 168, 176
technology(-ies). See also computer technology
    electricity, 84–85
    and employment, 77
    and reliance on risk control models, 161
telegraphy, 86–87
television, cable, 194
Temin, Peter, 113, 129, 134, 135, 143, 206n.31

Tempest, Rone, 100
Temporary Assistance for Needy
    Families (TANF), 167–168
Tenement Museum, 3
Tennessee Valley Authority (TVA), 53
Theory of Justice, A (Rawls), 191–192
"Thinking Clearly About Economic
    Inequality" (Wilkinson), 168
13 Bankers (Johnson & Kwak), 155–156,
    160, 188
Thompson, Michael J., 11
Thurow, Lester, 22
Tichenor, Daniel, 62
A Time for Truth (Simon), 123–124
Tocqueville, Alexis de, 42, 205n.15
too-big-to-fail banks, 187–188
top-income shares, 144–163
    and banking–trading distinction,
        158–159
    calculation of, 244–245n.17
    of corporate executives, 151–155
    and corporatizing of financial
        partnerships, 159–160
    data on, 144–146, 236n.4
    and deregulation, 160–162
    of entertainers and athletes, 162–163
    of financiers, 155–158
    patterns of, 24, 146–151
    in years before market crashes,
        205n.12
trade, 223–224n.5, 224n.7. See also
    international trade
Trade Adjustment Assistance, 106
trading (Wall Street), 158–159
Treaty of Detroit, 134–141, 152, 191
Tribune Company, 191
trickle-down economics, 108–109, 150
Trillin, Calvin, 161
truck drivers, 78–79
Truman, Harry S., 114, 132, 138
Truth in Lending Act, 160
tuition, 92–93, 185–186
Turkey, 4, 5
TVA (Tennessee Valley Authority), 53
two-income families, 53–54, 56
2008 financial crisis
    effects of, on bottom 20 percent,
        217n.24
    Great Divergence in, 168, 170
    income shares following, 4
    and reregulation of Wall Street,
        186

Undeniably Rich, 146–148, 150, 151
undocumented immigrants, 72–73
unemployment, 22–23, 116
Unequal Democracy (Bartels), 114, 116
unhappiness, inequality and, 173–174
"union density," 128–129, 137
unions, 53, 127. See also labor movement
United Auto Workers, 129–136, 140
United Food and Commercial Workers,
    125
United Kingdom, 14, 17, 57, 89, 150, 184
United States
    egalitarianism in, 19
    Gini coefficient of, 4, 5
    gross national income per capita of, 95
    income inequality in, 14
    and income inequality in Latin
        America, 27
    as land of opportunity, 28–29
    manufacturing in, 100
    single-parent households in, 56–57
    upward mobility in, 28–31, 166–167
university price controls, 185–186
unskilled labor, 67, 69–71
upward mobility, 28–43
    in American dream, 41–43
    enduring belief in, 27–29, 37–38
    intergenerational, 30–37, 167
    measuring, 28–31, 241n.3
    for middle class, 76
    opportunities for, 37–43, 166–167
Uruguay, 27
U.S. Steel, 135
U-shaped cycles, 16–19

Valenti, Jack, 65
Value Added Tax, 181
Vanderbilt, George, 3
"Vanishing Commons, The" (Rowe), 172
Vedder, Richard, 90, 93
Venezuela, 27
Vietnam draft, 90, 92
visas, guest-worker, 183–184
vocational training, 86
Vogel, David, 122
Volcker, Paul, 142
Voting Rights Act, 65

Wachovia, 81
wage premium
    after entry into World War II, 20
    for college graduates, 89–93

for high school graduates, 89–90
  reduction of, 184
wages
  controls on, 21
  decline in, 67–74
  differentials in, 22
  guideposts on, 135
  and international trade, 95–99, 225n.15
  and Mexican immigrants, 216n.20
  minimum, 18–21, 143
  and NAFTA, 224n.12
  negotiation of, 129, 132–133, 135, 191
  pre-World War II, 19, 20
  and profits, 177
  structure of, 146
Wagner Act, 131, 138–141
Walls, Jeannette, 75
Wall Street
  bankers vs. traders on, 158–159
  computer modeling on, 161
  in economy, 156
  Occupy Wall Street movement, 2, 147,
    167, 168, 177
  reregulation of, 186–188
  structure of, 157
  transformation of, 157–158
Walmart, 125–127, 136, 242–243n.8
Wal-Mart: The High Cost of Low Price
  (documentary), 126–127
Walmart effect, the, 136–137
War on Poverty, 208n.6
Warren, Elizabeth, 50, 54, 57
Watergate scandal, 120
wealth
  distribution of, 191–195, 244n.16
  and government policy, 18
  and productivity, 176–178
  and property ownership, 11–12
Wealth and Income of the People of the
  United States, The (King), 10, 12, 13,
  204n.2
Weather Underground, 194
weekly incomes, 210–211n.3
Welch, Finis, 165, 167
welfare assistance, 109, 167–168
Wells Fargo, 81
Wessel, David, 50, 51
Western, Bruce, 128
Westwood Capital, 159
Where Are All the Good Jobs Going?
  (Holzer, Lane, Rosenblum, and
  Andersson), 82–83

Which Side Are You On? (Geoghegan),
  140, 141
Whitehead, John, 159–160
WHO (World Health Organization), 172
Widick, B. J., 130
Wilkinson, Richard, 193
Wilkinson, Will, 168, 170–171
Williamson, Jeffrey, 67
Wilson, "Engine" Charlie, 132, 233n.7
Wilson, Woodrow, 11, 13, 63, 64
Winner-Take-All Politics (Hacker &
  Pierson), 112, 206n.31
Winner-Take-All Society (Frank & Cook),
  163
Winship, Scott, 207–208n.1
"Wisconsin Idea, the," 12–13
Wolfe, Tom, 27
women
  calculating average income of,
    210–211n.3
  in Great Divergence, 44–47, 49–50
  impact of, in labor force, 53, 57
  marriage patterns of, 55
  median incomes for, 44, 49,
    210–211n.3
  occupational employment share by
    education, 48
  in single-parent households, 56–57
  upward mobility for, 34, 167
Wood, Adrian, 96
Woods, Tiger, 162
Work of Nations, The (Reich), 79–80
Works Progress Administration (WPA),
  182
World Health Organization (WHO), 172
World War II era
  college attendance in, 212n.11
  in emergence of the Great Compres-
    sion, 179
  income distribution during, 19–23
  and income equality, 20
  intergenerational mobility in, 41,
    167
  top-income shares in, 148, 152
  wages in, 19, 20, 22
WPA (Works Progress Administration),
  182
Wright Brothers, 84
Wriston, Walter, 160

Yom Kippur War, 23
Yu, Kyoung-Hee, 105

A NOTE ON THE AUTHOR

Timothy Noah is a columnist at the *New Republic*. He wrote for *Slate* for a dozen years, and previously worked at the *Wall Street Journal*, the *U.S. News & World Report*, and the *Washington Monthly*. He edited two collections of the writings of his late wife, Marjorie Williams, including the *New York Times* bestseller *The Woman at the Washington Zoo*. Noah received the 2011 Hillman Prize, the highest award for public-service magazine journalism, for the series in *Slate* that forms the basis of *The Great Divergence*.